P9-DXH-244

P9-DXH-244

HISTORY!

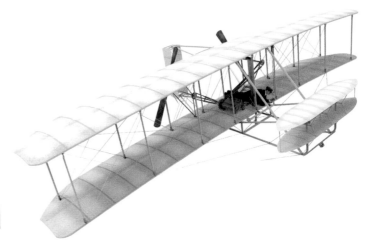

WITHDRAWN

DK SMITHSONIAN
HISTORY!

Senior Art Editor Smiljka Surla
Senior Editors Sam Atkinson, Shaila Brown
Designers Mik Gates, Joe Lawrence, Mark Lloyd
Project Editors Claire Gell, Francesco Piscitelli, Amanda Wyatt
US Editors Megan Douglass, Lori Hand
Consultant Philip Parker
Contributors Peter Chrisp, Alexander Cox, Susan Kennedy, Sally Regan
3-D Illustrators Art Agency, Peter Bull Art Studio, KJA Artists, Arran Lewis, Brendan McCaffrey, Sofian Moumene, SJC Illustration
Additional Illustrations Beehive, Peter Bull Art Studio, Gus Scott, Mohd Zishan
Cartography Ed Merritt
DK Media Archive Romaine Werblow
Picture Researchers Nic Dean, Myriam Megharbi
Managing Editor Lisa Gillespie
Managing Art Editor Owen Peyton Jones
Producer, Pre-Production Andy Hilliard
Senior Producer Meskerem Berhane
DTP Designers Nand Kishor Acharya, Syed Md Farhan
Jacket Designer Surabhi Wadhwa-Gandhi, Tanya Mehrotra
Jackets Design Development Manager Sophia MTT
Jackets Senior DTP Designer Harish Aggarwal
Jackets Editorial Coordinator Priyanka Sharma
Jackets Editor Emma Dawson
Publisher Andrew Macintyre
Art Director Karen Self
Associate Publishing Director Liz Wheeler
Design Director Phil Ormerod
Publishing Director Jonathan Metcalf

First American Edition, 2019
Published in the United States by DK Publishing
1450 Broadway, Suite 801, New York, NY 10018
Copyright © 2019 Dorling Kindersley Limited
DK, a Division of Penguin Random House LLC
19 20 21 22 23 10 9 8 7 6 5 4 3 2 1
001–312735–Aug/2019

All rights reserved.
Without limiting the rights under the copyright reserved above,
no part of this publication may be reproduced, stored in or introduced
into a retrieval system, or transmitted, in any form, or by any means
(electronic, mechanical, photocopying, recording, or otherwise),
without the prior written permission of the copyright owner.
A catalog record for this book is available from
the Library of Congress.
ISBN 978-1-4654-8175-7

DK books are available at special discounts when
purchased in bulk for sales promotions, premiums,
fund-raising, or educational use. For details, contact:
DK Publishing Special Markets, 1450 Broadway,
Suite 801, New York, NY 10018
SpecialSales@dk.com

Printed and bound in the United Arab Emirates

A WORLD OF IDEAS:
SEE ALL THERE IS TO KNOW
www.dk.com

Smithsonian
THE SMITHSONIAN

Established in 1846, the Smithsonian is the world's
largest museum and research complex, dedicated to
public education, national service, and scholarship in the
arts, sciences, and history. It includes 19 museums and galleries
and the National Zoological Park. The total number of artifacts, works of art,
and specimens in the Smithsonian's collection is estimated at 154 million.

CONTENTS

THE ANCIENT WORLD

THE ANCIENT WORLD

Humans first evolved in Africa about 300,000 years ago, and began to spread across the globe around 100,000 years later. From around 9000 BCE, some groups of humans developed farming and settled the first towns. Eventually, great civilizations sprang up in several different areas of the world. The oldest were in the Middle East and Egypt, with other civilizations forming in Europe, India, and China.

268–232 BCE: Ashoka the Great
Ashoka expanded the Mauryan Empire in India, and ordered the construction of many Buddhist monuments.

CAPITAL (TOP) OF AN ASHOKA PILLAR FROM A MONASTERY AT SARNATH

221–210 BCE: Qin Shi Huangdi
The king of Qin united the states of China for the first time, taking the title "Qin Shi Huangdi" ("First Emperor of Qin"). He was buried with thousands of model soldiers known as the Terra-Cotta Army.

206 BCE–220 CE: The Han Dynasty
The Han Dynasty ruled China for more than 400 years. In that time, the Chinese invented paper, the wheelbarrow, and the magnetic compass.

CHINESE WHEELBARROW

336–323 BCE: Alexander's empire
Alexander the Great of Macedon united Greece under his rule before conquering the Persian Empire and invading India. His empire collapsed after his death in 323 BCE.

ALEXANDER THE GREAT

c. 450–100 BCE: La Tène Culture
A high point of Celtic civilization, the La Tène culture is named after an archaeological site found in La Tène in Switzerland. Its people produced intricate metalwork in bronze and gold.

THE BATTERSEA SHIELD

Timeline of the ancient world

Early humans lived in small groups, moving from place to place to find new sources of food. But with the development of farming, many groups began to settle down in fertile areas, forming larger communities.

The earliest towns and cities were built in Mesopotamia (in modern-day Iraq) and along the Nile in Egypt, more than 5,000 years ago. Centuries later, the cultures of the Greeks, Phoenicians, and Romans developed around the edges of the Mediterranean Sea. In Asia, civilizations sprang up on the shores of the Persian Gulf, around the Indus River in modern-day Pakistan, and along the Yangtze River in China. Ancient regions traded with each other, but they also competed for land and resources, leading to war, and the creation of the world's first empires.

STATUES OF RAMSES II AT ABU SIMBEL

c. 1550–1069 BCE: The New Kingdom
In New Kingdom Egypt, pharaohs were buried in hidden tombs in the Valley of the Kings. The New Kingdom pharaoh Ramses II ruled over Egypt for 66 years, and commanded the building of many statues in his image.

2055–1710 BCE: The Middle Kingdom
After a period of division, Egypt united under the pharaohs of the Middle Kingdom. Much of what we know about Egyptian daily life comes from art of this period.

MIDDLE KINGDOM TOMB MODEL

SAHELANTHROPUS TCHADENSIS

7–6 million years ago:
Sahelanthropus tchadensis
The earliest human ancestors to walk upright, *Sahelanthropus tchadensis* may have spent as much time up in the trees as they did on the ground.

HOMO ERECTUS

1.89 million years ago:
Homo erectus
Homo erectus were the first human ancestors to have similar bodies and limb sizes to those of modern humans. They used fire and developed hand-ax tools.

200,000 to 18,400 years ago:
Humans spread across the world
Modern humans traveled out of East Africa and eventually spread to every continent apart from Antarctica.

HUNTING A MAMMOTH IN NORTH AMERICA

27 BCE: The Roman Empire
Augustus became the first of many Roman emperors. At its greatest extent in 117 CE, the Roman Empire stretched from Spain and Britain to modern-day Syria and the Red Sea.

EMPEROR AUGUSTUS

9 CE: Germanic tribes defeat Rome
An alliance of Germanic tribes under the chieftain Arminius defeated Roman armies at the Battle of Teutoburg Forest.

ARMINIUS

476 CE: Fall of the Western Roman Empire
In 286 CE, the Roman Empire had split into western and eastern halves. In 476 CE, Romulus Augustulus, the last Western Roman Emperor, was overthrown by a Germanic king.

ROMULUS AUGUSTULUS

492–479 BCE: The Greco-Persian Wars
Darius I of the Persian Empire and his son Xerxes I launched invasions of Greece. Darius was defeated by an Athenian army, Xerxes by an alliance of city-states.

PERSIAN AND GREEK WARRIORS

c. 500–336 BCE: Classical Greece
The Greeks of the Classical Age made great advancements in philosophy, politics, and science, and developed the first theaters. Classical Greek culture spread throughout the Mediterranean.

ROMAN SOLDIER

c. 1200 BCE: The Phoenicians
The seafaring Phoenician civilization, based in modern-day Lebanon in the Middle East, began to dominate trade across the Mediterranean.

PHOENICIAN CARGO SHIP

559–330 BCE: The Persian Empire
The Persians of the Middle East conquered many lands, and their empire stretched from Egypt to northwest India. The Persians allowed conquered peoples to keep their customs and religions.

c. 510 BCE: The Roman Republic
The Romans overthrew their king, establishing the Roman Republic. It was governed by elected officials and the Senate, a council of nobles. Under the Republic, Rome became a great power across the Mediterranean.

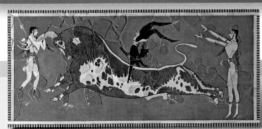

PAINTING OF BULL LEAPING, KNOSSOS

From c. 2500 BCE: The Indus trade with Mesopotamia
The people of the Indus Valley civilization in ancient India created trade routes with other cultures, such as the Sumerians of Mesopotamia.

INDUS STATUE OF A BULL

2900–1450 BCE: Minoan civilization
The earliest civilization in Europe, the Minoans built palaces such as Knossos on their island home of Crete, and set up trading centers across the Mediterranean.

KHAFRA

c. 9000 BCE: The first farmers
Some groups began to settle down and produce their own food rather than living by hunting and gathering. They grew plants to eat and tamed animals for meat and to work the land.

EARLY FARMING AX

c. 3300–3100 BCE: First cities in Mesopotamia
The earliest cities were established in Mesopotamia in the Middle East. The Mesopotamians developed rulership, religion, and a form of writing, known today as cuneiform, that was written on clay tablets.

CUNEIFORM TABLET

2686–2181 BCE: The Old Kingdom
During the period known as the Old Kingdom, the ancient Egyptians constructed pyramid tombs and other monuments for their pharaohs (ancient Egyptian rulers). The three greatest pyramids were the tombs of the pharaohs Khufu, Khafra, and Menkaure.

SAHELANTHROPUS TCHADENSIS

Region: Africa

Period: 7–6 million years ago

The earliest apes that walked upright, *Sahelanthropus tchadensis* lived in western Central Africa, in a region of lakes, forests, and grassy woodland. Although they could walk upright, they may have spent just as much time in the trees as on the ground.

AUSTRALOPITHECUS AFARENSIS

Region: Africa

Period: 3.85–2.95 million years ago

Like their ancestors *Sahelanthropus, Australopithecus afarensis* could still climb trees, but they were better adapted to living in East Africa's grasslands. Their improved upright stance meant they could run faster and see predators and prey across open plains.

HOMO HABILIS

Region: Africa

Period: 2.4–1.4 million years ago

Homo habilis (meaning "handy man") had brains that were 50 percent larger than those of *Australopithecus.* They made simple stone choppers by striking river pebbles with other stones to make a cutting edge.

Human ancestors

Modern humans are the only survivors of a family of apes that walked upright. These apes are called hominins, and they first appeared in Africa around seven million years ago.

Hominins diverged from other primates that would later evolve into human's closest living relative, the chimpanzee. There were many species of hominins, but only some are the ancestors of modern humans. Over millions of years, they began to walk on two legs, evolved increasingly larger brains, started to make tools, and learned to control fire. These adaptations, as well as many others, were passed on to modern humans.

Standing upright
Like today's humans, *Homo erectus* would have stood upright.

Long legs
Homo erectus could run away from predators using their long legs.

Eyes
Homo erectus may have evolved whites to their eyes, which would have improved their vision.

Cooked meat
Homo erectus ate meat, and may have also cooked it. This increased energy intake and fueled brain growth.

Staying cool
Homo erectus could keep cool better than earlier hominins as they had less body hair and bigger sweat glands.

Fire
Fire provided warmth, light, and protection from predators.

Humans were the only species in their
family to spread all over the world.

99% The percentage of DNA humans share with
their closest living relative, the chimpanzee.

11

HOMO ERECTUS

Region: Africa, Asia
Period: 1.8 million years ago–143,000 years ago

Homo erectus (meaning "upright man") were the first hominins with similar bodies and limb sizes to those of modern humans. They learned to control fire and invented a new kind of stone tool, a hand ax with a diamond-shaped blade.

Child
Homo erectus had a short childhood and reached puberty by the age of 12.

Digging tool
Homo erectus may have used sticks to dig for roots and tubers to eat.

Strong jaw
Strong muscles in *Homo erectus'* mouth helped to chew tough food.

Hand tool
Homo erectus used diamond-shaped tools to skin their prey.

Sculptures
Modern scientists have discovered that *Homo erectus* sculpted figures out of rock.

HOMO HEIDELBERGENSIS

Region: Europe, Africa
Period: 700,000–200,000 years ago

Homo heidelbergensis were named after Heidelberg in Germany, where their remains were first found in 1908. They hunted large animals, such as elephants, using spears. They were the first hominins to adapt to colder climates and build shelters.

HOMO NEANDERTHALENSIS

Region: Europe, Asia
Period: 400,000–40,000 years ago

Neanderthals, modern humans' closest relatives, were named after the Neander valley in Germany where fossils were discovered in 1856. Neanderthals were skilled toolmakers, wore clothes of animal skin, painted cave art, and buried their dead.

HOMO SAPIENS

Region: Worldwide
Period: 300,000 years ago–present

Our species, *Homo sapiens* (meaning "thinking man"), is the most versatile hominin. From African origins, we spread throughout the world, eventually replacing all other hominin species. We developed language and writing, which allowed us to communicate and work together in large groups.

12 the ancient world ○ **OUT OF AFRICA**

200,000 The **number of years** it took for **humans to spread all over the world,** except Antarctica.

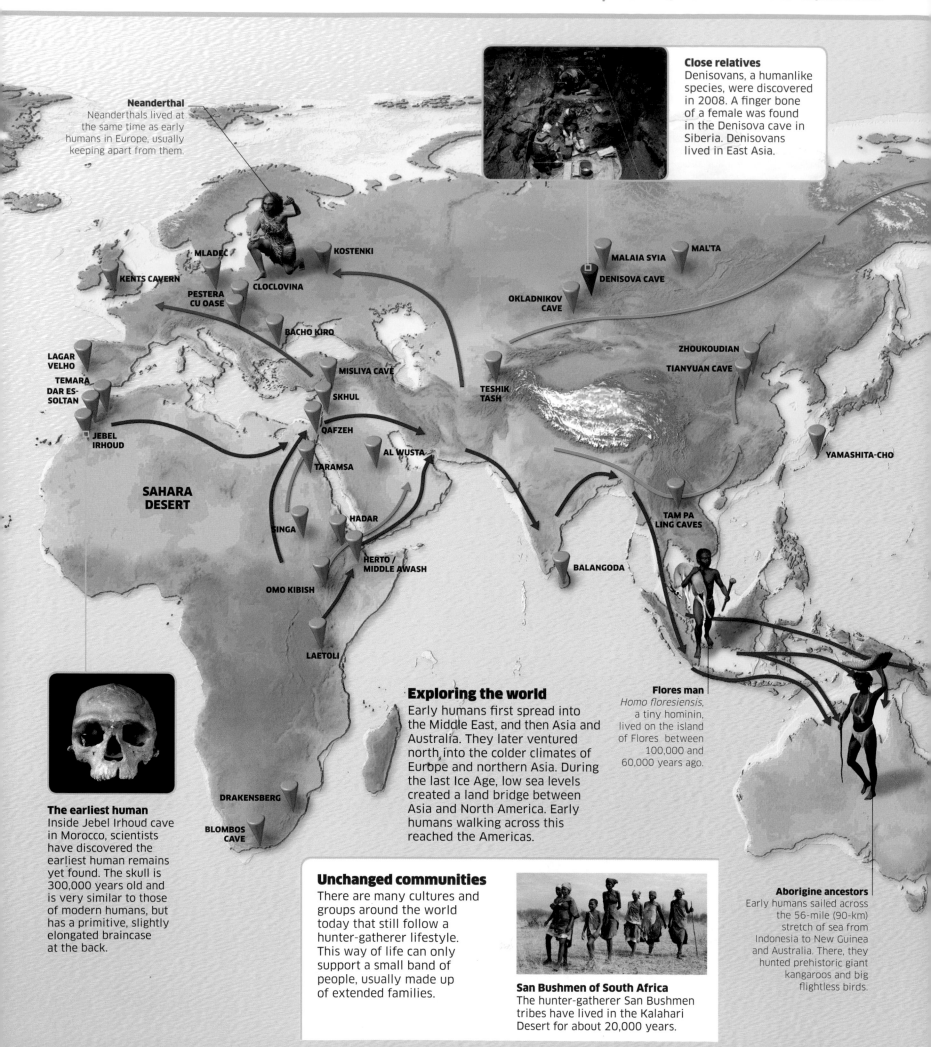

Close relatives
Denisovans, a humanlike species, were discovered in 2008. A finger bone of a female was found in the Denisova cave in Siberia. Denisovans lived in East Asia.

Neanderthal
Neanderthals lived at the same time as early humans in Europe, usually keeping apart from them.

MLADEC
KOSTENKI
MALAIA SYIA
MAL'TA
DENISOVA CAVE
KENTS CAVERN
CLOCLOVINA
OKLADNIKOV CAVE
PESTERA CU OASE
BACHO KIRO
ZHOUKOUDIAN
TIANYUAN CAVE
LAGAR VELHO
MISLIYA CAVE
TEMARA DAR ES-SOLTAN
SKHUL
TESHIK TASH
JEBEL IRHOUD
QAFZEH
AL WUSTA
YAMASHITA-CHO
TARAMSA

SAHARA DESERT

SINGA
HADAR
TAM PA LING CAVES
HERTO / MIDDLE AWASH
BALANGODA
OMO KIBISH

Flores man
Homo floresiensis, a tiny hominin, lived on the island of Flores between 100,000 and 60,000 years ago.

Exploring the world
Early humans first spread into the Middle East, and then Asia and Australia. They later ventured north into the colder climates of Europe and northern Asia. During the last Ice Age, low sea levels created a land bridge between Asia and North America. Early humans walking across this reached the Americas.

LAETOLI

DRAKENSBERG

BLOMBOS CAVE

The earliest human
Inside Jebel Irhoud cave in Morocco, scientists have discovered the earliest human remains yet found. The skull is 300,000 years old and is very similar to those of modern humans, but has a primitive, slightly elongated braincase at the back.

Unchanged communities
There are many cultures and groups around the world today that still follow a hunter-gatherer lifestyle. This way of life can only support a small band of people, usually made up of extended families.

San Bushmen of South Africa
The hunter-gatherer San Bushmen tribes have lived in the Kalahari Desert for about 20,000 years.

Aborigine ancestors
Early humans sailed across the 56-mile (90-km) stretch of sea from Indonesia to New Guinea and Australia. There, they hunted prehistoric giant kangaroos and big flightless birds.

Humans sailed to Australia
on rafts made of bamboo.

Early humans reached some large islands, such as modern-day
Britain and the islands of Japan, by walking over land bridges.

13

Hunting
Early humans walked across
a land bridge from Asia to
North America, possibly
following herds of animals.

Out of Africa

The first humans evolved in Africa 300,000 years ago. When the climate in the previously impassable Sahara Desert briefly turned wetter 100,000 years later, they started to explore elsewhere.

When humans migrated out of Africa, they shared the planet with several different kinds of humanlike species called hominins. The most common were the Neanderthals in Europe and western Asia and the Denisovans in East Asia. All early humans were hunter-gatherers. They moved from place to place as they searched for fresh sources of food. This lifestyle meant early humans were great travelers. Humans' ability to travel and adapt to changing environments meant they survived while all other hominins went extinct by about 40,000 years ago. Over many generations, early humans gradually traveled further and further. By 15,000 years ago, humans had spread into every continent (except Antarctica).

CALGARY

MANIS

ANZICK
CHILD

PAISLEY
5-MILE
POINT

MEADOWCROFT

BUTTERMILK CREEK
COMPLEX

Using tools
The earliest known
North Americans were
the Clovis people.
They were toolmakers,
and made distinctive
diamond shaped blades.

YUCATAN
CAVES

Key

→ Between 194,000 and
88,000 years ago

→ Between 120,000 and
45,000 years ago

→ Between 80,000 and
40,000 years ago

→ Between 50,000 and
25,000 years ago

→ Between 18,000 and
15,000 years ago

▮ Land during low
sea levels

▼ Fossil sites of
early humans

HUACA PRIETA

PEDRA FURADA

CUNCAICHA

CUEVA BAUTISTA

MONTE
VERDE

Mixing populations

Scientists have studied and compared DNA of modern humans and DNA extracted from the remains of other hominin species. They have discovered that we share many genes with these hominins. As early humans left Africa and came into contact with other hominins, we interbred with them. Modern humans are the result of this interbreeding.

NEANDERTHAL

HUMANS

Early humans

Earth was undergoing an Ice Age between 60,000 and 40,000 years ago. Early humans living in Europe and northern Asia at that time experienced a cold and dry climate, and much of Europe and Asia were covered with steppes (treeless grasslands).

Early humans lived in small groups of between 25 and 50 people. They kept on the move and lived in temporary shelters. There were no leaders, and men and women were equally important. While men hunted large animals, women gathered plant foods and cared for children. Early humans made a wide range of tools, including bone needles for sewing and harpoons for fishing. Because they traveled from place to place, early humans came into contact with a range of foods and as a result they had a varied diet. They were also very adaptable to changes in the climate.

Hunting woolly mammoths

During the Ice Age, early humans hunted woolly mammoths and other large mammals on the steppes of Europe and Asia. Mammoths provided them with meat, skin for clothing, and bones and tusks to build shelters and make spears.

Hut
Some early humans made huts from mammoth bones and skin.

Spear
These early humans made spears tipped with mammoth-tusk blades.

Clothes
Early humans wore thick clothing sewn together from animal skin and furs.

CAVE ART

About 40,000 years ago, early humans started to paint animals in caves. Cave art has been found in Europe, Africa, and Australia. Early humans painted using fingers smeared with red ocher (clay) and sticks dipped in charcoal. Prehistoric art is evidence for the first humans' ability to imagine and create.

Lascaux cave paintings
These 20,000-year-old paintings of horses and aurochs (wild cattle) are from the Lascaux cave in France.

73,000 years old—the **age of the earliest drawing discovered** so far.

Humans' **close relatives, the Neanderthals, also painted cave art**.

15

Tusks
Mammoths used their tusks, which could grow up to 16 ft (5 m) long, to defend themselves against attacking humans.

Fur
Mammoths were covered with a coat of long hair over a thick layer of fat.

43,000-year-old flutes made from ivory and bone found in Germany in 2012 are the earliest known musical instruments.

Jewelry
Early humans wore necklaces made from animal bones and teeth, sea shells, or beads. Necklaces made of sea shells have been found far from the sea, showing that early humans traveled great distances.

Hunters
To bring down large animals, early humans hunted together in groups.

CLOTHING

Early humans wore clothing made from animal skins, sewn together with bone needles. Clothes were worn for display as well as for protection from the cold. A man buried 30,000 years ago near modern-day Sunghir in Russia was found wearing around 3,000 mammoth ivory beads, which had been sewn onto his clothing. He also wore a cap decorated with fox teeth.

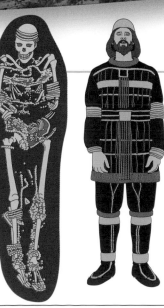

LANGUAGE

Humans have a hyoid bone that anchors the tongue, allowing them to make a wide range of vocal sounds. Neanderthals also had a hyoid bone. Although both species were capable of speech, it is likely that early humans used language in more complex ways.

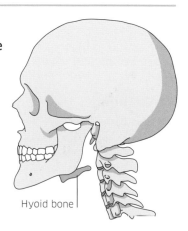

Hyoid bone

16 the ancient world • THE FIRST FARMERS

35,000 years ago—**dogs** were **first tamed** by humans.

The first farmers

By around 9000 BCE, the way humans lived had begun to change. Instead of constantly being on the move, hunting wild animals and gathering wild plants, humans started to produce their own sources of food by farming.

People started to plant seeds in fertile soil and grow crops. They also learned to domesticate (tame and raise) animals, such as sheep and goats, for food or to help them tend to crops. This was the beginning of farming. Farming could produce much more food than hunting and gathering, so many humans started to settle down in permanent villages to be close to their crops. If farmers produced more food than they needed at the time, they stored it to be eaten when food was hard to come by. This meant that farming produced more reliable supplies of food than hunting and gathering.

CHANGE IN DIET

Though farming was more productive than hunting and gathering, farmers ate a less varied diet. Early farmers lived on a few staple crops, such as grain, which lacked important vitamins and minerals. Early farmers were prone to diseases caused by a lack of nutrition.

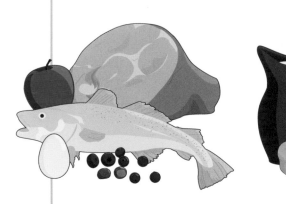

What hunter-gatherers ate
Hunter-gatherers had a varied diet, including red meat, fish, and plants rich in nutrients.

What farmers ate
Farmers had a small selection of foods, such as grains, which they ate every day.

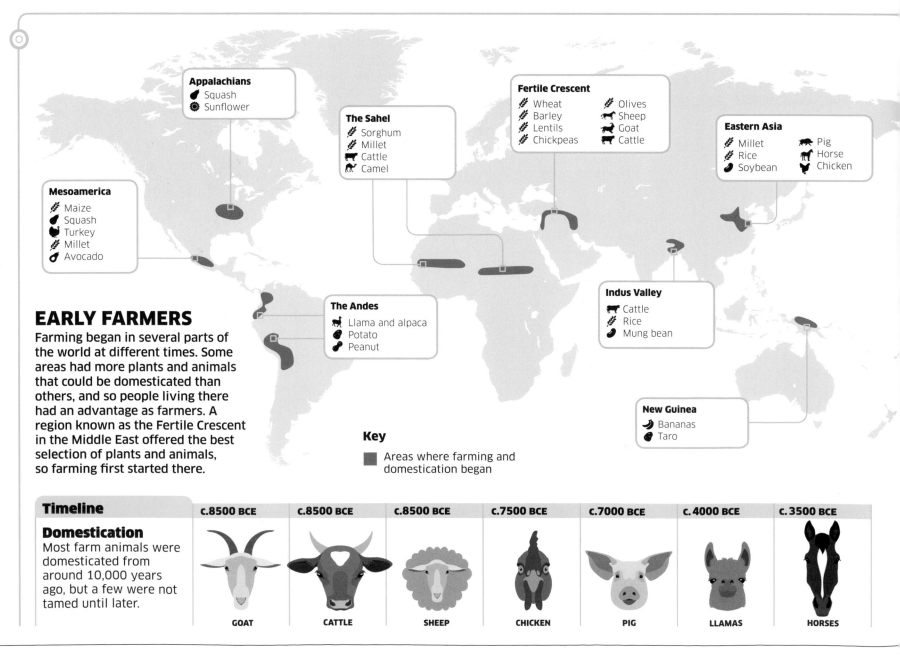

Appalachians
- Squash
- Sunflower

The Sahel
- Sorghum
- Millet
- Cattle
- Camel

Fertile Crescent
- Wheat
- Barley
- Lentils
- Chickpeas
- Olives
- Sheep
- Goat
- Cattle

Eastern Asia
- Millet
- Rice
- Soybean
- Pig
- Horse
- Chicken

Mesoamerica
- Maize
- Squash
- Turkey
- Millet
- Avocado

The Andes
- Llama and alpaca
- Potato
- Peanut

Indus Valley
- Cattle
- Rice
- Mung bean

New Guinea
- Bananas
- Taro

EARLY FARMERS

Farming began in several parts of the world at different times. Some areas had more plants and animals that could be domesticated than others, and so people living there had an advantage as farmers. A region known as the Fertile Crescent in the Middle East offered the best selection of plants and animals, so farming first started there.

Key

■ Areas where farming and domestication began

Timeline	c.8500 BCE	c.8500 BCE	c.8500 BCE	c.7500 BCE	c.7000 BCE	c.4000 BCE	c.3500 BCE
Domestication Most farm animals were domesticated from around 10,000 years ago, but a few were not tamed until later.	GOAT	CATTLE	SHEEP	CHICKEN	PIG	LLAMAS	HORSES

EARLY TOOLS

Living in one place allowed people to use heavier tools, as they didn't have to carry them around. They also began to make pottery, which was too fragile and heavy for wandering tribes to transport. Early farmers sharpened pieces of flint to make sickles and axes.

Pottery
Pots allowed people to boil food, make stews, and store and contain food.

Sickle
Farmers harvested grains using sickles that had blades of flint.

Ax
Stone-bladed axes were used to cut down trees and clear the land for growing crops.

Quern
People ground grain using two stones, which together were called a quern.

MEASURING TIME

Farmers needed to know when to plant their crops. They measured the passing seasons by keeping track of the sun and the stars. In Egypt, farming depended on the yearly flooding of the Nile River. Egyptian farmers learned that when they saw the bright star Sirius rising each August, the Nile flood would soon follow.

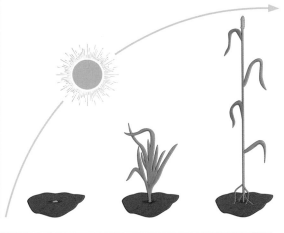

WILD SHEEP

DOMESTIC SHEEP

Selective breeding

When farmers bred animals, they picked those that were easiest to manage to mate with each other. Domesticated animals became smaller and less aggressive than their wild ancestors. Farmers also desired certain qualities in their animals. They picked wild sheep with the thickest fur and smallest horns for breeding. Over time, the wild sheep's descendants gained thick, woolly coats and their horns got even smaller.

FIRST SETTLEMENTS

Farming villages grew bigger until they became towns. The first town appeared in West Asia 10,000 years ago. The people of these early towns kept sheep, goats, and cattle and grew wheat, barley, and pulses. Towns were also craft centers, where textiles, pottery, and jewelry were manufactured.

Entrance
Houses were entered through the roof.

Loom
Craftwork, such as weaving, took place on the rooftops.

House
Made of mud and bricks, houses were tightly packed together.

Cattle
Cattle were kept in pens and used for carrying heavy items or food.

Çatalhöyük
One of the world's earliest towns was Çatalhöyük in modern-day Turkey, lasting from 7400 to 6200 BCE. It had a population of several thousand people.

Population growth

As people settled in one place and started to produce more food than they could eat, populations grew.

Cooperation

Farmers had to learn to cooperate with one another. Many farmers working together on large farms could produce more food.

Warfare

There was a sharp rise in violent conflict as different groups fought to defend their food and land.

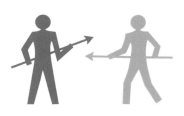

Göbekli Tepe

The earliest megalithic structure that has been discovered, Göbekli Tepe in present-day Turkey, was built in c. 10,000 BCE and is made up of at least 20 circular structures. Only two structures are shown here. Unlike later megaliths, it was built by hunter-gatherers who had only just started to farm.

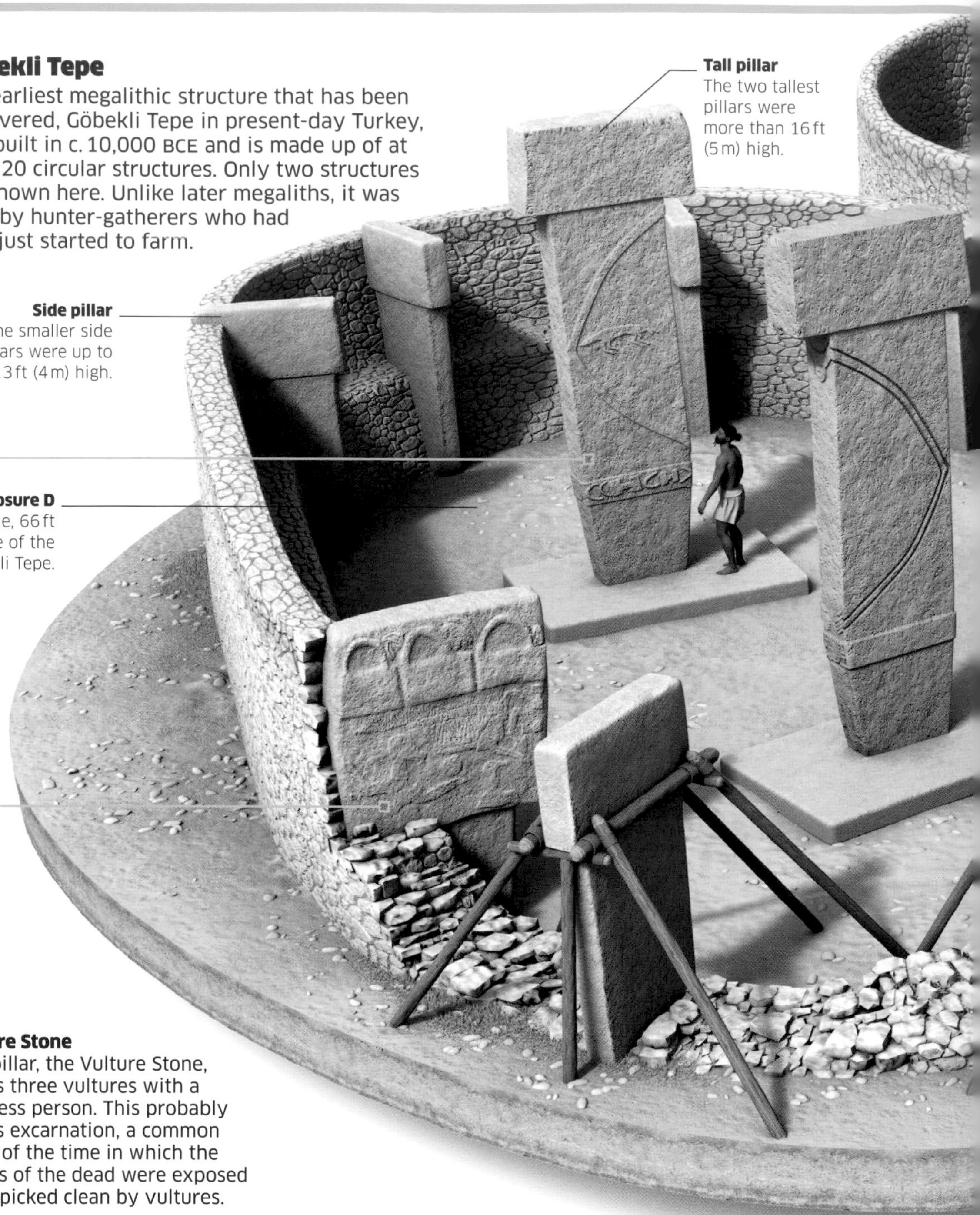

Tall pillar
The two tallest pillars were more than 16 ft (5 m) high.

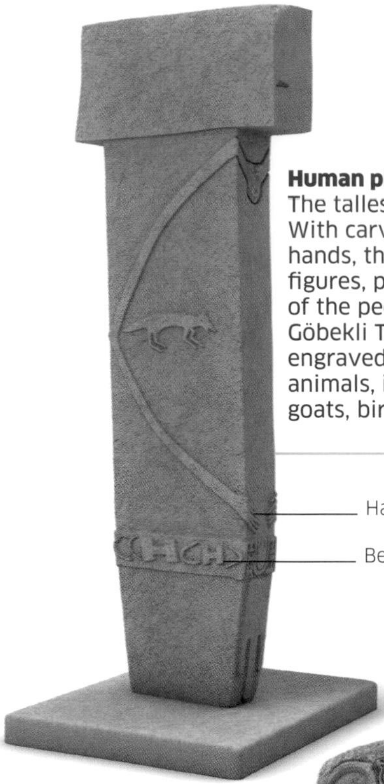

Human pillar
The tallest pillars are T-shaped. With carved belts, arms, and hands, these represent human figures, possibly the ancestors of the people who made Göbekli Tepe. Many stones are engraved with images of wild animals, including lions, snakes, goats, birds, and insects.

Hand

Belt

Side pillar
The smaller side pillars were up to 13 ft (4 m) high.

Enclosure D
This circular temple, 66 ft (20 m) across, is one of the biggest at Göbekli Tepe.

The vulture may be holding the head of a person.

A scorpion climbs up toward the vultures.

Headless body

Vulture Stone
This pillar, the Vulture Stone, shows three vultures with a headless person. This probably shows excarnation, a common ritual of the time in which the bodies of the dead were exposed to be picked clean by vultures.

CARNAC

Location: France
Date: 4500–3300 BCE

At Carnac, early people erected more than 3,000 standing stones in rows that stretch for many miles. The stones are 3 ft (0.9 m) to 7¾ ft (2.4 m) tall. Their purpose remains a mystery, but it is possible that each stone represents an ancestor whose spirit was thought to live on inside it.

GGANTIJA

Location: Malta
Date: c. 3600–3200 BCE

Early people built the temple of Ggantija in Malta so that the structure aligned with the sunrise during the equinoxes (when day and night are equal in length). On these dates, in March and September, the rising sun illuminates the temple's central chamber.

NEWGRANGE

Location: Ireland
Date: c. 3200 BCE

Newgrange contains a long, underground passage that leads to a central burial chamber. Early people carefully designed Newgrange so that, on the winter solstice (the shortest day of the year), the rising sun would shine through the passage and light up the burial chamber.

140 miles (225 km)—the **distance** some **stones** were **moved** from **Wales** to **Stonehenge**.

19

Inner wall
This enclosure featured a secondary wall.

Entrance
Early people could enter this enclosure through a short corridor.

Wooden rollers
The stones were hauled to the site, maybe with the help of wooden rollers. Though quarried nearby, they had to be dragged uphill over rough, rocky ground.

Carver
Each pillar was carved with designs before it was put into place.

Clothes
Early people likely wore simple clothes such as cloths.

Walls
Like the pillars, the walls were made of blocks of local limestone with clay mortar.

Ancient megaliths

Around 12,000 years ago, people started to build the world's first large monuments called megaliths (Greek for "big stone").

Megaliths can be found all over the world. In Europe and western Asia, they were built to be communal tombs, and alignments of standing stones whose purpose remains a mystery. Others may have been temples. They are the first instances of permanent structures. Early people were probably strongly aware of their ancestors, who were felt to still be present after their deaths. Standing stones may have been set up to honor or worship them. Builders often aligned their megaliths with sunrises and sunsets at certain times of the year—but the reasons for this are not yet known.

RUJM EL-HIRI
Location: Syria/Israel
Date: 3000–2700 BCE

Rujm el-Hiri is made up of five circular stone walls that encircle one another, the largest measuring 525 ft (160 m) across. Its purpose remains a mystery, though some features line up with the sunrise during specific dates of the year. Early people later built a burial ground that stands in the center.

STONEHENGE
Location: England
Date: 3000–2000 BCE

At Stonehenge, builders set up huge, locally quarried stones in a circle of trilithons (two upright stones and a horizontal stone on top). This enclosed a circle of smaller stones that are thought to come from Wales, more than a hundred miles away. Like Newgrange, it is aligned with the winter solstice sunrise.

KOREAN DOLMEN FIELDS
Location: North and South Korea
Date: c. 700–200 BCE

A dolmen is a tomb made of three or more huge stones arranged to resemble a table, commonly covered with a mound of earth. Though the earliest dolmens are found in western Europe, many more were built in Korea. The earth mounds that once covered the dolmens have since been worn away by wind and rain.

NINEVEH

ASSUR

The god Ashur
The main temple to the chief god of the Assyrians, Ashur, was based in Assur, the original capital city of the empire. Ashur was sometimes depicted as an archer inside a winged disk.

Royal hunt
Assyrian king Ashurbanipal's palace at Nineveh was decorated with reliefs showing him hunting lions. Killing lions was seen as a way of displaying royal power.

Hammurabi's law code
In 1754 BCE, King Hammurabi of Babylon had a famous law code carved onto a stele (a stone slab). At the top it showed the king receiving the laws from Shamash, god of justice.

BABYLON

AKKAD

EUPHRATES

Mesopotamia

The word Mesopotamia means "the land between two rivers" in ancient Greek. This word is now used to refer to a region of the ancient Middle East around the Tigris and Euphrates rivers, in modern-day Iraq. The people who lived here in ancient times, known today as the Mesopotamians, built the world's first cities more than 5,000 years ago.

The inhabitants of early Mesopotamia were not a unified people. The first cities were built in Sumer, a region of southern Mesopotamia. The Sumerians were later conquered by people from empires in the north—the Akkadians, the Babylonians, and the Assyrians. Through these conflicts, the people of Mesopotamia developed the first armies, but they also invented many of the fundamental features of civilization, such as monarchies and organized religion.

Sargon of Akkad
Historians believe this copper head shows Sargon of Akkad, the first ruler of the Akkadian Empire, or possibly his grandson, Naram-Sin.

Timeline

The history of Mesopotamia

Various empires sprang up in ancient Mesopotamia through a series of conflicts over thousands of years. Cities fought with each other for dominance, while foreign peoples arrived as invaders. The last invasion was by the Persians, who took control of the region and made it a part of their empire.

c. 6000–4000 BCE

First farmers
Farming people from northern Mesopotamia moved south, into the flat southern plains of Sumer. They worked together to irrigate their fields, building canals, dykes, and reservoirs to store water. Over time, villages grew larger, and some people began to specialize in a single trade or craft. By 4500 BCE, the Mesopotamians had developed the potter's wheel.

c. 3300–3100 BCE

City-states emerge
Around a dozen cities emerged in Sumer. Each was governed by an ensi (ruler) who claimed to reign on behalf of the local god. The Sumerians developed a writing system known today as cuneiform (meaning "wedge-shaped"), made up of marks imprinted on clay tablets.

CUNEIFORM TABLET

c. 3000 BCE

Sumerian bronze
The Sumerians learned that by mixing two soft metals, copper and tin, they could create a harder metal, called bronze. They used it to make tools, weapons, and pots, and to create sculptures. The land of Mesopotamia had no metals that could be mined from under the earth, so the tin and copper needed to make bronze had to be imported from other lands.

c. 2325 BCE

The Akkadian Empire
King Sargon of Akkad conquered all of Sumer, establishing the Akkadian Empire. The language of Akkadian, which is related to modern-day Arabic and Hebrew, gradually replaced Sumerian. Even the Sumerian gods were given new Akkadian names. For example, Nanna, chief god of Ur, was renamed Sin.

The tombs of the **kings and queens** of the city of Ur were filled with **many treasures**.

907 The **number of signs** in the Assyrian **cuneiform language**.

21

Mesopotamian empires

Assyria in the north and Babylon further south created large empires that covered the whole of Mesopotamia. These two empires battled for control of the region. This map shows the growth of the Assyrian Empire from 859–669 BCE, and the extent of the Babylonian Empire when it finally fell to the invading armies of the Persian Empire in 539 BCE.

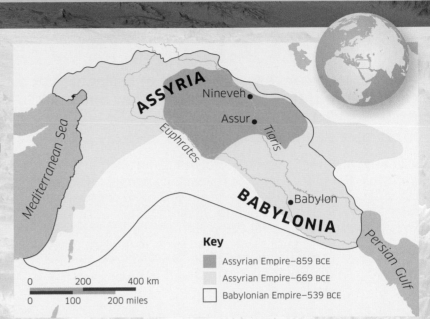

Key

	Assyrian Empire–859 BCE
	Assyrian Empire–669 BCE
	Babylonian Empire–539 BCE

ZAGROS MOUNTAINS

TIGRIS

Battle of Lagash
One of the earliest recorded battles was fought between the cities of Lagash and Umma in around 2450 BCE. Lagash won the battle.

Ancient Mesopotamia
The fertile lands around the Tigris and Euphrates were ideal for farming, and the people of ancient Mesopotamia built their cities close to the rivers and the coast. However, the lands of Mesopotamia lacked many raw materials. Stone, timber, and metals all had to be imported from distant lands.

Ziggurat of Ur
Each Sumerian city had its own patron god, worshipped in a huge temple called a ziggurat. The ziggurat of Ur was the temple of Nanna, the moon god.

LAGASH

UMMA

URUK

UR

PERSIAN GULF

Gilgamesh
The *Epic of Gilgamesh*, written before 2000 BCE, is the world's oldest surviving story. It tells of the adventures of Gilgamesh, a mythical king of Uruk.

---

c. 1900 BCE

The Babylonian Empire
The Amorites, a people from the western deserts, conquered most of Mesopotamia. They ruled from the city of Babylon, and the empire they created is known as the Babylonian Empire. Even after the Amorite Dynasty was overthrown, in 1595 BCE, Babylon remained an important city.

c. 1595–1530 BCE

HITTITES ON A CHARIOT

Hittites and Kassites
Two foreign peoples, the Hittites and Kassites, invaded Babylonia, introducing fast chariots pulled by horses. The Kassites ruled Babylon for around 500 years.

c. 911–609 BCE

GUARDIAN STATUE AT AN ASSYRIAN ROYAL PALACE AT DUR-SHARRUKIN

The Assyrian Empire
The warlike Assyrians from the north conquered Mesopotamia, creating an empire stretching from Egypt to modern-day Iran. They spoke Aramaic, which became the standard language across the Middle East.

612 BCE

The fall of Assyria
The cruelty of the Assyrians led to widespread rebellions against their rule. They were finally overthrown by Nabopolassar, the ruler of Babylon, in alliance with the Medes people from the east of Mesopotamia. In 612 BCE, Nabopolassar destroyed the Assyrian cities. Babylon became the capital of a second Babylonian empire.

539 BCE

Babylon conquered
King Cyrus the Great of Persia conquered the Babylonian Empire. Cyrus named himself "king of Babylon, king of Sumer and Akkad, king of the four quarters of the world." Under his rule, Babylon remained the most important Mesopotamian city.

Ancient Egypt

Five thousand years ago, the people of ancient Egypt created the world's first united state. They invented writing, created beautiful works of art, and built tombs and temples, some of which still stand today.

Ancient Egypt was the world's longest lasting and most stable civilization. For more than 3,000 years, its people spoke the same language, worshipped the same gods, and dressed in similar linen clothing. Throughout this time, they were led by rulers, called pharaohs, who were seen as living representatives of the gods. Life in Egypt followed an orderly pattern of work and religious festivals, with the cycle of the Egyptian year governed by the annual flooding of the Nile River.

EMPIRE ON THE NILE

The ancient Egyptians built their empire in the desert alongside the Nile River. For most of their history, the desert landscape protected the Egyptians from foreign invaders. Originally, there were two states: Upper Egypt in the south, and Lower Egypt in the north. Long after Egypt was united, a pharaoh could still be called "Lord of the Two Lands" and symbolized this by wearing a double crown.

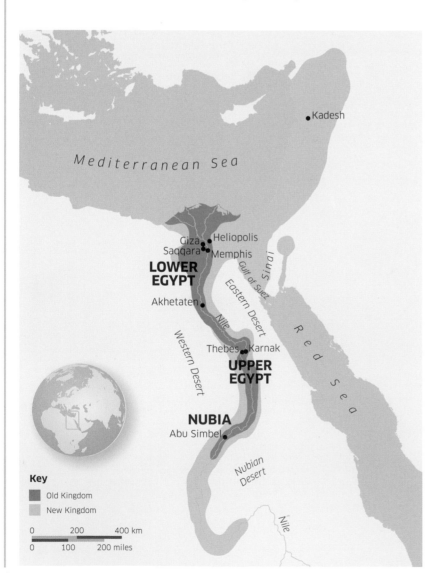

Mediterranean Sea

Kadesh

Giza • Heliopolis
Saqqara • Memphis
LOWER EGYPT
Akhetaten •

Gulf of Suez
Sinai
Eastern Desert
Western Desert
Nile

Thebes • Karnak
UPPER EGYPT

Red Sea

NUBIA
Abu Simbel •

Nubian Desert

Nile

Key
■ Old Kingdom
■ New Kingdom

0   200   400 km
0   100   200 miles

POWERFUL PHARAOHS

Every pharaoh wanted to be remembered long after their own time. They built statues of themselves and filled temples with reliefs showing them conducting religious ceremonies or leading their armies. After their deaths, they were worshipped as gods.

Khafra
Pharaoh Khafra (2558–2532 BCE) built the Great Sphinx—a statue of a lion with the pharaoh's own face.

TOMBS OF THE PHARAOHS

The dead pharaohs of the Old Kingdom were buried in massive stone tombs called pyramids, but the New Kingdom pharaohs were buried in tombs hidden underground.

Early pyramids

The first pyramid was built for Pharaoh Djoser around 2650 BCE, and is thought to have been designed by Imhotep, Djoser's vizier (chief minister).

IMHOTEP

Djoser's pyramid
Historians believe that this pyramid, built with stepped levels, was the first large structure in the world to be made of stone rather than mud bricks.

Pharaoh, meaning "**great house**", was a respectful way of referring to the king.

479 ft (146 m)—the height of Pharaoh Khufu's pyramid.

23

Mentuhotep II
Reuniting Egypt after a period of strife, Mentuhotep II (2055–2004 BCE) founded the Middle Kingdom.

Hatshepsut
A powerful queen, Hatshepsut (1473–1458 BCE) ruled Egypt in her own right as pharaoh.

Thutmose III
The warrior king Thutmose III (1479–1426 BCE) conquered an empire in Asia.

Great Pyramid of Khufu
After Djoser, pharaohs built pyramids with smooth sides. The largest was Khufu's pyramid at Giza, which is still the world's biggest stone building. This is also the only pyramid with a burial chamber high up inside the structure rather than at the bottom.

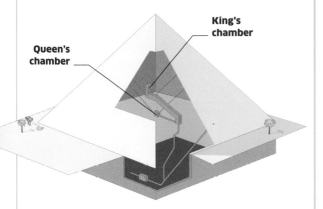

King's chamber

Queen's chamber

Inside the pyramid
Khufu's pyramid has a complex internal structure with at least three chambers, a grand gallery, and two mysterious air shafts.

The Valley of the Kings
The burial place of New Kingdom pharaohs was the Valley of the Kings, in the desert west of their capital, Thebes. These tombs were almost all robbed of their treasures in ancient times.

Treasures of Tutankhamun
The only unrobbed tomb was that of Tutankhamun, a pharaoh in the 14th century BCE. His tomb was found by British archaeologist Howard Carter in 1922, still filled with treasures.

DEATH MASK OF TUTANKHAMUN

HIEROGLYPHICS
Around 3300 BCE, the Egyptians invented the world's first writing system, now called hieroglyphics. They used picture signs that stood for ideas, sounds, and words, which could also be made up of a combination of signs. Scribes could write either from left to right or right to left. Hieroglyphics were read depending on which way the faces of the symbols were looking; if they faced the right, the text was read from right to left.

MUMMY

FESTIVAL

RIVER

TOMB

PRIEST

Cartouche
A cartouche is an oval with a horizontal line at one end. Cartouches were used to show that the text within them was a royal title—in this case the name of Pharaoh Ramses II.

History of ancient Egypt
Egypt's long history is divided into three main periods: the Old, Middle, and New kingdoms. Ancient Egyptian historians recorded the names of pharaohs and listed them in numbered dynasties.

c. 3100 BCE — Egypt united
Previously two kingdoms, Egypt was first united by the pharaoh Narmer, commemorated on this palette wearing the crowns of Upper and Lower Egypt.

NARMER PALETTE

2686–2181 BCE — The Old Kingdom
During the Old Kingdom, pharaohs ruled from Memphis and built pyramid tombs and monuments at Giza. Huge numbers of people built the pyramids.

GREAT SPHINX OF GIZA

2055–1710 BCE — The Middle Kingdom
After a 26-year period of division, Egypt was reunited by the pharaohs of the Middle Kingdom. The period is remembered for beautiful art and poetry, much of which depicted Egyptian daily life.

1650 BCE — Kingdom invaded
The Hyksos moved into northern Egypt from western Asia, destroying the Middle Kingdom. They ruled the north while Egyptian pharaohs ruled the south.

c. 1550 BCE — The New Kingdom begins
Ahmose, ruler of Thebes, drove out the Hyksos and reunited Egypt, founding the New Kingdom. The Theban god Amun became the chief Egyptian god.

1352–1336 BCE — Sun worship
The pharaoh Akhenaten introduced a new religion, making the Egyptians worship the Aten, the solar disk. He built a new capital called Akhetaten, with open-air temples for sun worship.

WORSHIPPING THE SUN

1279–1213 BCE — The great pharaoh
Ramses II ruled for 66 years and fathered around 100 children. He famously fought a battle at Kadesh against the Hittites that he claimed to have won single-handedly from his chariot.

664–332 BCE — Late Period
Egypt's power waned as the country was conquered by a series of foreign powers. Three thousand years of Egyptian rule ended in 332 BCE, when Egypt was conquered by Alexander the Great.

24 the ancient world ○ EGYPTIAN RELIGION

The name **Ramses** means "born of Ra," another name for the sun god Re.

Egyptian gods and goddesses

There were many Egyptian gods, who might be depicted in different forms, as humans, animals, or a mixture of the two. Over time, some gods were combined, creating new gods. In the New Kingdom, for example, Re, the sun god, merged with Horus, becoming Re-Horakhty.

Osiris
Usually depicted as a mummy, the king of the dead's green skin represented new life.

Isis
A protector, magician, and mother, Isis was crowned with a sun disk or cattle horns.

Set
The god of the desert, disorder, and storms, Set was depicted with the head of an animal.

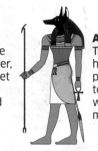

Anubis
The jackal-headed Anubis protected tombs and watched over mummification.

Thoth
The god of writing had the head of an ibis, a bird whose beak resembled a reed pen.

Bast
The protector goddess had the head of a cat, an animal that killed pests in the home.

The Egyptian afterlife

Egyptians believed that they could live again in Osiris's kingdom after death—yet their souls would still need a physical body, kept in a tomb, as a place to live. Those who could afford it therefore had their bodies preserved by mummification.

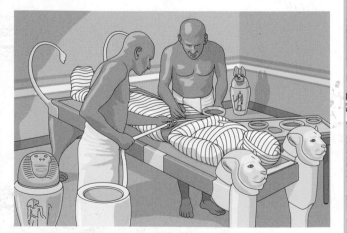

Preserving the dead
After the inner organs were removed, the body was dried with natron (a salt), then stuffed and wrapped in bandages.

Re-Horakhty
A statue of Re-Horakhty stands in the alcove above the entrance.

Royal family
Around the pharaoh's legs stand small statues of his wife, mother, and children.

Royal wedding
A carving in stone depicts Ramses' wedding to a Hittite princess.

Abu Simbel

South of Egypt, in Nubia, Pharaoh Ramses II had a great temple carved out of solid rock. It was dedicated to the gods Ptah, Amun, and Re-Horakhty, and to the pharaoh himself, who was worshipped alongside them. By claiming equal status with the gods, Ramses meant to impress the Nubians with his great power.

2,000 At least this many **gods were worshipped** by the ancient Egyptians.

65 ft (20m)—the height of each of the **four statues of Ramses**.

25

Sanctuary
The temple was aligned so that twice a year, during February and October, the rising sun shone into the sanctuary, lighting up the statues of Re-Horakhty, Ramses, and Amun. The statue of Ptah, on the left of this image, was always shrouded in darkness.

Side chambers
These were used for storing documents, ritual tools, food, and sacrifices.

Pharaoh's crowns
Ramses wears the double crown of Upper (southern) and Lower (northern) Egypt.

Small pillared hall
Each day, priests brought offerings to this small hall in front of the sanctuary.

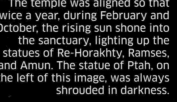

"**Ramses, chosen of Re, beloved of Amun, given life forever.**"

Abu Simbel inscription

Large pillared hall
The hall is lined with eight 30 ft (9m) tall statues of Ramses, depicted as Osiris.

Egyptian religion

The Egyptians believed that they lived in a well-ordered world, overseen by gods, and ruled by the gods' earthly representative, the pharaoh. It was the gods who made the Nile flood, the sun rise, and the plants grow in the fields.

The great pharaoh
Ramses II ruled Egypt for 66 years, giving him time to commission more statues of himself than any other pharaoh. Wanting to be remembered, he even had his name carved on earlier kings' monuments. It is no wonder that he later became known as Ramses the Great.

The pharaoh was seen as a son of the gods in heaven as well as the earthly form of Horus, the sky god. After death, he united with Osiris, god of the dead. As chief priest, the pharaoh made sure that the gods continued to watch over Egypt. The gods all had their own centers of worship. Ptah, the creator god, had his temple in Memphis, while Re, the sun god, was worshipped at Heliopolis.

26 the ancient world ◦ **EGYPTIAN DAILY LIFE**

20,000 The number of **towns and villages** according to **ancient Egyptian records**.

The cycle of the Nile

The annual Nile flood was caused by summer rains in Ethiopia, to the south of Egypt. The flood left behind black silt, which was perfect for growing crops. Farmers did not need fertilizers because their soil was replaced each year. Their year was divided into three seasons: *akhet* (flood), *peret* (growth), and *shomu* (harvest).

FLOOD

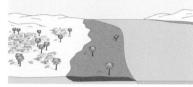

GROWTH

HARVEST

Egyptian clothing

For most of ancient Egyptian history, people dressed in plain white linen clothes. Men wore a *shenti* (a short kilt) and women wore long dresses. Decorated clothes became more fashionable during the New Kingdom, but were only worn by the rich.

Roof spaces

Egyptian houses had flat roofs. Families would often sleep on the roof when the weather was hot.

Loom
Linen, from the flax plant, was woven into cloth using a horizontal loom.

Kiln
Pottery was fired over burning charcoal in the kiln.

Pottery
Potters, who were usually male, made pots using a slow-turning wheel.

Egyptian daily life

Most ancient Egyptians were farmers who lived in villages along the banks of the Nile. They usually worked on great estates, which were owned by the pharaoh, the temple priests, or the nobles.

Farming in Egypt depended on the Nile River, which flooded every summer, covering the fields. When the rains came, many farmers left their villages to work on building projects for the pharaoh. After the Nile waters sank, they returned to plow and plant their fields. A farmer's busiest time was during the harvest season, when everyone worked from sunrise to sunset, gathering the crops.

Food and drink
The men in this model from an Egyptian tomb are making bread, while the women are making beer. Ancient Egyptians also regularly ate fish, onions, and pulses.

34 years—the life expectancy for Egyptian men; for women it was 30.

The ancient Egyptians **believed** that even the **afterlife** included hard **work**.

27

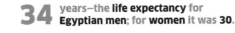

Counting grain
There were two types of granary: round or rectangular. In this model of a rectangular granary, officials called scribes record the amount of grain brought in by the peasants.

Dovecote
Pigeons and doves, both sources of meat, were housed in these mud-brick towers.

Shaduf
Water was lifted using a *shaduf*, a swinging pole with a counterweight on one end.

Draft animals
Egyptian cattle pulled plows and provided meat, leather, and milk.

Threshing
Farmers walked cattle over harvested grain to separate the seeds from the husks.

Building materials
While stone was used for temples and tombs, Egyptian houses were constructed from mud bricks. These were made by mixing wet mud and straw in wooden molds and leaving them out to dry in the sun.

Fishing
Egyptians fished with nets but also used harpoons and lines with hooks.

Reed boats
Small boats were made from bundles of papyrus reeds tied together.

Life by the Nile
Egyptian villages occupied a narrow strip of land between the Nile and the desert, with the fields alongside. Houses were small, with two or three rooms. People did not have much furniture; they sat on the ground or on low stools, and slept on straw mattresses. Apart from houses, the most important buildings were granaries, where grain was stored after harvest.

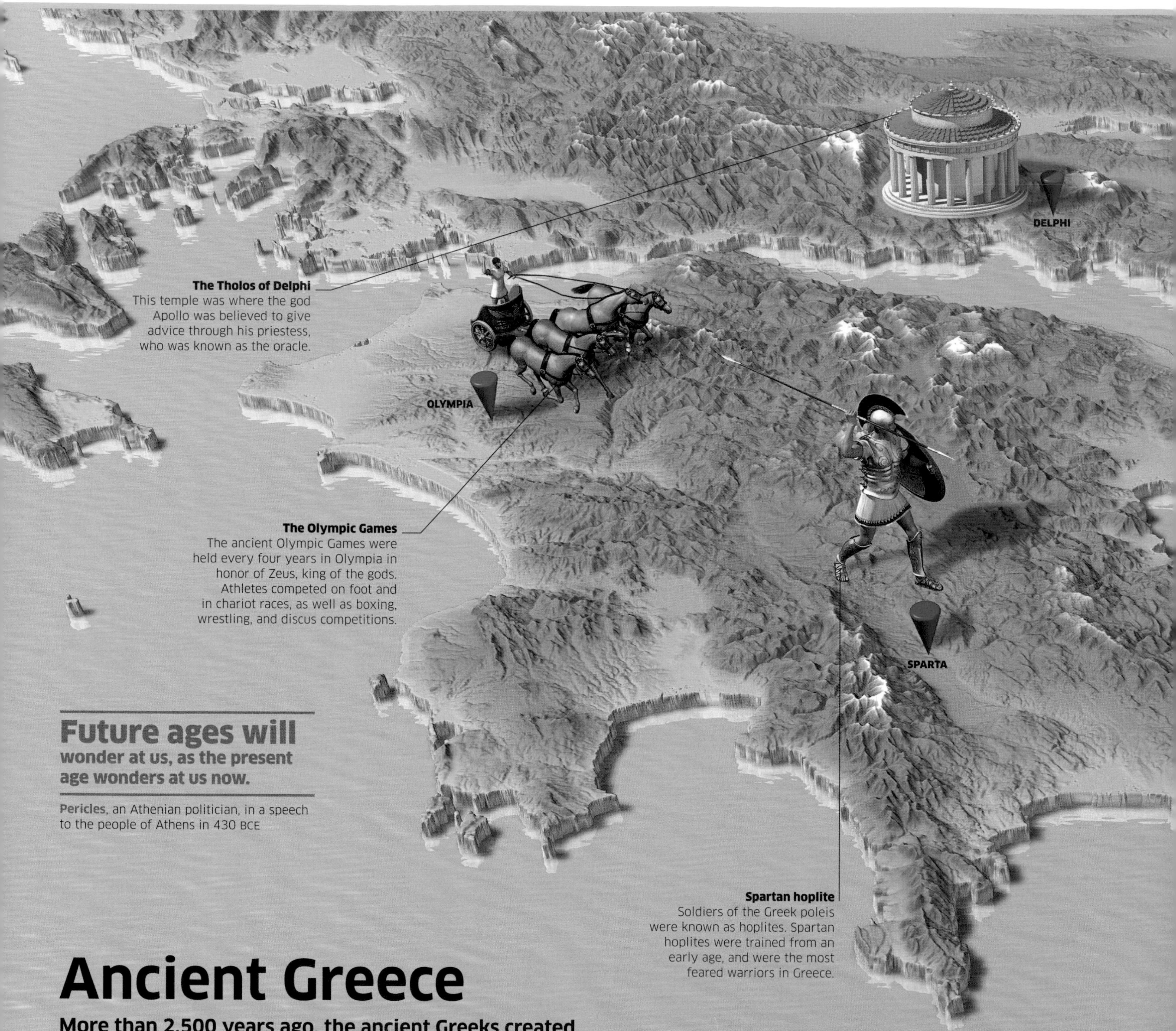

The Tholos of Delphi
This temple was where the god
Apollo was believed to give
advice through his priestess,
who was known as the oracle.

DELPHI

OLYMPIA

The Olympic Games
The ancient Olympic Games were
held every four years in Olympia in
honor of Zeus, king of the gods.
Athletes competed on foot and
in chariot races, as well as boxing,
wrestling, and discus competitions.

SPARTA

Future ages will
wonder at us, as the present
age wonders at us now.

Pericles, an Athenian politician, in a speech
to the people of Athens in 430 BCE

Spartan hoplite
Soldiers of the Greek poleis
were known as hoplites. Spartan
hoplites were trained from an
early age, and were the most
feared warriors in Greece.

Ancient Greece

**More than 2,500 years ago, the ancient Greeks created
one of the world's most influential civilizations. The
height of Greek culture is known as the Classical Age,
which lasted from around 500 BCE to 336 BCE.**

The Greeks were not a united people, but lived in more than
1,000 rival poleis, or city-states, which were often at war with
each other. But they did share a common sense of identity,
joining together to defend their homeland against invaders,
and to compete in athletic festivals, such as the Olympic Games.
The Greeks also developed philosophy, politics, science, history
writing, and theater in this period. The Classical Age ended
when Alexander the Great of Macedonia united the people of
Greece and conquered the neighboring Persian Empire.

City-states of central
and southern Greece

In the Classical Age, many of the
powerful poleis were clustered in
central Greece and the Peloponnese,
a peninsula in southern mainland
Greece. Each polis had its own
government, laws, coinage, and
calendar. The two leading poleis
were Athens, an artistic center and
great naval power, and Sparta,
whose male citizens spent all their
time training for warfare.

The Greeks established **colonies** all around the **Mediterranean** and the **Black Sea**.

1 The **number of events** held at the **first-ever Olympic Games**.

9,573 ft (2,918 m)—the **height of Mount Olympus**, which the ancient Greeks believed to be the **home of the gods**.

29

THEBES

The sphinx of Thebes
The symbol for the polis of Thebes was the sphinx, a monster that guarded the city in Greek mythology.

ATHENS

CORINTH

The Parthenon
At the center of a citadel rising above Athens stood the Parthenon, a temple to the goddess Athena. The Athenians took Athena as their patron god, and believed she watched over the city.

Corinthian coins
The city of Corinth was a major trading center during the Classical Age.

Key

■ Greek area of influence in 500 BCE

Sea of Marmara

MACEDON

Mount Olympus ▲

Aegean Sea

PERSIAN EMPIRE

GREECE

Ionian Sea

Peloponnese • Mycenae

Area of main map

Sea of Crete

Rhodes

Mediterranean Sea

• Knossos

Crete

0   100   200 km
0   50   100 miles

Greek influence

The poleis of Greece controlled all of the lands around the Aegean Sea by the beginning of the Classical Age in 500 BCE. They also set up colonies throughout the Mediterranean and the Black Sea.

Timeline

The ages of ancient Greece

Early influential Greek cultures sprang up on the island of Crete and in the city of Mycenae, but these civilizations both collapsed over time. Centuries later, the Classical Age revived the influence of Greece in the Mediterranean.

2900–1450 BCE

The Minoan Age
On the island of Crete, the Minoan civilization built large palaces decorated with images of bulls, which were sacred in Minoan religion. The Minoans also founded trading settlements across the eastern Mediterranean.

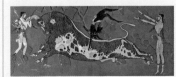

MINOAN BULL LEAPING WALL PAINTING

1600–1200 BCE

The Mycenaean Age
The Mycenaean civilization developed on the Greek mainland. The Mycenaeans were warlike and, around 1450 BCE, they conquered Crete, becoming the leading power in the eastern Mediterranean.

MYCENAEAN FUNERAL MASK

1200–800 BCE

The Dark Age
Mycenaean civilization collapsed around 1200 BCE, when all the major palaces were destroyed by unknown enemies. Greece entered a "dark age," in which writing was forgotten and long-distance trade declined. The Greek language broke up into several different dialects, and knowledge of ironworking spread.

800–500 BCE

The Archaic Age
The Archaic ("old") Age was a period when Greek civilization slowly recovered from the Dark Age. A new alphabet was introduced, trade revived, and the Greeks founded many colonies throughout the Mediterranean.

500–336 BCE

The Classical Age
During the Classical Age, Greek culture was at its height. Athens and Sparta joined together to defeat two invasions by the Persian Empire, in 490 and 480 BCE. The two cities later fought a long war against each other, in 431–404 BCE, in which most of Greece took sides. The final victor was Sparta.

Ancient Greek culture

During the Classical Age of Greece, between around 500 and 336 BCE, the Greek city-states produced some of history's most brilliant politicians, thinkers, and writers. The thoughts and ideas of these influential figures are still important today.

As Greece flourished, its citizens began to develop new ways of looking at the world. Thinkers asked more questions, poets and artists began to record what they saw, and astronomers tried to make sense of the universe. Even 2,500 years later, our understanding of subjects such as math, science, and architecture is based on the work of these great scholars.

GREEK PHILOSOPHY

Greek thinkers known as philosophers wanted to make sense of the world around them: from the way people behaved, to what made the seasons change, to the motions of the stars. In seeking knowledge and wisdom they created new ways of thinking and of testing ideas. Some of the greatest philosophers set up schools, which helped spread their ideas far and wide.

"KNOWLEDGE IS THE FOOD OF THE SOUL"
PLATO, *PROTAGORAS*, 5TH CENTURY BCE

DEMOCRACY

Around 508 BCE, the city of Athens developed a new system of government called democracy (meaning "rule by the people"). In Athenian democracy, citizens could vote on new laws to be introduced to the city. But democracy didn't include everyone: only adult men who were free (not slaves) were allowed to vote. Greek women would not win the right to vote until 1952.

The Pnyx
Athenian assemblies met at the Pnyx, a hill near the Acropolis. Pericles, a famous politician, is seen here giving a speech.

LITERATURE AND DRAMA

The earliest works of Greek literature were not written but performed, and were passed on from generation to generation by word of mouth. In the 6th century BCE, poets such as Sappho began to write their poems down. Dramatic plays dominated 5th-century literature, and the first historians—notably Herodotus—also began writing at around this time. Together, these writers created forms of literature that we still use today.

Voting for banishment

The Athenian lawgiver, Cleisthenes, introduced a new law called ostracism in around 506 BCE. This was designed to prevent any single individual becoming too powerful. If enough citizens voted in favor, a person could be sent into exile for ten years, but without losing his citizenship of Athens or property.

Voting stones
When voting to ostracize someone, voters would write the person's name on shards of pottery called *ostraka*. These would then be counted.

Homer

The most famous Greek poet was Homer, who lived in the 8th century BCE. We know nothing for certain about him, but tradition says that he was blind. His long poems, the *Iliad* and the *Odyssey*, would originally have been learned and passed on by word of mouth, and were not written down until hundreds of years later.

GREEK MYTHOLOGY

The Greek myths are a large collection of stories that were first used to explain the world as seen by the ancient Greeks. Some showed people how they should—and should not—behave. Others revealed how places and things were first created, and how the gods influenced the events in people's lives. With their heroes, gods, and monsters, many of these myths have been used by artists and writers for thousands of years, and still appeal to our imaginations.

Zeus
Zeus was "King of the Gods." He was also father of many of the lesser gods, goddesses, and heroic figures, including Aphrodite, Perseus, Apollo, and Helen of Troy.

Poseidon
Poseidon was brother of Zeus. As well as being god of the sea, he was thought to be responsible for earthquakes and other natural disasters.

30,000 The estimated **number of Athenian citizens** allowed to **vote**, out of a population of around 250,000.

90 The estimated **number of plays** written by **Aeschylus**. Only 7 have survived.

31

Thales
Thales was one of the first Greek philosophers. He figured out how to measure the height of the Egyptian pyramids, and believed that water was the substance from which all other things came.

Democritus
The investigations of Democritus into the natural world paved the way for the first scientists. One of the theories of Democritus was that all things were made of tiny, uncuttable particles.

Socrates
Socrates thought that the best way to discover the truth was to ask questions—though he didn't claim to know the answers. He wrote nothing down, and much of what we know of his work comes from his student, Plato.

Plato
Plato founded his own academy, or school, in Athens in 367 BCE. Many of his writings survive, and have been hugely influential, particularly on the subjects of religion and politics.

Aristotle
Like his teacher, Plato, Aristotle also founded a school, called the Lyceum. He wrote about many different subjects, from money to music, nature to poetry, and language to politics. He also tutored Alexander the Great.

A Greek theater
Greek plays were performed on a round stage, with the audience sitting on rows of seats built into surrounding hillsides. In the middle of the 5th century BCE, a "backdrop" was added behind the stage, where actors could change their costumes.

Drama and theaters
Greek drama reached its peak during the 5th century BCE with the tragedies of Aeschylus, Sophocles and Euripides, and the comedies of Aristophanes. Unfortunately, most of their plays have been lost. Performances took place in huge open-air theaters, with seating for thousands of people. The architects understood acoustics (how sound travels) so even people seated a long way from the stage could still hear the actors.

Homer's influence
Homer's inspirational stories have been told many times over, originally on pots and in paintings, and nowadays in films.

Athena
The goddess of wisdom, Athena is usually shown with a helmet and shield. She was not born, but sprang fully formed from the head of her father, Zeus.

Artemis
Often pictured with a wild deer, and carrying a bow or a quiver of arrows, Artemis was the goddess of hunting and of the moon. She also protected the young.

Hercules
The greatest of the Greek heroes, this lion-skin-wearing strongman is most famous for performing 12 "labors" as punishment for killing his wife and children.

Phoenician trade

Phoenician merchants sailed all around the Mediterranean searching for new markets to sell their products. They established many trading stations, several of which became great cities, including Cadiz and Cartagena in Spain and Palermo in Sicily. Others, such as Kition in Cyprus, survive only as ruins.

Key
→ Phoenician trade route
■ Phoenician homeland

The Phoenician alphabet

The Phoenicians' alphabet formed the basis of all later Western writing systems. Easy to learn, it had just 22 signs, all standing for consonants. It was adapted by the Greeks, who added signs for vowels.

aleph	beth	gimmel	daleth	he	waw
zayin	heth	teth	yodh	kaph	lamedh
mem	nun	samekh	ayin	pe	tsadi
qoph	res	sin	taw		**PHOENICIAN ALPHABET**

The Carthaginian Empire

The city of Carthage in North Africa broke away from Phoenician rule in c. 650 BCE and became the center of a Carthaginian Empire, controlling western Sicily, Corsica, Sardinia, and southern Spain. The rivalry of Carthage and Rome led to three wars, which the Romans called the Punic Wars.

First Punic War
During the First Punic War, Carthage fought Rome for control of the island of Sicily. Carthage lost, and Rome became a great naval power.

CARTHAGINIAN COIN SHOWING HANNIBAL

Second Punic War
The Carthaginian general Hannibal led an army, including elephants, from Spain to Italy. After three great victories, he was finally defeated by Rome, which became the dominant power in the Mediterranean.

Third Punic War
The Romans conquered and destroyed Carthage. They took control of all Carthaginian territory and enslaved or killed the entire population.

Timeline

264–241 BCE

218–201 BCE

149–146 BCE

The Phoenicians

The Phoenician civilization began in port cities on the coast of modern-day Lebanon, in the Middle East. Though they had no land empire, the Phoenicians became the leading seafaring merchants of the Mediterranean from 1200 BCE.

The main Phoenician cities were Byblos, Tyre, and Sidon, each ruled by a different monarch. The people of these cities did not see themselves as a single nation. It was the Greeks who called them Phoenicians—from *phoinos*, meaning "dark red," perhaps after their most expensive product, a dye known as Tyrian purple. The Phoenicians were the greatest navigators of the ancient world. Apart from their voyages across the Mediterranean, they explored the Atlantic coast of Europe and the west coast of Africa.

Horse's head
The figurehead may have honored Yam, the Phoenician sea god. Like the Greek sea god Poseidon, Yam was also worshipped as the god of horses.

Water container
This large amphora (pottery jar) contained water for the crew.

Ivory tusks
Ivory, taken from the tusks of elephants in North Africa, was carved into decorative panels by Phoenician craft workers.

Textiles
Rolls of textiles were dyed and woven in Phoenician workshops.

Anchor
The crew dropped the heavy anchor into the sea when they arrived at a port.

According to the Bible, **Phoenician cedar wood** was used to make the roof of **Solomon's Temple in Jerusalem**.

The Carthaginian explorer **Hanno the Navigator** explored the **west coast of Africa** in the 5th century BCE.

33

Phoenician merchant ship

With big, broad, rounded hulls, Phoenician merchant ships could carry large amounts of cargo. They were slow but stable, and could be sailed or, if the wind dropped, rowed. Reliefs from Assyria in the ancient Middle East show that the ships had horse figureheads at the front. The Greeks called these ships "hippoi" (horses).

Tyrian purple
This rich, purple-colored dye was one of the Phoenicians' most sought-after exports.

Square sail
With only a single sail, the ship had trouble sailing into the wind.

Steering oar
Two oars at the stern (the rear of the ship) were used to change the ship's direction.

Cedarwood logs
Phoenician cedar, prized for its aroma, was exported to Greece, Egypt, and Mesopotamia, where building timber was in short supply.

Amphora
These large pottery jars held olive oil or wine which were both produced all around the Mediterranean.

Luxury goods
Phoenician cities were centers of craft production, making glassware and ivory carvings. Craft workers were influenced by Mesopotamian and Egyptian art, and the Phoenicians spread these styles across the Mediterranean.

IVORY SPHINX

BEARDED HEAD PENDANT

GLASS AMPHORA

Copper ox hide ingots
Copper, from Cyprus, was mixed with tin to make a piece of bronze. With handles at each corner, the ingot's shape resembled an ox hide.

The people of the steppes

In the ancient world, the steppes (vast treeless plains) of Europe and Asia were home to tribes of nomads, who lived by moving from place to place to find fresh pastures for their horses, sheep, cattle, and goats.

The people of the steppes usually lived in small tribes. The power and speed of their horses made them feared warriors, so when they united, these groups of nomads became a deadly threat to the settled civilizations to the east and west. The greatest threat came from the Huns, who conquered large areas of Asia and Europe in the 4th and 5th centuries CE.

c. 3500-3000 BCE
The horse was first tamed on the steppes of Asia. This gave humans their first fast method of transportation.

215-212 BCE
The first emperor of China ordered the construction of a barrier along China's northern border. The Great Wall was built to prevent raids from the Xiongnu tribes that controlled much of north and central Asia in the 3rd century BCE.

c. 370 CE
Europeans first became aware of the Huns as they began to conquer their neighbors, sweeping west from lands beyond the Volga River in modern-day western Russia.

c. 900-200 BCE
The Scythians, a group of nomadic tribes who lived on the steppes to the north of the Black Sea, extended their control eastward across Siberia in northeast Russia to the borders of China.

1st century BCE
The nomadic Yuezhi people were united under the Kushan, who went on to conquer an empire that covered Afghanistan, parts of central Asia, and northern India. The Kushan Dynasty maintained control of these regions until the 3rd century CE.

441-453 CE
The leader of the Huns, Attila, launched a series of attacks to take control of lands in eastern and central Europe. But soon after Attila's death in 453 CE, his empire fell apart.

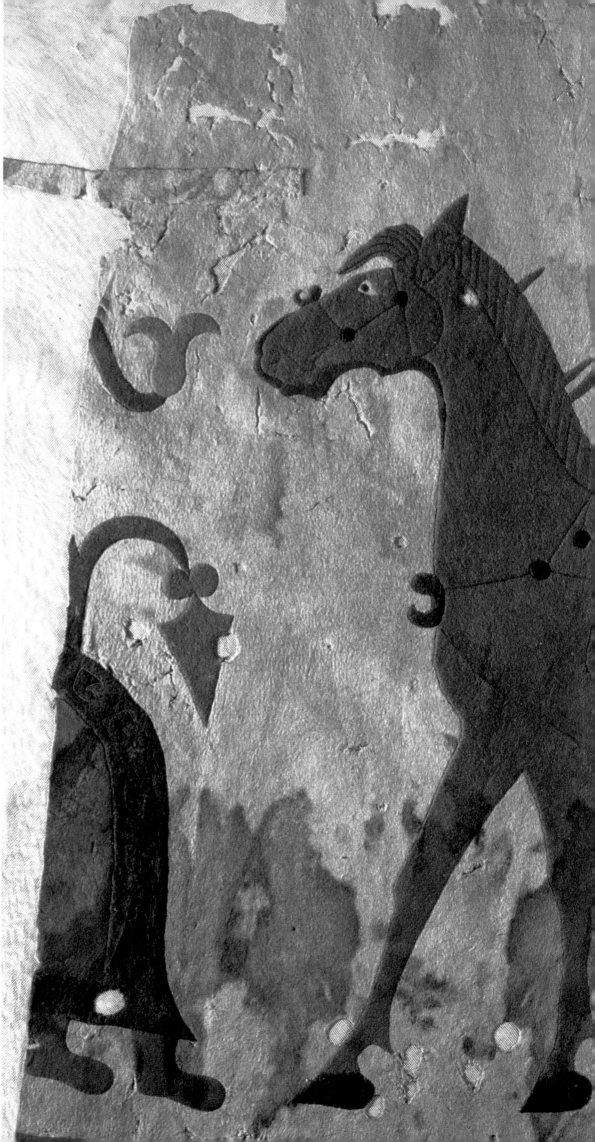

Mounted warrior
This hanging from a Scythian tomb in the Pazyryk Valley of Siberia shows a horse rider with a bow case by his leg. The short bow was a powerful weapon for the nomadic tribes of the steppes, and was used in warfare and hunting.

36 the ancient world ○ CELTIC EUROPE

4,147 The number of **hillforts** so far identified as built by the Celts in **Britain** and **Ireland**.

Celtic Europe

The ancient Celts were a people that lived in tribes across ancient mainland Europe and the British Isles. Celtic civilization was at its height between the 6th and 1st centuries BCE.

The word "Celt" comes from *keltoi*, the Greek name for a people who lived across Europe. The Romans called the Celts "Galli" (meaning "barbarians"), or Gauls, which led to areas they settled being called Gaul (France), Galicia (in Spain), and Galatia (Turkey). The Celts lived in hundreds of tribes, and did not see themselves as a single people. Despite this, they shared common religious beliefs and customs, and many were skilled artists, creating richly patterned metalwork. Their languages, such as Welsh and Gaelic, are still spoken today by people who see themselves as Celts.

CULTURES OF THE CELTS

Although the Celts were separate tribes, they shared the same customs and styles of art. Over time, these customs and styles changed, and new cultures emerged. All Celtic cultures were known for their skill at bronze metalwork.

Urnfield culture

The people of the Urnfield culture (c. 1300–750 BCE) were the ancestors of the Celts, and lived in east-central Europe and northern Italy. The culture was named for the funeral practices of its people—they cremated their dead and put the ashes in urns. The ashes of warrior rulers were buried with bronze weapons, armor, and ornaments.

Pottery urn
This urn from Taranto in Italy held the ashes of the dead.

Hallstatt culture

The first true Celtic culture according to modern historians, the Hallstatt culture is named after an ancient Celtic cemetery that was found in modern-day Austria. The Hallstatt people grew rich by trading, particularly in the salt they mined. Known for its bronze weapons and geometrical patterns, the culture spread across Europe, from the Loire River in modern-day France to the Danube River in central Europe. The Hallstatt did not cremate their dead, but buried people with offerings for the gods.

Hallstatt necklace
Found in modern-day Poland, this bronze necklace's linear patterning is typical of Hallstatt culture. It probably dates from the 6th century BCE.

La Tène culture

Celtic metalwork from around 450 BCE onward moved on from the geometric patterns of the Hallstatt culture to use flowing, curved lines. This new culture is named after La Tène in Switzerland, where Celts threw many gold and bronze items into a lake as offerings. The La Tène custom of leaving precious metalwork in water was widespread. The "Battersea shield," below, was found in the Thames River in 1857.

Shield cover
The Battersea shield is actually only a cover—it would have been attached to the front of a wooden shield. It is made of bronze and decorated with red glass.

CELTIC LIFE

Celtic tribes were ruled by chieftains, kings, and queens. There were different classes in Celtic society, with most land owned by warrior nobles and most people living as poor farmers. Others took on roles as bards (poets and singers), priests, craft workers, and merchants. The Celts also kept slaves, who had been captured in warfare.

Celtic homes

The typical Celtic home was a circular thatched structure called a roundhouse, which contained a single large room. The main difference between rich and poor Celts was the size of their roundhouse. In western Europe, there were many hillforts—villages of roundhouses surrounded by banks, ditches, and stockades (walls made of sharpened logs). From the 3rd century BCE, Celtic people in Europe began to build larger towns, which the Romans called *oppida*. Influenced by Roman building styles, many of these *oppida* were filled with rectangular houses rather than roundhouses.

Inside the roundhouse
This roundhouse at Castell Henlyss in Wales was excavated and reconstructed in the 1980s.

THE CELTS AND ROME

Much of what we know about the Celts comes from the writings of the ancient Romans, who fought them for centuries and eventually conquered most of Celtic Europe. The Romans first encountered the Celts in around 390 BCE, when a large number of Celtic tribes crossed the Alps into present-day northern Italy.

Gauls attack Rome

In 390 BCE, one of the Gallic (Celtic) tribes in Italy, the Senones, inflicted a humiliating defeat on Rome. After defeating the Romans in battle, the Senones captured and raided Rome itself. However, according to legend, they could not take the central Capitoline Hill because a flock of geese, sacred to the Roman goddess Juno, raised the alarm. The Romans paid the Senones in gold to leave the city.

ROMAN CARVING OF JUNO'S SACRED GEESE

The land the Romans called Gaul covered much of modern-day western Europe, including all of France, Luxembourg, and Belgium.

75,000 The estimated number of Romans and Britons killed by Boudicca's armies.

37

Celtic religion

Celts worshipped hundreds of gods. Different groups had their own gods, but there was some overlap—the Irish goddess Badb, for example, may have been inspired by the Gallic goddess Cathubodua. The Celts offered precious gifts to their gods in rivers, lakes, and pools—places seen as entrances to another world. Animals and people were also killed in elaborate ways and offered as sacrifices. In Britain and Gaul, sacrifices were carried out by priests called druids. Druidism was one of the few religions banned by the Romans.

God of the wild
The Gundestrup cauldron, a silver bowl found in a Danish bog, may depict Cernunnos, the horned nature god of the Celts. The bowl's design is influenced by a range of cultures.

Caesar conquers Gaul

Between 58 and 51 BCE, the Roman general Julius Caesar conquered Gaul in a series of wars. Caesar also led two expeditions across the sea to Britain in 55 and 54 BCE. He told the story of his campaigns in his book *The Gallic Wars*, in which he described Celtic society and customs. Caesar's final victory over the Gallic people was the capture of the *oppidum* Alesia in modern-day France, the stronghold of King Vercingetorix.

Gallic surrender
Vercingetorix surrendered to Caesar at Alesia. Caesar then took him to Rome, where he paraded the chained king in a triumphal procession before executing him.

Romans and Britons

In 43 CE, an army of the Roman emperor Claudius invaded Britain, quickly conquering the southeast. By 84 CE, the Romans ruled most of Britain, despite resistance from Celtic leaders. Unlike the Gauls, who gave up speaking their own languages, many Britons continued to speak Celtic languages rather than Latin. The Celtic way of life also continued in Scotland and Ireland, which were unconquered.

Warrior queen
In 60 CE, Queen Boudicca of the Iceni tribe, aided by her daughters, led a great uprising against Roman rule. Her army destroyed three Roman towns before it was defeated.

38 the ancient world ○ **THE PERSIAN EMPIRE**

10,000 The number of warriors in the elite Persian army known as the "Immortals."

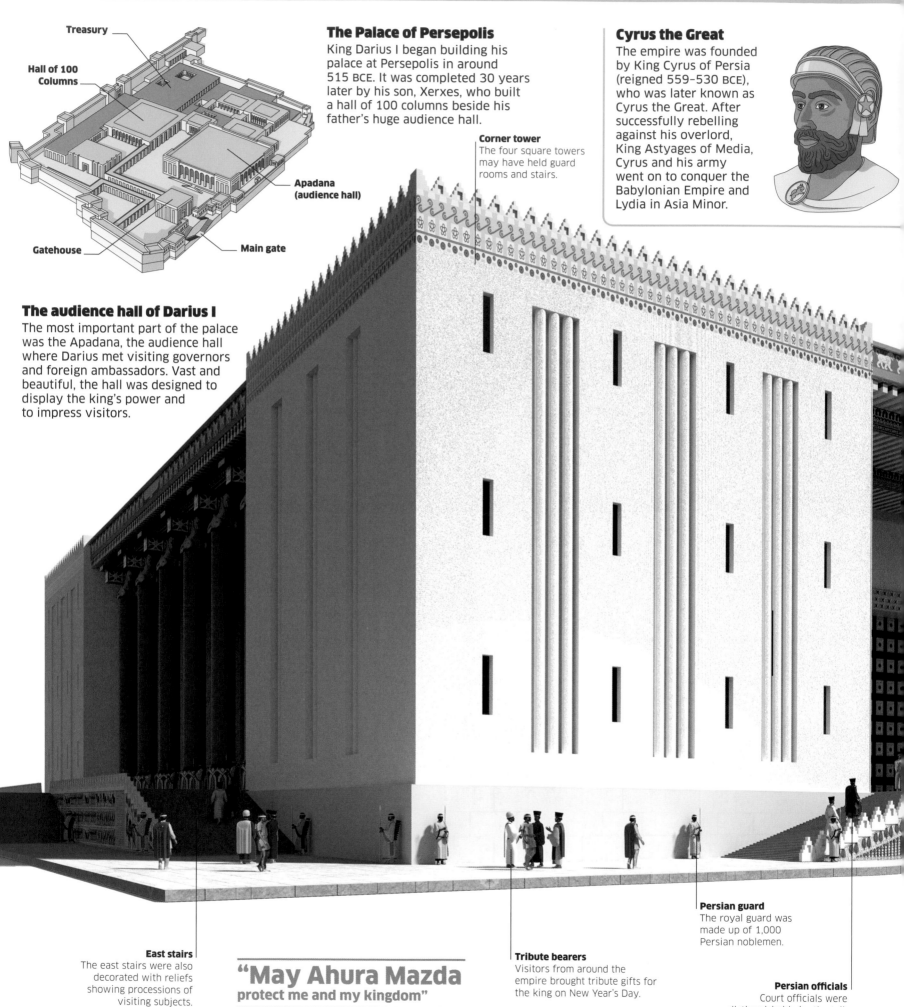

Treasury

Hall of 100 Columns

Gatehouse

Apadana (audience hall)

Main gate

The Palace of Persepolis

King Darius I began building his palace at Persepolis in around 515 BCE. It was completed 30 years later by his son, Xerxes, who built a hall of 100 columns beside his father's huge audience hall.

Cyrus the Great

The empire was founded by King Cyrus of Persia (reigned 559–530 BCE), who was later known as Cyrus the Great. After successfully rebelling against his overlord, King Astyages of Media, Cyrus and his army went on to conquer the Babylonian Empire and Lydia in Asia Minor.

Corner tower
The four square towers may have held guard rooms and stairs.

The audience hall of Darius I

The most important part of the palace was the Apadana, the audience hall where Darius met visiting governors and foreign ambassadors. Vast and beautiful, the hall was designed to display the king's power and to impress visitors.

East stairs
The east stairs were also decorated with reliefs showing processions of visiting subjects.

"May Ahura Mazda
protect me and my kingdom"

Darius I, in an inscription at Persepolis

Tribute bearers
Visitors from around the empire brought tribute gifts for the king on New Year's Day.

Persian guard
The royal guard was made up of 1,000 Persian noblemen.

Persian officials
Court officials were distinguishable by the tall, fluted hats that they wore.

Persepolis is a Greek name; it means "city of the Persians."

330 BCE The year of the **murder of Darius III, the last ruler** of the Persian Empire.

39

AHURA MAZDA

Persian religion

Persian kings claimed to rule on behalf of the supreme god, Ahura Mazda ("Wise Lord"). He was seen as the protector of the king and the empire, and was represented in art as a man rising from a winged disk. The ancient Persian religion is called Zoroastrianism.

Rise of the Persian Empire

Cyrus the Great's son, Cambyses II (reigned 529–522 BCE), conquered Egypt, and under Darius I (reigned 522–486 BCE), the Persian empire expanded into northwest India and Europe. It was Darius who organized the empire into satrapies. He also founded a new capital, Persepolis. This map shows the Persian Empire in c. 500 BCE, during the reign of Darius I.

MACEDONIA
THRACE
Black Sea
Caspian Sea
IONIA
LYDIA
LYCIA
Mediterranean Sea
MEDIA
Jerusalem
Babylon
Persepolis
EGYPT
Red Sea
Key
The Persian Empire, c.500 BCE
Arabian Sea

Bull carvings
The pillars were topped with carvings of double-headed bulls. The bull's strength was associated with kingship.

Pillars
The 72 columns, each 65.5 ft (20 m) high, supported the wooden beams of the roof.

The Persian Empire

Lasting from the 6th to the 4th centuries BCE, the Persian Empire was the world's first superpower. At its height, it spanned three continents, stretching from Egypt to northwest India.

The empire was divided into 20 satrapies (provinces). Each had a satrap (governor), usually a Persian noble appointed by the empire's Great King. The provinces paid tribute (gifts such as gold, ivory, or slaves) to the king, provided soldiers for his armies, and were harshly punished if they rebelled. Otherwise, they could manage their own affairs and, unusually for an ancient empire, the peoples living in the provinces were allowed to keep their native languages, customs, and religions.

Timeline

The Greco-Persian Wars
Darius ruled over many Greek cities. In 499 BCE, they rebelled against his rule, helped by western Greeks from Athens and Eretria. After crushing the rebellion, Darius vowed to conquer Greece itself.

492 BCE
Darius's first invasion of Greece
A Persian army led by Darius's son-in-law, Mardonius, crossed into Europe. The Persians conquered Thrace and the kingdom of Macedonia, which lay to the north of Greece.

490 BCE
Battle of Marathon
Darius sent another army by sea to invade Greece. The Persians captured many Greek islands and sacked Eretria, but were decisively defeated by an Athenian army at Marathon.

A PERSIAN (LEFT) FIGHTS A GREEK

480–479 BCE
Xerxes' second invasion
Darius's son Xerxes I also tried to conquer Greece. The Persians defeated the Greeks at Thermopylae and sacked Athens, but were beaten at sea at Salamis and on land at Plataea.

479–448 BCE
Peace of Callias
An alliance of Greek seafaring cities, led by Athens, set out to free the eastern Greeks from Persian rule. After Greek victories in Thrace and Ionia, the war finally ended in a peace treaty.

Royal scene
A relief on the north stairs (later moved to the treasury) showed Darius I in his inner court.

Wall of tribute bearers
Carved reliefs showed the peoples of the empire, in their national dress, bringing gifts. When tribute bearers approached the hall, they passed images of themselves.

The Hellenistic world

In the 4th century BCE, the conquests of Alexander the Great of Macedonia began a new period of ancient history. The Hellenistic Age (from *Hellene*, meaning "Greek") saw Greek culture spread south as far as Egypt and east to what is now modern-day Afghanistan.

In new Hellenistic cities, such as Alexandria in Egypt, people adopted Greek dress and worshipped Greek gods such as Zeus and Poseidon, though sometimes they gave them different names. Ancient Greek became the common language of the eastern Mediterranean and the Middle East. The influence of Greek art spread even further, with sculptors from the Indian subcontinent taking inspiration from Greek artistic forms in their depictions of the human body.

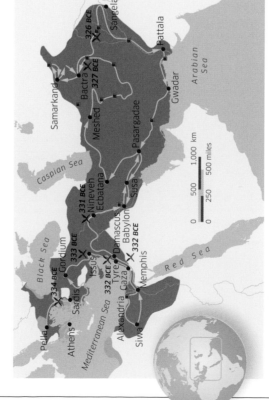

Cylindrical section
Inside this top portion of the lighthouse, which was probably 69ft (21m) high, a system of pulleys and ropes raised fuel up to the fire.

Octagonal section
The middle section of the lighthouse is believed to have been octagonal (eight-sided), and may have been 98ft (30m) high.

Merman
On each corner of the square section that formed the base of the tower stood a statue of the god Triton, messenger of the sea, who had a human upper body and a fish's tail.

Guiding light
The lighthouse was the only one of the Seven Wonders of the Ancient World to provide a practical benefit for people. Its light burned for centuries, saving the lives of countless seafarers by guiding them safely to the harbor of Alexandria.

"The first city of the civilized world"

Diodorus of Sicily on Alexandria, *Bibliotheca historica*, 1st century BCE

Statue of a god
On top of the lighthouse stood a statue of one of the Greek gods. It may have been Zeus, ruler of the gods; Poseidon, god of the sea; or Helios, the sun god.

Signaling mirror
During the daytime, a polished bronze mirror reflected the light of the sun's rays to signal to ships.

Fire chamber
At dusk, a large fire was lit to signal to ships, and was kept burning all through the night.

Alexander the Great

In 336 BCE, at the age of just 20, Alexander became king of Macedonia, an ancient kingdom bordering the city-states of Greece. After uniting Greece under his rule, Alexander led a vast army into Asia. In an unbroken series of victories, he conquered the Persian Empire and then invaded India. Alexander's empire was the largest the world had seen, yet it quickly fell apart on his death in 323 BCE.

A Greek hero
Greek coins of Alexander showed him wearing the lion skin of Hercules, a hero of Greek mythology.

Alexander's empire

Alexander's lasting legacy was the foundation of more than 30 new cities, which he established with Greeks and Macedonians. He called 20 of them Alexandria, after himself. The biggest was Alexandria in Egypt, a great port city on the Mediterranean coast.

Key

- Alexander's empire
- Dependent regions
- Alexander's route
- City founded by Alexander
- ✕ Significant battles

Sangela
326 BCE ✕
Pattala
327 BCE ✕
Bactra ✕
Samarkand
Gwadar
Arabian Sea
Meshed
Pasargadae
Caspian Sea
331 BCE ✕
Nineveh
Ecbatana
Susa
332 BCE ✕
Babylon
Gordium
333 BCE
Sardis
Issus ✕ 333 BCE
334 BCE ✕
Tyre ✕ 332 BCE
Damascus
Gaza ✕ 332 BCE
Athens
Pella
Alexandria
Memphis
Siwa
Black Sea
Mediterranean Sea
Red Sea

1,000 km
500 miles
500
250
0

Ptolemaic Egypt

After Alexander's death, his leading generals broke up his empire into separate kingdoms. Alexander's friend Ptolemy seized Egypt, where he made himself pharaoh. He was the first in a dynasty of Macedonian rulers, all called Ptolemy, while their queens were named Berenice or Cleopatra. On coins used throughout the kingdom, the Ptolemies were depicted in a Greek artistic style, while on temple walls they appeared as traditional Egyptian pharaohs.

Cleopatra VII

The last effective ruler of Ptolemaic Egypt was Cleopatra VII. After her death, the Roman Empire took control of Egypt.

The **lighthouse of Alexandria** is estimated to have been at least **360 ft (110 m)** high.

41

The Pharos of Alexandria

In the 3rd century BCE, the Greek rulers of Egypt built a great lighthouse on Pharos, a small island beside Alexandria's harbor. The lighthouse stood for more than 1,500 years. It was so famous that at the time of the Roman Empire the word *pharos* was used to mean lighthouse or beacon.

Square section
The base of the tower is thought to have been 200 ft (61 m) high. It would have contained storerooms, sleeping quarters, and even an observatory.

Defending the tower
Soldiers were garrisoned at the base of the lighthouse to protect it from attack.

Beast of burden
The inside of the lighthouse was filled with ramps to allow animals to pull carts of fuel to the top for the fire.

Protective base
A base that rose 20 ft (6 m) above the island protected the lighthouse from sea storms.

Causeway
Supplies were delivered to the lighthouse by a causeway that connected the island to Alexandria.

Ancient wonders

The Pharos of Alexandria was one of the Seven Wonders of the World, a list of spectacular sights and monuments compiled by Greek travel writers in the 2nd century BCE. All of the seven wonders were located within the borders of the Hellenistic world of Greece, Egypt, and West Asia.

The Great Pyramid of Giza
Built for Pharaoh Khufu in 2589–2566 BCE, the Great Pyramid is the only wonder that still survives to this day.

The Hanging Gardens of Babylon
This tiered garden, praised as a feat of engineering, may not have existed in reality.

The Temple of Artemis at Ephesus
This ancient temple burned down twice before being rebuilt in 324 BCE, and was twice the size of any other Greek temple.

The Statue of Zeus at Olympia
Around 435 BCE, the Greek sculptor Phidias created this 43-ft- (13-m-) high gold and ivory statue of the king of the gods.

The Colossus of Rhodes
Erected in 280 BCE, this 108-ft- (33-m-) high bronze statue of the sun god, Helios, towered over Rhodes harbor.

The Mausoleum at Halicarnassus
This massive tomb was built for King Mausolus of Caria in the Persian Empire in c.350 BCE.

Ancient India

In South Asia, one of the world's first great civilizations, the Indus, flourished from around 2800 BCE. More than 2,000 years later, the Mauryans, followed centuries later by the Guptas, carved out their own empires in the region.

The people of the Indus Valley, in modern-day Pakistan, built the world's first planned cities, with sophisticated water supplies and drainage systems. But by 1800 BCE, the Indus civilization had declined, possibly due to flooding or war. It was not until the Mauryan Empire arose in around 321 BCE that the majority of India became united for the first time. After the fall of the Mauryans, the Gupta Empire emerged in the 4th century CE, and began a golden age of Indian art and science. Ancient India was also the birthplace of what are now two of the world's major religions—Hinduism and Buddhism.

c. 2500 BCE
The people of the Indus Valley began to trade with the Sumerians of Mesopotamia in the Middle East.

321–303 BCE
Inspired by Alexander the Great's invasion of India in 326–325 BCE, Chandragupta Maurya conquered northern India, founding the Mauryan Empire.

320–330 CE
Chandragupta I conquered northwest India, founding the Gupta Empire. Though the Guptas were Hindus, they also promoted Buddhism.

c. 1500 BCE
After the fall of the Indus, a people known as the Indo-Aryans migrated from central Asia into India. They spoke Sanskrit, and this language began to spread all over the region. Sanskrit hymns, called Vedas, are the earliest Hindu texts.

268–232 BCE
After expanding the Mauryan Empire, Ashoka the Great, the third emperor, gave up warfare. He converted to Buddhism and sent missionaries to spread the religion to Sri Lanka and central Asia.

380–415 CE
Chandragupta II ruled the Gupta Empire. He was a patron of the arts and sciences, and astronomers and mathematicians of the Gupta Empire were the most advanced in the world at the time.

Gateway to the Great Stupa at Sanchi
Ashoka the Great built many stupas—sacred mounds holding relics of the Buddha and other Buddhist teachers. The stupas at Sanchi in central India were improved upon by later rulers. This carved gateway to the Great Stupa at Sanchi was constructed in the 1st century BCE.

Weapons
The warriors originally carried a mixture of long-reach thrusting weapons, swords, and bows.

Clay figures
The statues were crafted from clay that was found close to the burial site.

Baked statues
Once assembled, the clay figures were baked in a kiln to harden them into shape.

Shang and Zhou

The Qin unified China, but they were not its first rulers. The Shang Dynasty (c. 1600–1046 BCE) of northern China developed the first Chinese writing. The Zhou (1046–256 BCE) conquered the Shang, and during their rule Chinese writing became closer to the script in use today.

Zhou bronze
The Zhou crafted beautiful bronze vessels for use in ceremonial rituals.

Black lacquer
After firing, the statues were covered with lacquer, a varnish that formed a base layer before painting.

The Warring States period

At the beginning of the Warring States period (475–221 BCE), China was divided into many small kingdoms, which were constantly at war. By the 3rd century BCE, only seven states remained. Between 230 and 221 BCE, the western state of Qin conquered each of the other kingdoms in turn.

Painted figures
The final stage of building each soldier was to paint it in bright colors.

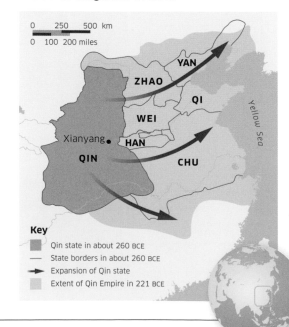

| 0 | 250 | 500 km |
| 0 | 100 | 200 miles |

YAN
ZHAO
QI
WEI
Xianyang
HAN
QIN
CHU
Yellow Sea

Key
- Qin state in about 260 BCE
- State borders in about 260 BCE
- Expansion of Qin state
- Extent of Qin Empire in 221 BCE

China's first emperor

In the 3rd century BCE, the state of Qin was one of seven warring kingdoms in the region known today as China. By 221 BCE, Qin had conquered the neighboring kingdoms and ruled over a unified state. The king of Qin took the title Shi Huangdi—First Emperor.

Qin Shi Huangdi compelled everyone in China to adopt the same writing system and coins, and he standardized units of weight and measurement across the empire. He forced laborers to build networks of roads and canals throughout China, and a great wall to protect the northern border against invasion. Yet his rule was so harsh and unpopular that the Qin Dynasty lasted just four years after his death in 210 BCE.

c. 40,000 bronze weapons were buried with the **Terra-Cotta Army**.

670 terra-cotta **statues of horses** were buried with the army. **45**

The Terra-Cotta Army

Qin Shi Huangdi was buried in a massive tomb. Pits were dug nearby, and more than 7,000 life-size statues of warriors were buried inside. The statues were made of terra-cotta, a form of pottery, but many of the statues carried real weapons. The warriors were buried with the emperor to protect him in the afterlife.

Bronze spearhead
Wooden spears were tipped with a bronze blade.

Long-reach weapon
The *ge* was made from a bronze, dagger-shaped blade mounted on a wooden pole.

Bun
Ordinary soldiers wore their hair tied up in a bun pointing to the right.

Official
One small pit of statues buried with the emperor did not contain soldiers, but a group of officials from the emperor's court.

Headwear
The shape of an officer's headgear showed their rank.

Armor
Ancient Chinese armor was made from pieces of leather sewn together.

There were eight different basic head molds.

Arms, hands, and armor were molded separately.

The bottom of the gowns were hand-built with strips of clay.

The legs and base were the first parts to be modeled.

Swords
Swords had bronze blades, but were covered in a coating to prevent rust.

"Brandishing his long whip, the
First Emperor
drove the world before him"

Jia Yi, *The Faults of Qin*, c. 170 BCE

Modeling the figures

The figures were made in sections, using molds for the heads and limbs. Artists then hand-shaped the noses, mouths, eyes, and facial hair. Each warrior's face was different, and they may even have been portraits of real people.

Han China

After the death of China's first emperor in 210 BCE, rebel leader Liu Bang overthrew the Qin Dynasty and established the Han Dynasty in 202 BCE. The Han ruled China for more than 400 years, and established many of the traditions and values of Chinese culture.

The Han emperors promoted Confucianism, a philosophy that everyone had a place in society. They also improved the Chinese government and created the Taichu (traditional Chinese) calendar that is still in use today. The Han established new overland trade routes called the Silk Road to link China with the eastern provinces of the Roman Empire.

◎ EMPEROR GAOZU

In the early 3rd century BCE, the Chinese rebelled against the hated Qin Dynasty. Liu Bang, who came from a peasant family, became a rebel leader and raised an army to take the Qin capital Xianyang. Liu Bang took control of China and renamed himself Emperor Gaozu. He built a new capital at Chang'an, simplified Chinese government, and employed Confucian scholars.

◎ INVENTIONS

During the Han Dynasty, the Chinese invented paper, a seismometer (an instrument for detecting earthquakes), the wheelbarrow, and the magnetic compass, among other things. China's metalworkers were the most skilled in the world at the time. They built furnaces so hot that they could melt iron into liquid, which they then poured into molds to make a range of weapons and tools.

Earthquake detector
In 132 CE, Han scholar Zhang Heng created an egg-shaped copper container that detected vibrations from the Earth. A ball would drop from one of the dragons' heads into one of the frogs' mouths, which would tell the Han in which direction the earthquake had happened.

Paper
In around 105 CE, court official Cai Lun made the first paper using bark, bamboo fibers, and water. This was cheaper to produce than sheets of bamboo or silk.

Magnetic compass
The first magnetic compass was a metal spoon, balanced on a plate, that always pointed south.

Wheelbarrow
Han wheelbarrows had a single central wheel that supported the whole weight of the load. The Han called wheelbarrows "wooden oxen."

1,500 miles (2,400 km)–the **length of the Grand Canal** built by **Han Emperor Yang** between the years 605 and 611.

4,000 miles (6,400 km)–the approximate **total length** of the **Silk Road** from **China to Europe**.

47

TRADE

Chinese craft workers made beautiful silk, pottery, and metalwork. These goods were traded across Asia along the Silk Road. The art of making silk from silkworm cocoons was a closely guarded Chinese secret. Rich Romans loved silk, but they had no idea how it was made.

Bronze art
The Han made many works of art from bronze. Han emperors often filled their tombs with bronze sculptures and ornaments.

Silk
Han noblewoman Lady Dai was buried in a tomb with an intricately painted silk banner.

HAN GOVERNMENT

In the early years of the Han Dynasty, Chinese government officials were appointed on recommendations from nobles and senior officials. But in 165 BCE, Emperor Wen introduced a new system in which applicants had to pass examinations in order to be appointed, allowing more people to work in government than ever before. However, only the children of wealthy families could afford to be educated and take the exam.

Confucian scholars

The Han emperors followed the principles set down by Confucius, a Chinese philosopher of the 5th and 6th centuries BCE. Confucius believed that people should treat those above their rank with respect and those below their rank with fairness. The relationship between ruler and subject was considered the most important in Han society, and many emperors employed Confucian scholars at their courts. In 124 BCE, Emperor Wu established the Imperial University, which trained scholar officials in Confucian texts.

Scholars at the imperial court
Han emperors invited leading scholars to serve as advisers at their courts. Here, the Han emperor Hsien Ti is shown with a group of scholars, who are translating classical texts.

AFTER THE HAN

In the 2nd century CE, disastrous floods, a plague of locusts, and famine devastated China, and desperate peasants rebelled against the Han. Emperors sent armies to end the rebellions, but the army generals changed sides and instead became local warlords. Han rule began to break down and, in 220 CE, the last emperor, Xian, gave up the throne.

The Three Kingdoms

From 220 to 280 CE, China was divided into three kingdoms, Shu in the west, Wei in the north, and Wu in the east. The ruler of each kingdom claimed to be the emperor of China, and they were constantly at war with one another. Wei was the most powerful kingdom, and conquered Shu in 263 CE.

Wu founder
The kingdom of Wu was founded by Emperor Dadi, who ruled from 222 to 252 CE.

Jin Dynasty

In 265 CE, a Wei general seized power and was proclaimed emperor of the Jin Dynasty. He conquered the eastern Wu kingdom in 280 CE and briefly reunited most of China. The Jin Dynasty was invaded by neighboring kingdoms and fell in 316 CE.

Calligraphy
Under the Jin, calligraphy flourished. Wang Xizhi was the greatest Jin calligrapher.

Southern and Northern dynasties

In 386 CE, northern China was reunited under the Northern Wei Dynasty. Meanwhile, the southern region of modern-day China was ruled by a series of dynasties. A new religion, Buddhism, introduced by merchants and missionaries from Central Asia, spread widely across China.

NORTHERN WEI BUDDHIST SCULPTURE

Sui Dynasty

In 588 CE, China was reunited by Emperor Wen, who established the short-lived Sui Dynasty. The second and last Sui ruler, Emperor Yang, ruled from 614 to 618 CE. He forced 5 million people to build a canal linking the Yellow and Yangtze rivers.

The Grand Canal
Emperor Yang's Grand Canal, linking China's two great rivers, remains the world's longest canal today.

48 the ancient world ○ **ANCIENT ROME**

The Roman language, called **Latin**, formed the basis for many **modern European languages**.

Ancient Rome

From its beginnings as a group of settlements on the banks of the Tiber River in Italy in the 8th century BCE, Rome grew to become an empire that spanned much of Europe and the lands around the Mediterranean Sea.

At its peak, the Roman Empire stretched from the western coast of Spain to modern-day Syria, and from the north of England to the banks of the Red Sea, incorporating up to a quarter of the world's population. Known for its military and engineering brilliance, the influence of Roman civilization is still felt to this day, with its law, art, literature, architecture, and politics still shaping much of the world around us.

EARLY ROME

According to legend, Rome was founded by Romulus and Remus, half-human sons of the god Mars. Archaeologists suggest that the first settlement, located at a ford on the Tiber River, dated to around the 8th century BCE. Early Rome was especially influenced by the Etruscan people, who spread to northern Italy from Lydia (in modern-day Turkey). The Etruscans brought knowledge of sewage systems, art, the toga, and chariot racing to Rome. The city was even ruled by Etruscan kings until the founding of the Republic.

Etruscan tomb painting
The Etruscans were known for their beautiful wall art, as well as statues made of bronze and terra-cotta.

THE ROMAN REPUBLIC

According to early Roman historians, the Roman Republic was founded in around 509 BCE, when the last Roman king, Tarquin the Proud, was overthrown. The monarchy was replaced with a system of elected officials (magistrates), led by two consuls, who worked alongside a council of nobles called the Senate.

Roman engineering

The Romans were skilled and innovative engineers. Rome's armies were able to cover huge distances using a network of roads so well-built that some are still in use today. The Romans built aqueducts to carry water to towns and cities, and they constructed bridges over rivers. They also designed effective mills, pumps, siege engines, dams, and even under floor heating.

Roads
Roman roads were made up of five layers, and designed to last. Parts of some Roman roads still survive today.

Aqueducts
Romans built colossal aqueducts to take water from lakes to public baths, fountains, houses, and mills.

Julius Caesar

After winning support as a brilliant general in the Roman army, Julius Caesar won power in Rome after defeating his political rival, Pompey, in a civil war. He became the most powerful man in Rome, but was murdered in 44 BCE by a group of senators who feared he would make himself king.

The murder of Caesar
On March 15 (known as the "Ides of March" in the Roman calendar), Caesar was stabbed to death by a group of Senators called the "Liberators."

Timeline

Ancient Rome
In its history, Rome experienced three different forms of government: monarchy, republic, and empire. Under each, its influence gradually grew.

753 BCE

Founding of Rome
Little is known of the early history of Rome. According to legend, Rome was founded by twin brothers Romulus and Remus. During an argument, Romulus murdered his brother and he became the first king, giving the city his name.

C. 509 BCE

Rome becomes a republic
After its last king was overthrown, Rome adopted a new form of government, the republic, which was governed by magistrates and consuls. The Roman Republic lasted until the beginning of the Roman Empire in 27 CE.

264–146 BCE

Carthaginian Wars
The North African city of Carthage, in modern-day Tunisia, was the greatest rival of the Roman Republic. Between 264 and 146 BCE, Rome and Carthage fought three wars. Rome ultimately destroyed Carthage, burning the city to the ground.

73–71 BCE

Spartacus revolts
Romans relied upon slave labor, but between 135 and 71 BCE, the Republic had three major slave rebellions. The last was led by Spartacus, a gladiator-general.

58–50 BCE

Julius Caesar in Gaul and Britain
Between 58 and 50 BCE, Julius Caesar conquered the Celtic tribes of ancient Gaul, adding most of modern-day France and Belgium to the Roman Republic. He also invaded Britain in 55 and 54 BCE, but with little success.

27 BCE

Rome becomes an empire
After Caesar's murder in 44 BCE, his great-nephew, Octavian, hunted down the assassins and defeated them. He fought his rivals to become the first emperor of Rome. He took the title Augustus, which means "majestic."

1 million There were at least **this many people** living in the city of Rome by the **1st century CE**.

No women, even the free born, could **vote or hold office** in ancient Rome.

49

THE ROMAN EMPIRE

At its greatest extent in 117 CE, the Roman Empire covered around 2 million sq miles (5 million sq km) and included tens of millions of people.

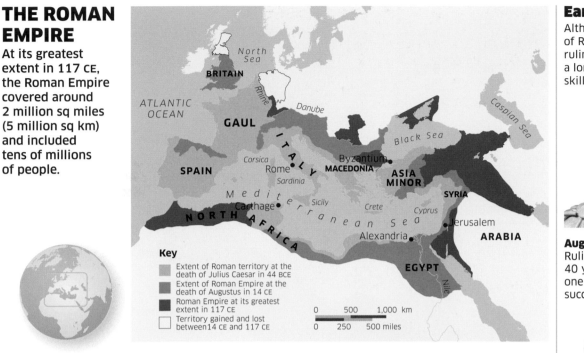

Key
- Extent of Roman territory at the death of Julius Caesar in 44 BCE
- Extent of Roman Empire at the death of Augustus in 14 CE
- Roman Empire at its greatest extent in 117 CE
- Territory gained and lost between 14 CE and 117 CE

0   500   1,000 km
0   250   500 miles

Emperor
The most powerful person in the Roman Empire.

Senators
Rich and powerful lawmakers who governed Rome.

Equestrians
Noble families, who were often wealthy and influential.

Plebeians
Working people, such as laborers and merchants.

Freedmen
Former slaves who had been granted freedom.

Slaves
Slaves had no rights, and were owned by their masters.

Roman society

The people of the Roman empire had different rights depending on their place in society. At the bottom were slaves, who often came from conquered foreign nations outside of Rome. At the top were the noble-born families of the equestrians and senators, as well as the emperor.

Heart of the empire

At its height, the Roman Empire stretched 2,500 miles (4,000 km) east to west and 2,300 miles (3,700 km) north to south. The central hub of this vast civilization was the city of Rome, which by the 1st century CE had more than 1 million inhabitants.

Rome in 100 CE
By the end of the 1st century CE, the city of Rome was filled with palaces, temples, theaters, public baths, monuments, and amphitheaters.

Early emperors of Rome

Although Julius Caesar never became emperor of Rome, his adopted son and heir Octavian did, ruling with the title Augustus. He was the first in a long line of emperors. Some were strong and skilled statesmen, but others abused their power.

Augustus (27 BCE–14 CE)
Ruling for more than 40 years, Augustus was one of Rome's most successful emperors.

Caligula (37–41 CE)
Known for his cruelty, Caligula was one of many Roman emperors to be assassinated.

Claudius (41–54 CE)
A great administrator, Claudius expanded the Roman Empire by conquering Britain.

Nero (54–68 CE)
Later Roman historians gave Nero a reputation for being a cruel and selfish emperor.

Trajan (98–117 CE)
The soldier-emperor Trajan expanded the Roman Empire to its greatest extent.

Hadrian (117–138 CE)
In Hadrian's reign, a massive wall was built in Britain to mark the limit of the empire.

---

70 CE

The Colosseum is begun
Titus Flavius Vespasianus, known as Vespasian, founded the Flavian Dynasty in 69 CE. He ruled for 10 years, but is best known for beginning construction of the Colosseum in Rome. He was the first Roman emperor to pass the throne on to his son.

113 CE

Trajan's column
This marble column in Rome celebrates the military victories of Emperor Trajan. It was completed in 113 CE and inspired many later victory and memorial columns, such as Nelson's Column in Trafalgar Square, London.

From 122 CE

Hadrian's Wall
Built to protect Roman Britain from northern tribes in modern-day Scotland, Hadrian's Wall was 73 miles (118 km) long. The wall had a fort every 5 miles (8 km) along its length.

286 CE

The Eastern and Western Roman empires
Near the end of the 3rd century CE, the vast Roman Empire split in two, with the western half ruled from Milan and Ravenna and the eastern half ruled from Nicomedia at first and later from Constantinople (modern-day Istanbul).

312–330 CE

The rule of Constantine
The emperor Constantine founded the city of Constantinople, which became the capital of the Eastern Roman Empire. He also became the first emperor to convert to Christianity, but only did so on his deathbed.

476 CE

The fall of Rome
From the late 4th century CE, the Western Roman Empire declined in power, unable to prevent the advance of powerful tribes from western and central Europe. The last western emperor, Romulus Augustulus, was overthrown by a Germanic king in 476 CE.

50 the ancient world ○ THE ROMAN ARMY

Even with their packs, legionnaires could march 22 miles (35 km) in five hours.

The Roman army

The army of the Roman Empire was the most effective fighting force of the ancient world. Unlike most of their enemies, Roman soldiers were highly trained and made their living from being in the army.

The finest soldiers were heavily armed citizen foot soldiers called legionaires. They joined up at the age of about 18, and served for the next 25 years. Constant training, and marching with heavy equipment, kept them fit. Legionaires were laborers as well as fighters. They built temporary camps, as well as forts and roads. Alongside the legionaires were noncitizen soldiers called auxiliaries (helpers), who were lightly armed and fought as archers, slingshot wielders, and cavalry (soldiers on horseback).

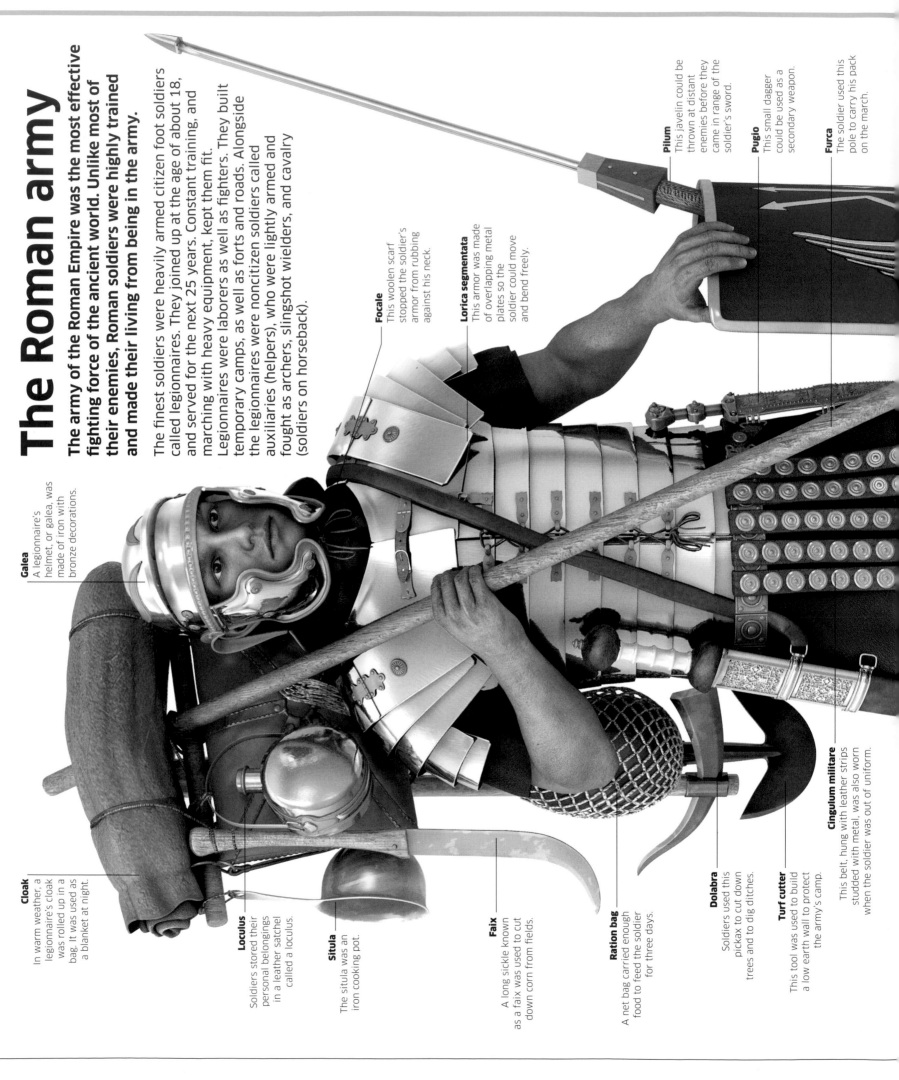

Galea
A legionnaire's helmet, or galea, was made of iron with bronze decorations.

Cloak
In warm weather, a legionaire's cloak was rolled up in a bag. It was used as a blanket at night.

Loculus
Soldiers stored their personal belongings in a leather satchel called a loculus.

Situla
The situla was an iron cooking pot.

Faix
A long sickle known as a faix was used to cut down corn from fields.

Ration bag
A net bag carried enough food to feed the soldier for three days.

Dolabra
Soldiers used this pickax to cut down trees and to dig ditches.

Turf cutter
This tool was used to build a low earth wall to protect the army's camp.

Cingulum militare
This belt, hung with leather strips studded with metal, was also worn when the soldier was out of uniform.

Focale
This woolen scarf stopped the soldier's armor from rubbing against his neck.

Lorica segmentata
This armor was made of overlapping metal plates so the soldier could move and bend freely.

Pilum
This javelin could be thrown at distant enemies before they came in range of the soldier's sword.

Pugio
This small dagger could be used as a secondary weapon.

Furca
The soldier used this pole to carry his pack on the march.

375,000 The **total number of soldiers** in the **Roman army** in 117 CE.

165,000 The number of **legionnaires** in the **Roman army** in 117 CE.

51

Tunic
Soldiers wore a short-sleeved, knee-length woolen tunic underneath their armor.

Scutum
This rectangular curved shield was made of wood covered in leather.

Roman cavalry
The soldiers who made up the Roman cavalry were skilled horse riders who were able to fight from the back of a horse.

Cavalry unit
Each legion was supported by a cavalry unit made up of 120 skilled horse riders.

Lesser cohorts
The second to tenth cohorts were made up of 500 men each, with the tenth cohort being the least experienced.

First cohort
The first cohort was made up of 800 men, who were the most experienced soldiers in the legion.

Marching equipment
On the march, each legionnaire carried his own equipment and supplies, in a "sarcina" (pack) carried on a pole slung over his shoulder. The sarcina included food rations and a sickle for reaping corn, as well as a pickax and turf cutter to help build a new camp at the end of every day's march.

Gladius
The gladius was a short, stabbing sword used in close-quarters fighting.

"Then they advance, all
marching in silence
and in good order, each man
keeping his place
in the ranks, as if in face of the enemy ..."

Josephus, Description of the Roman Army, 70 CE

Caligae
The soles of these heavy sandals were reinforced with iron nails.

A Roman Legion
The Roman army was split into legions. In 117 CE, when the Roman Empire reached its greatest extent, there were 30 Roman legions spread throughout the empire. Each had a number and a name, which might have been the country its soldiers came from or a nickname, such as "Fulminata" (lightning hurler). One legion was made up of 5,500 men, split into 10 divisions called cohorts. These cohorts in turn were divided into centuries, smaller units of 100 men. Each legion also had a unit of cavalry, who served as scouts and messengers.

Roman daily life

There were big differences between the lives of rich and poor people in the Roman Empire. While the wealthy had lives of luxury, the poor often lived in small rooms in badly built slum blocks.

In a traditional upper-class Roman family, the oldest male was known as the paterfamilias (father of the family). He often owned a town house, called a domus, and a country house, or villa. While the villa was a place to relax and go hunting, the domus was where the paterfamilias did business and socialized. Every morning he received a stream of visitors, who were often less wealthy Romans coming to ask favors. The family was served by many slaves, who did all the housework, acting as maids and cooks. The slaves lived in small, simple rooms around the courtyard at the back of the domus.

Atrium
The atrium (entrance hall), where visitors were greeted, was the most public part of the house. The compluvium, an opening in the roof, let in light. Beneath, rainwater collected in the impluvium, an ornamental pool.

A Roman domus
The plan for this Roman domus is based on evidence found at Pompeii, where many houses were preserved when they were buried by a volcanic eruption in 79 CE.

Ianua and vestibulum
The front door (ianua) opened into a small entryway (vestibulum) that was closed off from the main domus.

Taberna
The parts of the domus facing the street were rented out as tabernas (shops). These were often run by former slaves of the family.

Peristylum
Romans loved gardens, and a domus often had a peristylum, a courtyard filled with plants or sometimes featuring a small pool.

Latrina
The latrina (toilet) was cleaned out using waste water from the kitchen.

Culina
Slaves cooked all the meals, which were prepared over a charcoal fire in the culina (kitchen).

Tablinum
At the center of the domus, the tablinum was an office, where the paterfamilias conducted his business.

Triclinium
The dining room (triclinium) was named after the three couches on which diners reclined to eat. They leaned on their left elbow and ate with their right hand.

High-rise living
In Rome and other big cities, the poor lived in towering apartment blocks called insulae (meaning "islands"). Often badly and cheaply built, they were at constant risk of fire and sudden collapse. The tallest could reach nine stories in height.

Cubiculum
The cubiculum (bedroom) was not just where family members slept. It was also a place for private meetings with important visitors.

Lararium
Every home had a small shrine called a lararium, where offerings were made each day to the gods who watched over the family.

Concrete walls
A Roman invention, concrete was a cheap building material. Early concrete was made of rubble held together with a material called lime (which means "sticking"). Volcanic ash was added to the mix to help prevent cracks.

54 the ancient world ○ **GERMANIC PEOPLES**

3 The number of days the Visigoths spent plundering Rome.

Germanic peoples

In 250 BCE, hundreds of tribes were living in a region known to the Romans as Germania (in Scandinavia and eastern Europe). Many were nomads and migrated across large distances, forming new kingdoms and battling old empires as they roamed across the continent.

Germanic people settled across modern-day Germany, Scandinavia, France, Britain, Spain, and North Africa. They lived outside and near the borders of the Roman Empire. The Germanic tribes were not united and often fought among themselves, as well as with the Roman Empire. During the 4th and 5th centuries CE, after several rebellions and wars, the tribes contributed to the fall of the Western Roman Empire. Over the next 300 years, small Germanic kingdoms formed across Europe and would later grow into some of the major European kingdoms of the medieval period.

GERMANIC PAGANISM

The many Germanic tribes had their own religious beliefs. They worshipped many gods that represented nature and the world around them. These beliefs are collectively known as Germanic paganism. They also believed in supernatural beings, such as elves, sprites, and dragons. As the tribes migrated across Europe, each tribe's religious beliefs changed over time.

Torslunda plates
Cast in bronze, the Torslunda plates were found in Sweden in 1870. Historians think that they show scenes from Germanic mythology.

RELATIONSHIP WITH ROME

For more than 600 years, the Germanic tribes were at odds with the Roman Empire. In the 4th century CE, people known as the Huns migrated into Germania, forcing several tribes to move into lands occupied by the Roman Empire. Some tribes settled peacefully and traded with the Romans, as well as adopting their values and traditions. But they started to rebel and invade more land, and also attacked Rome several times.

Chieftain Arminius
In 9 CE, in Teutoburg Forest in modern-day western Germany, chieftain Arminius defeated invading Roman legions.

GERMANIC TRIBES

The Germanic people formed many tribes across Europe, from Scandinavia in the north to the Black Sea in the south. After the fall of the Roman Empire in 476 CE, some of these tribes established the first Germanic kingdoms.

Vandals

The Vandal tribe of Scandinavia migrated through mainland Europe. They settled in North Africa in the 5th century CE, where chieftain Genseric started the Vandal Kingdom.

VANDALS PLUNDER ROME, 455 CE

Suebi

The Suebi were a collection of tribes, including the Marcomanni, Quadi, and Lombards. They settled along the banks of the Elbe River in central Europe, as well as venturing west to modern-day Spain where some tribes established the Kingdom of the Suebi.

SUEBIAN STATUE OF A PRAYING MAN

Goths

The Goths were made up of two tribal groups—the eastern Goths, known as the Ostrogoths, and the western Goths, known as the Visigoths. In 410 CE, Goth leader Alaric I successfully attacked and plundered Rome. In the late 5th century, Theodoric the Great formed an Ostrogothic empire in modern-day Italy.

THE MAUSOLEUM OF THEODORIC

Some **Germanic warriors** believed that **pendants** worn on their swords could **heal wounds**.

Germanic **prophets**, known as **soothsayers**, performed **rituals at sacred locations**, such as groves.

55

WARFARE AND WEAPONS

Germanic warriors were fearless fighters. They used iron to make swords, but iron was scarce, and their swords were weaker than the steel weapons used by the Roman Empire. They were also armed with lances, wooden clubs, and darts. It was rare for a Germanic warrior to wear armor, and most carried a shield made from wicker or wooden planks.

Sutton Hoo helmet
A 7th-century Germanic helmet discovered at a burial site called Sutton Hoo in Britain was made from iron and copper.

KINGS AND CHIEFTAINS

Germanic tribes were ruled by skilled warriors. These chieftains led by example and gained reputations as fierce warlords. After centuries of war with the declining Roman Empire, the nomadic tribes settled and claimed land. Their rulers changed from chieftains into monarchs, reigning over their new territories.

Germanic chieftain
Clovis I was a chieftain before he became the first king of the Franks in 482 CE. He was baptized as a Christian in 496 CE.

GERMANIC SOCIETY

At first, Germanic tribes were clan-based, with related families forming small settlements of wooden houses. They grew crops and reared animals for food. Over the centuries, as populations grew and the need for protection increased, military chieftains and lords came to power, with younger warriors pledging loyalty to their leader.

Mead hall
Large one-room buildings called mead halls, also known as feasting halls, were places where tribespeople and warriors celebrated with their lord or chieftain.

People in Germanic society had a value in gold known as weregild based **on their social status.** If they were killed or injured, their family would receive payment from the attacker.

Anglo-Saxons
The Anglo-Saxon tribes migrated from northern Germany into Britain from the 5th to the 6th centuries. Several Anglo-Saxon languages merged and became known as "Old English."

ANGLO-SAXON PENDANT, 600 CE

Lombards
From the 6th to the 8th centuries, the Lombard tribe split from the Suebi tribes and started the Kingdom of the Lombards, occupying most of modern-day Italy.

LOTHAR I, KING OF THE LOMBARDS

Franks
The Franks spread from modern-day western Germany into Belgium and France. Charlemagne formed the Carolingian Empire, one of the most powerful kingdoms in western Europe.

CHARLEMAGNE, KING OF THE FRANKS

THE MEDIEVAL WORLD

In the 1,000 years between the 5th and 15th centuries, the collapse of the Roman Empire fractured Europe into rival kingdoms. China, and new Islamic empires spreading from the Middle East, went through golden ages of art and science. In Japan, warlords took over the empire, eventually leading to a century of civil war. New cultures emerged in the Americas, Africa, Southeast Asia, and the Pacific.

SAMURAI ARMOR AND WEAPONS

c. 1190: Mesa Verde Cliff Palace
The ancestral Pueblo, a people of southwest North America, built a settlement now known as Cliff Palace in a rock face at Mesa Verde in modern-day Colorado.

ANCESTRAL PUEBLO WOVEN BASKET

13th century: Maori arrive in New Zealand
The Polynesian people known as the Maori settled on the islands of New Zealand, which they called Aotearoa, meaning "land of the long white cloud."

MAORI MASK

1185: Warlords rule Japan
With the support of his samurai armies, the military leader Minamoto Yoritomo came to power in Japan. This led to more than 400 years of conflict as rival warlords fought for control of Japan.

12th century: Great Zimbabwe
The Kingdom of Zimbabwe in southeast Africa built a capital city known as Great Zimbabwe. Its towers were the tallest structures in sub-Saharan Africa until the arrival of Europeans in the 15th century.

BIRD SCULPTURE AT GREAT ZIMBABWE

KRAK DES CHEVALIERS

Timeline of the medieval world

In Europe, with the fall of the Roman Empire, ancient knowledge was lost and regional rulers fought each other for dominance. But across Asia and the Americas, old and new empires continued to expand and flourish.

Belief in Christianity took hold across Europe, while the new religion of Islam quickly spread out from the Middle East into North Africa and southern Spain. Conflict between the two religions led to centuries of warfare. Elsewhere, the great cultures of China and India spread their influence into Southeast Asia, while the Pacific Islands were settled by Polynesians. Great civilizations arose in the Americas, isolated from the rest of the world until the arrival of Europeans in the 15th century.

CHARLEMAGNE

802–1431: The Khmer Empire
The people of the Khmer Empire in Southeast Asia constructed hundreds of temples at their capital city of Angkor, in modern-day Cambodia.

ANGKOR TEMPLE SCULPTURE

800: The Holy Roman Empire
Charlemagne was crowned the first emperor of the Holy Roman Empire, a group of territories in west and central Europe.

794–1185: The Heian Period
During the Heian Period, a high point of Japanese culture, literature and the arts flourished at the imperial court and Buddhism continued to spread throughout Japan.

HEIAN PERIOD BUDDHIST STATUE

527–565: Justinian I
The eastern portion of the Roman Empire survived the fall of Rome in 476 CE, and continued on as the Byzantine Empire. One of its most successful emperors, Justinian I, led many campaigns to conquer parts of North Africa and Italy.

JUSTINIAN I

MISSISSIPPIAN CULTURE DECORATED POT

From c. 700: Mississippian culture
In North America, Native American tribes living in the Mississippi Valley region built giant earth mounds and traded in pottery and woven items.

JABAL AL-NOUR

c. 610: Islam begins
According to Islamic belief, the prophet Muhammad began preaching Islam after being visited by an angel at a cave in a mountain now known as Jabal al-Nour (the "Mountain of the Light").

MONGOL QUIVER

1206–1368: The Mongol Empire
The Mongol tribes of Central Asia, united under the leadership of Genghis Khan, conquered large areas of Asia, the Middle East, and Europe, creating one of the largest empires in history.

SONGHAI TOMB

c. 1335–1591: The Songhai Empire
The Muslim Songhai Empire was one of the largest states in African history. It controlled all trade along the Niger River in West Africa.

1368–1644: The Ming Dynasty
Ming China produced highly prized porcelain pottery. The Ming also took on great building projects, such as the Forbidden City in Beijing and the rebuilding of the Great Wall of China.

MING PORCELAIN VASE

1095–1291: The Crusades
Christian armies from Europe set out on a series of holy wars known as the Crusades. Their aim was to conquer cities in the Holy Land (in the Middle East) that were under Muslim control. The Crusaders built or captured many castles, such as Krak des Chevaliers.

HAGIA SOPHIA

1054: The East–West Schism
The Roman Catholic Church and the Eastern Orthodox Church separated in an event known to historians as the East–West Schism. The Hagia Sophia cathedral in Constantinople became the center of Orthodox Christianity.

960–1279: The Song Dynasty
During the Song Dynasty, the Chinese economy boomed and the population of China doubled from 50 million to 100 million. Like the Tang emperors before them, the Song were great patrons of the arts.

SONG DYNASTY COIN

c.1000: Vikings land in America
The Viking explorer Leif Erikson and his crew became the first Europeans to set foot on the east coast of North America. They named the area they explored Vinland, after the grapevines they found there.

LEIF ERIKSON

793: The Vikings raid Lindisfarne
A seafaring people from Scandinavia known as the Vikings raided a Christian monastery on Lindisfarne, an island off the coast of England. For the next three centuries, the Vikings launched attacks against coastal settlements throughout Europe.

VIKING HELMET

THE CITY OF BAGHDAD

750–1258: The Abbasid Dynasty
The Abbasids oversaw a period of learning, art, and culture across the Islamic world. They ruled from the new city of Baghdad.

618–907: The Tang Dynasty
Under the rulers of the Tang Dynasty, China experienced a Golden Age of cultural and artistic achievement. The Tang set up academies to promote arts such as pottery making, scroll painting, and poetry.

THE MEZQUITA OF CÓRDOBA

c. 718–1492: The Spanish Reconquista
The Moors, an Islamic people of North Africa, invaded southern Spain in the 8th century. They converted many churches, such as the Mezquita in Córdoba, into mosques. The Spanish drove out the Moors after a series of wars known as the Reconquista ("reconquest").

TANG STATUE OF A DANCER

Timeline

Medieval Christianity

As empires rose and kingdoms fell, Christianity endured and became increasingly powerful. Christianity helped to build kingdoms, mighty institutions, and spread new ways of thinking. However, it also sparked violent wars and created divides between empires and cultures.

313–380 CE

Christianity endorsed by Rome
At first, Romans treated Christians with violence, as the Christians refused to worship Roman gods. However, in 313 CE, attitudes started to change when Emperor Constantine I granted religious freedom to all Christians in the Roman Empire. Later, in 380 CE, Emperor Theodosius I made Christianity the official religion of the Roman Empire.

597

AUGUSTINE OF CANTERBURY

Augustine of Canterbury
A group of monks led by Augustine journeyed from Rome to England on a mission to spread Christianity in 597. Augustine became the first Archbishop of Canterbury, converting thousands of English people to Christianity, including King Ethelbert of Kent.

711–1492

Spanish Reconquista
At the start of the 8th century, Muslim people known as Moors invaded modern-day Spain and Portugal. From the early 8th century to the end of the 15th century, the Christian kingdoms of Spain battled the Muslim Moor armies for control of the region. The conflict lasted for more than 700 years and is known as the Spanish Reconquista.

The power of the Church

From its beginnings in the 1st century CE, the religion of Christianity began to spread from the Middle East, eventually reaching Europe. The teachings of the Christian Church became a part of everyday life.

For its first 1,000 years, the Church was unified and was led from Rome by a religious leader known as the Pope. This Roman Catholic Church influenced all aspects of medieval society, from the courts of kings and queens to the daily routines of peasants. As it grew in power, the Church gained wealth and began to control large areas of land. It built elaborate places of worship, helped care for the sick, and provided education. It also helped raise armies for war and influenced powerful monarchs.

Aachen Cathedral
Built under the rule of Charlemagne in the late 8th century, Aachen Cathedral is the oldest cathedral in northern Europe and was inspired by eastern Roman architecture.

AACHEN

Joan of Arc
Joan of Arc, a peasant girl, believed she was chosen by God to help drive the invading English from France. In 1429, she led French armies against English troops and helped win many battles.

AVIGNON

Palais des Papes
Between 1309 and 1377, Pope Clement V temporarily moved the headquarters of the Roman Catholic Church from Rome to the Palais des Papes in Avignon in France because of political unrest in Rome.

The Mezquita
When the Muslim Moors invaded modern-day Spain in the 8th century, they captured Christian cathedrals such as the Mezquita in Córdoba. It was adapted into an elaborate mosque. In the 13th century, when Christians regained Córdoba, it was converted back into a cathedral.

CÓRDOBA

30 The **number of years** it took to **build** the **Old St. Peter's Basilica in Rome**.

1.3 billion The **approximate number** of **Catholics** in the world today.

61

800

HOLY ROMAN EMPEROR CHARLEMAGNE

Charlemagne crowned
In 800 CE, the Frankish king, Charlemagne, was crowned Holy Roman Emperor by Pope Leo III. Charlemagne's Holy Roman Empire included most of western and central Europe.

1054

The East–West Schism
In the middle of the 11th century, the Roman Catholic Church, based in Rome, and the Eastern Orthodox Church, based in Constantinople, separated. This was caused by years of arguments over interpretations of the Bible and cultural differences between the Roman West and the Greek East.

1084–c. 1250

Different factions emerge
During the 11th to the 13th centuries, several religious orders emerged from monasteries throughout Europe and the Middle East. These new orders, such as the Cistercians, Carthusians, and Carmelites, focused on a solitary existence, taking vows of silence and living simple, disciplined, and spiritual lives.

1095–1291

The Crusades
In 1095, Pope Urban II called for the Christian armies of Europe to invade the sacred cities of the Holy Land in the Middle East, which were at that time under the control of Muslim empires. Over the next 200 years, several wars between Christian and Muslim armies, known as the Crusades, raged across the Middle East.

1455

The Gutenberg Bible
During the Printing Revolution, the first mass-produced book was a Bible made by printing pioneer Johannes Gutenberg. It had 1,286 pages that filled two volumes. The expensive Bibles were bought by wealthy church leaders.

GUTENBERG BIBLE

Christian Europe
The Roman Catholic Church was based in Rome, with its headquarters at Old St. Peter's Basilica from the 4th century CE. The building was demolished and replaced with the current St. Peter's Basilica in the 16th century. The Eastern Orthodox Church, which split from Rome in the 11th century, was based in the city of Constantinople (modern-day Istanbul).

Old St. Peter's Basilica
Old St. Peter's Basilica was built in the 4th century CE. It was one of the most important centers of the Roman Catholic Church and the largest church in the world. It became a sacred destination for pilgrimage and religious ceremonies.

Vladimir the Great's baptism
The Grand Prince of Kiev, Vladimir the Great, converted to Christianity in 988 CE and helped spread the religion across eastern Europe.

CHERSONESUS

Hagia Sophia
Built during the reign of Byzantine ruler Justinian I in the 6th century, the Hagia Sophia cathedral in Constantinople was the center of Orthodox Christianity.

CONSTANTINOPLE

ROME

Montecassino
The hilltop monastery at Montecassino was founded in the 6th century. It is home to one of the first orders of monks–the Benedictines.

The Byzantine Empire

In 395 CE, the Roman Empire was divided in two. The Western Roman Empire was captured by barbarians in 476 CE, but the Eastern Roman Empire survived, and became known as the Byzantine Empire.

The Byzantine Empire was named after Byzantium, the original name of its capital, Constantinople (now Istanbul in present-day Turkey). At its height, the Byzantine Empire stretched from southern Spain to the Middle East. Its people were devoutly Christian, spoke Greek, and referred to themselves as Romans. The Byzantine Empire was invaded by barbarians and nearby empires many times, but it endured for almost 1,500 years.

527–565
Emperor Justinian I was crowned in 527. During his reign, he led many successful military campaigns to conquer parts of North Africa and Italy.

976–1025
Emperor Basil II ruled over a golden age in which the Byzantine Empire grew wealthy, produced great works of art and literature, and strengthened its military might.

1095–1204
The Byzantine Empire allied with European kings during the Crusades, a series of military campaigns against the Muslim empires.

1204–1453
The Byzantine Empire grew even weaker after constant invasions. Now just a city-state, Constantinople was conquered by the Ottoman Turks in 1453.

600–900
The Byzantine Empire lost some of its territory to nearby Muslim empires and to invaders from Europe and Persia.

1054
The Byzantine Empire split from the Roman Catholic Church and formed the Eastern Orthodox Church.

1204
The Byzantine Empire's alliance with European kings dissolved and the Crusaders attacked and plundered the city of Constantinople. The empire became severely weakened.

Byzantine empress
This mosaic depicts Empress Theodora (in the middle wearing a brown robe and a jeweled crown decorated with sapphires and emeralds) and other ladies of the Byzantine royal court. Theodora married Emperor Justinian I, and together they ruled over the Byzantine Empire.

EARLY JAPAN

From 11,000 BCE, during the Jomon Period, clans of people lived in small settlements on the islands of Japan and created simple pottery. Around 10,000 years later, in the Yayoi Period, the clans mined bronze and iron, and farmed rice.

The Kofun Period (300–552 CE)

The Kofun Period is now known for the elaborate burial mounds that were built for the era's leaders. The tombs were created in several designs, including special keyhole shapes. *Haniwa*—cylinder-shaped figurines crafted from clay—were buried with the dead.

DAISEN KOFUN NEAR OSAKA, THE LARGEST KOFUN TOMB IN JAPAN

The Asuka Period (552–710)

Japanese society began to change during the Asuka Period. Buddhism arrived from Korea and started to spread with the help of the Soga clan, who rose to power and dominated Japan until 645.

A new name
During the Asuka Period, the islands became known as Nippon, which means "land of the rising sun."

The Nara Period (710–794)

During the short Nara Period, Buddhism grew in popularity and became a mainstream religion across Japan. Large Buddhist temples were built, such as the one at Todaiji. The era was also known for its poetry and historical literature.

NARA BUDDHIST STATUE

The Heian Period (794–1185)

The Heian Period was the high point of the imperial court and early Japanese culture. Literature flourished, with female writers such as Murasaki Shikibu and Sei Shonagon producing works that are still read today.

MURASAKI SHIKIBU WRITING *THE TALE OF GENJI*, c. 1020

Medieval Japan

From the end of the 12th century to the beginning of the 17th century, Japan experienced a turbulent period of civil war, power struggles, and foreign intervention.

Military leaders came to power in Japan, supposedly ruling in the name of the emperor. These leaders took control of the country, setting up military governments, called shogunates, that ruled Japan for more than 400 years. The leaders of these governments were known as the shoguns, and they commanded armies of loyal warriors known as samurai. Warfare between the samurai clans broke out regularly, as rival leaders competed for control. Yet among the civil wars and social chaos, Japanese culture and art continued to flourish.

JAPANESE SOCIETY

Under the samurai, everyone in Japan had different rights and privileges, depending upon their role in society. The social system was similar to that of Europe, but here, peasants were seen as an important part of society, because farmers and fishermen provided food for everyone to eat. Merchants were looked on less favorably, as they produced nothing and profited from the work of others.

Emperor
Although the emperor was seen by the Japanese as the supreme ruler, he lacked any real power.

Shogun
Officially the emperor's second-in-command, the shogun made most of the political decisions.

Daimyo
Influential landowners, the daimyo swore loyalty to the shogun and employed samurai to guard their land.

Samurai
These elite Japanese warriors served and protected their masters and their community, living by a code of honor.

Peasants and craftworkers
The samurai protected those below them in return for food, weapons, armor, and other goods.

Merchants and servants
All classes of the community were served by people who bought and sold goods.

ERA OF THE SHOGUNS

During the Heian period, wealthy landowners hired warriors to protect their land. These warriors became known as the samurai. After the Genpei War, in the late 12th century, the victorious Minamoto clan set up the first shogunate (a government controlled by a military dictator) and claimed power. Over the next 400 years, civil wars raged across Japan as rival clans tirelessly battled each other for territory and power.

Castles

Japanese castles were initially built in important strategic positions, such as along trade routes and next to major rivers. They later became the official residences of lords and their samurai followers. The castle itself stood at the heart of a complex of buildings that were built to govern the local lands.

Himeji Castle
The Himeji Castle complex was made up of more than 80 buildings and was protected by an imposing stone base and several moats.

THE UNIFICATION OF JAPAN

During the second half of the 16th century, three influential daimyo, Oda Nobunaga, Toyotomi Hideyoshi, and Tokugawa Ieyasu, helped bring an end to the civil wars, and finally united the warring clans of Japan. Tokugawa Ieyasu established the last shogunate of Japan, bringing all of the regional lords under his control.

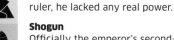

10% The estimated amount of the **Japanese population** that belonged to the **samurai class**.

7 The **number of virtues** the samurai were expected to possess. They included **honesty, courage, loyalty,** and **honor**.

65

The samurai

The name samurai means "one who serves." The samurai were soldiers who loyally supported their shoguns and protected the lands of their lords. They followed a strict code of conduct, known as Bushido. The sword was an important part of samurai culture and represented their status.

Culture and the arts

New traditions and art forms developed during the medieval period. Decorative arts, such as garden design, flower arranging, and calligraphy (handwriting) flourished. The rituals of the tea ceremony, originally from China, took on a distinctly Japanese form. Plays and performance arts, such as Noh dance-dramas, also became popular.

Masks
Noh masks were crafted from wood. They were carved so that, depending on the position of the actor and the stage lighting, the expressions and moods looked different to the audience.

MASK OF AN OLD MAN

MASK OF A WOMAN

14TH-CENTURY SAMURAI ARMOR AND WEAPONS

Timeline

Japan under the samurai

When Minamoto Yoritomo became the first shogun, the elite warrior class of samurai rose to power. This led to more than 400 years of conflict as rival samurai warlords battled with each other for power.

1192
Minamoto Yoritomo becomes shogun
After defeating rival clans, Minamoto Yoritomo established the Kamakura Shogunate, taking the political power away from the emperor. Yoritomo's authority relied on the samurai.

1274 and 1281
The Mongols invade
Having conquered China, Mongol leader Kublai Khan set his sights on Japan. He amassed a huge fleet and tried to invade by sea on two occasions. However, the samurai and a series of devastating storms made the Mongols retreat both times.

1331–1333
Genko War
Emperor Go-Daigo attacked the Kamakura Shogunate with the help of the shogun's rivals. A civil war broke out, known as the Genko War, and the Kamakura Shogunate was defeated.

1338
Ashikaga Shogunate
The Kamakura Shogunate were betrayed by one of their own generals, Ashikaga Takauji, who then stole power from Emperor Go-Daigo and established the Ashikaga Shogunate in Kyoto.

1467–1477
Onin War
The Onin War started an era of civil war and unrest across Japan known as the Sengoku or "Warring States" period. Japan divided into regional warring clans battling for dominance.

1543
Japanese firearms
When Portuguese sailors arrived in Japan with firearms, Japanese engineers studied the weapons and started to manufacture them. This changed how battles were fought.

Oda Nobunaga

Using new firearms, based on those brought to Japan by Portuguese sailors, Oda Nobunaga and his samurai defeated many rival clans and overthrew the Ashikaga Shogunate. By the time of his death in 1582, Nobunaga had united nearly half of Japan.

Toyotomi Hideyoshi

Toyotomi Hideyoshi took over as Oda Nobunaga's successor after Nobunaga's death. He continued the attempt to conquer all of Japan and eventually unified all of the clans. In 1585, he became the Chancellor to the Emperor, and later, the Chief Imperial Minister.

Tokugawa Ieyasu

After Toyotomi Hideyoshi's death, another civil war broke out as rival clans tried to claim power. In 1600, Hideyoshi's powerful advisor, Tokugawa Ieyasu, won the Battle of Sekigahara. He took lands away from his previous enemies, placed his allies in strategic positions, and established an era of peace across Japan.

66 the medieval world ○ **THE EARLY ISLAMIC WORLD**

62 million—the **population** of the Islamic **empire** during the **reign** of the Umayyads.

The Mezquita
Islamic people known as theMoors arrived in Spain from Morocco in 711. The Islamic influence on Spanish architecture can be seen in the red-and-white archways inside the Mezquita's prayer hall in Córdoba.

CÓRDOBA

TANGIER

CAIRO

The Islamic empire
At its height in the mid-8th century, the early Islamic states formed one of the largest empires the world had ever seen, stretching for more than 5,000 miles (8,000 km) from modern-day Spain across North Africa, through the Middle East, and into Asia.

City of the Dead
This network of tombs, crypts, and mausoleums in Cairo was built during the Islamic conquests of Egypt.

Ibn Battuta
The great explorer Ibn Battuta (1304–1369) traveled the world for nearly half of his life. His journey of around 75,000 miles (120,000 km) took him through modern-day Turkey, Crimea, Asia, India, China, and Africa.

The early Islamic world

The religion of Islam was founded by the prophet Muhammad in the Middle East in the early 7th century. Within just 100 years, powerful Muslim armies had spread the influence of the new religion across three continents, creating an Islamic empire.

Over the following centuries, the Islamic empire continued to expand its borders in Asia, Africa, and Europe. The empire was ruled by a series of caliphs ("successors" of Muhammad), many of whom encouraged the development of new ideas in science, math, and medicine. Travelers and merchants from the Islamic world journeyed far and wide, spreading their culture and beliefs around the world.

Pioneering scientist
Ibn al-Haytham (965–1040), also known as Alhazen, was one of the world's first physicists. He performed many experiments that helped establish the idea of the scientific method.

During the **9th** and **10th centuries**, the **Islamic empire** established some of the **world's first universities**.

29 The **number of years Ibn Battuta** spent **traveling the world**.

67

Early Islamic leaders

According to Muslim belief, Islam was founded in 610 when a merchant named Muhammad saw a vision of an angel in a cave. The angel dictated to Muhammad the word of Allah (God), which he wrote down as the Quran, Islam's holy book. Muhammad went on to unite the tribes of Arabia under Islam.

UTHMAN IBN AFFAN, SECOND CALIPH

The first rulers

When Muhammad died in 632, the first Islamic government, known as a caliphate, was created. The first four caliphs were leaders who had been taught by Muhammad.

The Umayyads

In the mid-7th century, the Umayyad Dynasty took control of the caliphate and expanded its lands to Spain and Central Asia.

UMAYYAD GREAT MOSQUE

The Abbasids

The Abbasid Dynasty came to power in 750 and encouraged learning, art, and culture. They began to lose power during the 13th century after the Mongol Empire destroyed Baghdad, their capital.

ABBASID ART

FATIMID TEXTILE

The Fatimids

During the 10th century, a rival clan to the Abbasids, the Fatimids, claimed to be descendants of Muhammad's daughter, and rose to power across North Africa and the Middle East.

The Mamluks

The Mamluks were slave warriors before they overthrew their masters, the Abbasids, and took over the caliphate. They were formidable soldiers, defeating the Mongols.

MAMLUK POTTERY

Timeline

632–661	661–750	750–1258	909–1171	1250–1517

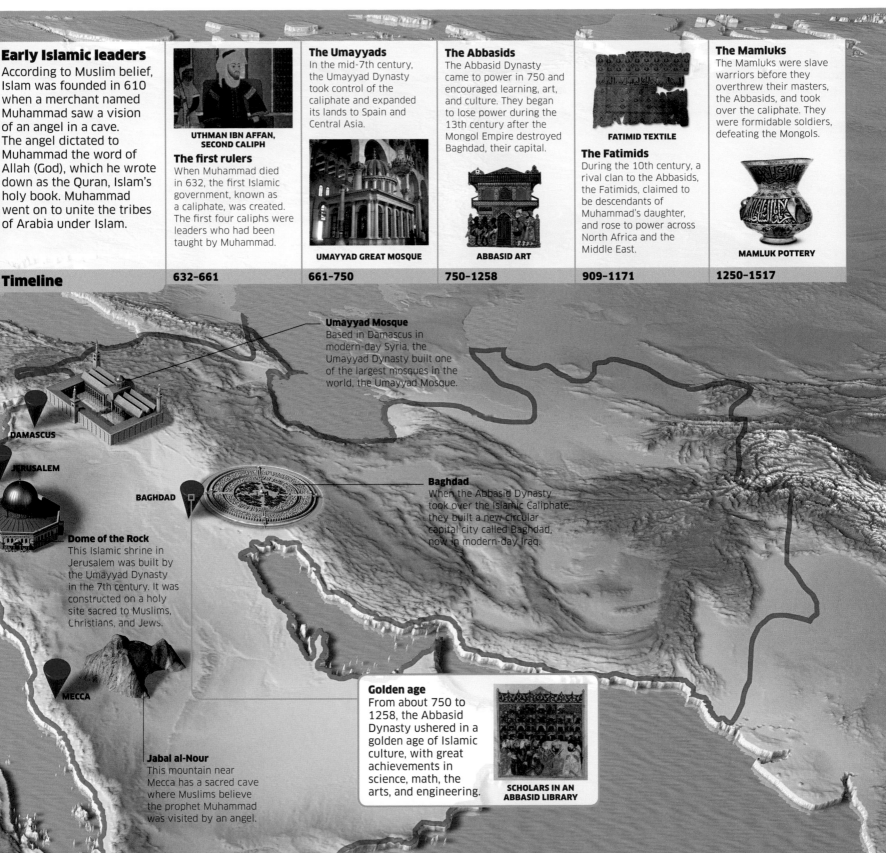

Umayyad Mosque
Based in Damascus in modern-day Syria, the Umayyad Dynasty built one of the largest mosques in the world, the Umayyad Mosque.

DAMASCUS

JERUSALEM

BAGHDAD

Baghdad
When the Abbasid Dynasty took over the Islamic Caliphate, they built a new circular capital city called Baghdad, now in modern-day Iraq.

Dome of the Rock
This Islamic shrine in Jerusalem was built by the Umayyad Dynasty in the 7th century. It was constructed on a holy site sacred to Muslims, Christians, and Jews.

MECCA

Jabal al-Nour
This mountain near Mecca has a sacred cave where Muslims believe the prophet Muhammad was visited by an angel.

Golden age
From about 750 to 1258, the Abbasid Dynasty ushered in a golden age of Islamic culture, with great achievements in science, math, the arts, and engineering.

SCHOLARS IN AN ABBASID LIBRARY

> "I constantly sought knowledge **and truth.**"
>
> Alhazen, Islamic scientist, *Book of Optics*, 1021

68 the medieval world ○ **THE VIKINGS**

870 The year **Iceland was discovered** by a Viking who set sail from Norway.

The Vikings

The Vikings, a seafaring people from Scandinavia, ventured beyond their homeland in search of land, raw materials, and lured by the promise of gold and silver.

From the 8th to the 11th centuries, the Vikings' fearsome reputation spread as they raided and plundered settlements across Europe. But they weren't just pirates—the Vikings were excellent shipbuilders, sailors, and navigators, too. They were daring explorers, sailing as far west as North America and traveling overland as far east as Baghdad in present-day Iraq. They also created new trade routes, selling animal furs, crafts, and slaves.

Kitchen
A fire in the hearth burned all day and night for cooking and warmth. Cooking cauldrons were either hung from the ceiling or suspended from a tripod. Once the Sun had set at the end of the day, families gathered together to eat.

Viking longhouse
When they were not at sea, Vikings lived a rural life in large, narrow homes known as longhouses. Several families lived inside a longhouse, alongside their animals. There was little privacy, but it was cozy and warm.

Smoke holes
Gaps in the roof allowed smoke from the fire to escape.

Growing crops
Crops included wheat, rye, barley, and oats, as well as onions, cabbages, and peas.

Chopping firewood
Lots of dry firewood was needed to keep the fire burning inside the longhouse.

Longhouse floor
The floor was made from compacted earth.

Wattle and daub walls
Walls were made of interwoven branches, covered in a mixture of clay, soil, sand, and straw.

Important Vikings were buried in boats, along with their weapons and valuables.

841 The year **Viking explorers first settled in Dublin, Ireland.**

Some longships had enough space to **carry horses** as well as crew.

69

Barn animals
Vikings kept their animals and tools in a barn area at one end of the longhouse.

Roof materials
Roofs were made from materials such as wooden tiles, thatched reed, or turf.

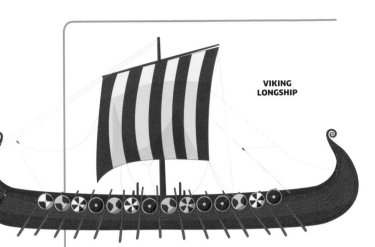

VIKING LONGSHIP

Adventurous explorers

The Vikings used their navigational skills to explore far-reaching lands, sailing fast wooden longships huge distances. Each ship had a large sail as well as 24–50 oars with a crew of at least as many people. One group of Viking explorers crossed the Atlantic Ocean, stopping in Scotland and Iceland before reaching Greenland in 982. In about 1000, Leif Eriksson was the first European to make landfall on the east coast of North America.

Viking warriors

In 793, Viking raiders destroyed a Christian monastery on Lindisfarne, an island off the northeast coast of England. This violent raid shocked the Christian world. For the next three centuries, Viking raiders terrorized Europe, looting enough treasure to fill their ships, taking slaves, and setting up bases from which to attack new targets. They demanded enormous payments in return for leaving areas in peace.

VIKING HELMET

Prized animals
Sheep, cows, goats, and poultry supplied meat, eggs, and milk for food, as well as wool for clothing.

Sleeping areas
The Vikings ate, worked, and slept on raised wooden platforms that ran alongside the walls of the longhouse. They used animal furs and blankets to keep warm and comfortable. Longhouses had little furniture—only the richest families had chairs or beds.

Weaving garments
Viking women spent part of each day making clothes. They used wool or flax on a weaving loom to make fabric, which they then fashioned into clothing. Vikings wore simple tunics, sometimes embellished with patterns or fur trimmings.

Gods and religion

The Vikings worshipped many different gods, such as the one-eyed Odin, the super-strong thunder god Thor, and the mischief-maker Loki. Around campfires, they told stories through songs and poems about the gods and their epic battles against giants and monsters. Over time, as the Vikings settled across Europe, they began to convert to Christianity.

Storage space
Locked wooden chests stored clothing, blankets, and family valuables.

Thor's hammer
Thor was the favorite god of farmers and peasants. His hammer protected him against his enemies.

Medieval Europe

Between around 720 and 1400, many European nations were organized on the feudal system, in which different levels of society, from kings and queens to peasants, had obligations to each other for military protection, the rights to farm land, and food.

Feudalism affected everyone living in northern and western Europe. Rulers needed armies to defend their kingdoms, so they shared their land with lords, who would supply them with trained and armored knights in return. For the next 700 years the knight became one of the most important soldiers in the army of European monarchs.

Jousting tournaments

To train and show off their combat skills, knights took part in elaborate tournaments. They would battle each other in a joust, exhibitions of swordplay, and show off their horse-riding skills.

Plate armor

By the 15th century, improved weaponry, such as crossbows, and advances in making armor meant knights replaced chain mail with suits of armor made from metal plates. This meant they were better protected, although it was heavier than chain mail.

Coat of arms

A knight's shield was decorated with his personal coat of arms, so other soldiers could identify its owner.

Scabbard

The knight stored his sword in a leather pouch that had been shaped to fit the weapon.

Chain mail

A knight wore a shirt of chain, known as a hauberk. It was made up of small interlinking metal rings and was an effective defense against most medieval weapons.

Helmet

The knight's helmet was made of metal and often had a hinged visor and holes to allow him to breathe.

Shield

A knight carried a shield made of wood or metal to protect him during battles and tournaments.

Sword

Knights mainly used swords in battle, but they also used lances, maces, and war hammers.

Warhorse

The knight's combat horse was bred for strength, stamina, and speed.

The **word "knight"** comes from an Old English word **meaning "servant."**

3,000 The **number of knights** that attended the **largest tournament,** at **Lagny-sur-Marne, France,** in **1179.**

71

Bard

A knight's horse wore special armor, called a bard, which was very expensive and heavy.

Stirrup

The stirrup supported the knight's foot, allowing him to balance and fight, even on a charging horse.

Knight of the realm

A knight was usually of noble birth and began his training from the age of seven. He started as a page, helping to care for another knight's horse and equipment. At around the age of 13, he became a squire, starting combat training and assisting his knight during battle. He eventually became a knight himself at the age of 21.

The feudal system

The king allowed lords to hold areas of the king's lands (known as "fiefs") in exchange for money and the promise of fighting men during times of war. The lords then leased parts of their fief to noble knights. Knights were in charge of law and justice in their land. Serfs (peasants) worked the land for the knights, producing food and supplies in exchange for a place to live. Some serfs worked for free, others paid rent—but no serf was allowed to leave the fief without the permission of their lord.

Monarch

A king and queen owned all the land in their kingdom.

Lords and ladies

Lords and ladies received land (often a manor house) and peasants from the monarchs in exchange for loyalty and military aid.

Knights

Knights received food, protection, and land from lords ir exchange for loyalty and military service.

Serfs

Serfs received food, protection, and a place to live from knights in exchange for work and rent.

The Black Death

During the middle of the 14th century, a plague known as the Black Death spread across Europe, killing millions. Suddenly, there were fewer peasants to work the land and the demand for peasants rose. Peasants realized they could choose where and for whom they worked, which led to feudalism's decline.

DOMINANT EMPIRES

The mix of cultures and religions created tensions between the kingdoms of Southeast Asia, leading to rivalry, war, and the rise and fall of several empires throughout the region's history. However, from the 11th century onward, a group of large empires—the Khmer (see right), Champa, Srivijaya, Pagan, and Dai-Viet—were locked in a power struggle to dominate the area.

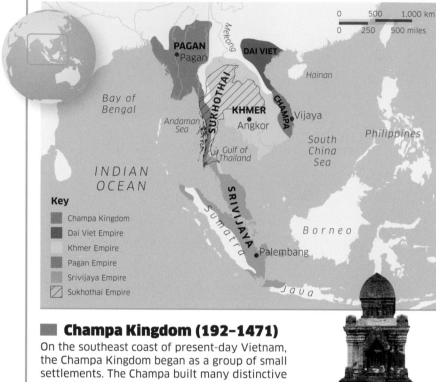

Key
- Champa Kingdom
- Dai Viet Empire
- Khmer Empire
- Pagan Empire
- Srivijaya Empire
- Sukhothai Empire

◼ Champa Kingdom (192–1471)

On the southeast coast of present-day Vietnam, the Champa Kingdom began as a group of small settlements. The Champa built many distinctive red-brick temple-towers, and survived several attacks from their more powerful neighbors.

ANCIENT HINDU TEMPLE AT MY SON COMPLEX, VIETNAM

SRIVIJAYAN METAL COINS

◼ Srivijaya Empire (c.650–1288)

This sea-based empire had its capital on the Indonesian island of Sumatra. It controlled all sea trade to India and China, before losing its dominance to the seafaring Indian Chola Dynasty.

◼ Pagan Empire (849–1287)

Built on the Irrawaddy River in present-day Myanmar, Pagan started out as a city-state, but later united the surrounding states to form an empire. Its people built thousands of Buddhist temples.

BUDDHA STATUE AT SULAMANI TEMPLE, MYANMAR

◼ Dai Viet Empire (939–1804)

Around what is now present-day Hanoi in Vietnam, the Dai-Viet Empire emerged in the 10th century. It created foreign trade routes, and survived invasions from the powerful Mongol and Khmer empires.

BUST OF DAI VIET MILITARY COMMANDER TRAN HUNG DAO

▨ Sukhothai Empire (1238–1438)

In the early 13th century, Sukhothai separated from the Khmer Empire and became the first independent Thai state in the region. The new empire spread from what is now present-day Thailand into Laos and Myanmar.

SUKHOTHAI STONEWARE DISH

Empires of Southeast Asia

From the 2nd century CE, contact with the cultures of India, China, Europe, and the Middle East transformed the tribes and settlements in the jungles of Southeast Asia into great city-states, kingdoms, and empires.

Early Southeast Asian societies were shaped by the politics, religions, art, and architecture of their neighbors, India and China. European and Arab merchants later brought their own culture to the region. By combining these influences in different ways, Southeast Asia developed many distinct cultures. Some became empires, building huge cities and thousands of temples, as well as seaports to trade with the rest of the world.

◎ THE KHMER EMPIRE

The Khmer Empire (802–1431) was one of the largest and most powerful in the region. Stretching from present-day south China to Malaysia, the Khmer Empire used the Mekong River for trade and travel. The Khmer people were great builders and constructed roads, canals, and reservoirs. The capital of the empire was based in Angkor, which, at its peak, was the largest city in the world. It had hundreds of temples, including Angkor Wat.

"The suffering of **the people** is the suffering of the **emperor.**"

Emperor Jayavarman VII, 1181–1218

Angkor Wat

Originally a Hindu temple, Angkor Wat was built in the early 12th century by thousands of workers for Suryavarman II, the ruler of the Khmer Empire. It was a large complex that covered an area of 0.75 square miles (2 square km).

Main entrance
The main entrance, to the west of the complex, had lion statues guarding a stone causeway.

Ancient shrine
Eight towers surrounding Angkor Wat are thought to have been part of an old shrine.

Water barrier
The moat around the complex was about 650 ft (200 m) wide.

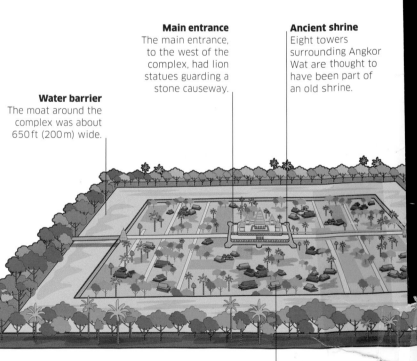

Khmer homes
The Khmer people probably lived in thatched houses surrounding the temple.

1 million The **number of people** that lived in **Angkor** during the 12th century.

200 The **number of wall paintings** decorating **Angkor Wat.**

73

RELIGIOUS INFLUENCE

The empires of Southeast Asia were influenced by the religions of India, China, the Middle East, and Europe, as traders, conquerors, and pilgrims traveled through the region. Four of the world's major religions—Hinduism, Buddhism, Islam, and Christianity—have all been important in the history of Southeast Asia.

Hinduism from the 1st century
Hindu culture spread overland from India in the northwest, as well as by sea when Indian sailors began to visit the region.

Buddhism from the 6th century
Both Indian and Chinese cultures brought Buddhism to a few empires. Some Hindu temples later became Buddhist.

Islam from the 10th century
Arab merchants traveled the long trade routes from the Middle East to East Asia, bringing Islam to the region.

Christianity from the 16th century
Portuguese traders brought Christianity to the area. Dutch, English, and German missionaries helped spread the new faith.

MALACCA AND THE SPICE ISLANDS

In the 15th century, the city-state of Malacca was formed in what is now present-day Malaysia. It soon became the main port for the region's spice trade. In the 16th century, Europeans arrived, looking to trade in nutmeg, mace, cloves, and pepper.

Central tower
The 215-ft (65-m) central tower of the temple was accessed by a steep staircase.

Laterite core
A hard, red-colored rock called laterite formed the core of the buildings.

Towers
The four outer towers and the central tower of the temple are thought to symbolize Mount Meru from Hindu mythology.

Intricate design
The intricate decorative features on the temple buildings were carved from soft sandstone, and then adorned with gold.

Vishnu statue
The temple was built in honor of the many-armed Hindu god Vishnu, who had a giant statue in the central tower. The statue was later moved near the entrance.

KHMER WOMEN PARTICIPATED IN TRADE AND SERVED AS BODYGUARDS FOR THE KING

Cultures of North America

Before the arrival of Europeans from the late 15th century onward, several distinct cultures developed across the different landscapes of North America.

In their early history, North American tribes relied on their environment for food–they hunted, fished, and gathered seeds and nuts to eat. Later, some tribes began to farm the land, growing crops and rearing animals for food, clothing, and tools. Some of the tribes were nomadic, and followed food sources such as migrating bison herds. Others settled by rivers or built structures into mountainsides. Many tribes were experts in basket weaving, pottery, and sculpting, creating unique works of art.

Basket weaving
The Ancestral Pueblo were expert basket makers. They weaved intricate patterns into their baskets, which were used to gather crops, nuts, and berries. The baskets were also used for cooking.

ANCESTRAL PUEBLO
Date: From 1500 BCE

Originally hunter-gatherers, the tribes of the Ancestral Pueblo culture that lived in the mountainous regions of the modern-day states of Arizona, New Mexico, Colorado, and Utah eventually became farmers. They built some of their settlements in large sheltered cliff faces, such as the Cliff Palace at Mesa Verde.

Hunter
The Ancestral Pueblo hunted animals to supplement the crop harvest.

Grinding corn
Corn was ground down using a rounded stone called a mano and a flat stone plate called a metate.

Crafting pots
Pottery was made from long coils of clay. Pots were decorated with geometric patterns.

Turkeys
Domesticated turkeys were reared for food, and their feathers and bones were used to decorate clothing and make tools.

ADENA CULTURE
Date: c. 1000–100 BCE

The Adena culture was a collection of tribes that lived in western and central North America. They were hunter-gatherers, following animal herds and farming simple crops. They used tools, created pottery, and built large earth mounds, which were used as places to meet and for ceremonies.

SERPENT MOUND IN MODERN-DAY OHIO

HOPEWELL CULTURE
Date: c. 200 BCE–500 CE

A collection of societies and tribes that arose from the Adena culture, the Hopewell culture spread along the rivers of eastern North America. They were skilled sculptors and developed a large network of trade routes along rivers and streams.

SCULPTURE OF A DUCK AND FISH

MISSISSIPPIAN CULTURE
Date: c. 700–1600

The tribes of the Mississippian culture were mostly farmers, who grew corn, squash, and beans. They lived in small towns in the Mississippi Valley and the surrounding areas, constructing houses and buildings on top of earth mounds and platforms. They also sculpted and carved unique works of art and decorated pottery.

DECORATED POT

c. 100 The number of people that lived at the **Mesa Verde Cliff Palace**.

50 million people were living in North America by the late 1400s.

75

Homes
Multi-story homes were made from sandstone and mortar, and accessed by ladders.

Storing crops
Small rooms at the back of the Cliff Palace were used to store crops.

Farming the land
Ancestral Pueblo farmed crops such as corn and beans on the fertile ground above and behind the cliff face. They built dams to ensure their crops got enough water.

Family
Many families occupied the Cliff Palace, with several generations living together.

Kiva
Built underground, large circular chambers known as kiva were used for important community meetings and religious ceremonies. They were accessed through a hole in the roof that also let out smoke from a fire pit below.

Tools
The Ancestral Pueblo did not use metal—they crafted tools from animal bones and stone.

GREAT PLAINS HUNTERS
Date: From at least 10,000 BCE

The many tribes of the Great Plains of central North America were hunter-gatherers who followed herds of migrating bison. They crafted bison remains into everyday items, such as headdresses. The people of the Great Plains were nomads and lived in cone-shaped tepees (tents) that were easy to build, pull down, and transport.

AMERICAN BISON

THE NORTHWEST COAST
Date: From c. 9000 BCE

The tribes that lived along the Pacific coastline of western North America relied on the ocean for food. They used trees from coastal forests to make canoes and houses. The Makah tribe carved images in stone (called petroglyphs) showing hunters, priests, whales, and ships, which can still be seen today.

MAKAH PETROGLYPH IN MODERN-DAY WASHINGTON STATE

DORSET AND THULE PEOPLE
Date: From c. 500 BCE

The tribes of the Dorset and Thule cultures lived in the Arctic regions of North America. They adapted to living in cold climates, making houses from bones and clothing from furs and animal skins. The Dorset tribes hunted seals, while the Thule tribes used harpoons and skin-covered canoes to hunt whales.

THULE HOUSE IN MODERN-DAY ONTARIO IN CANADA

China's Golden Age

In the 7th century, after a period of 400 years in which China was divided into rival clans, the Tang Dynasty unified the country and ushered in a cultural and creative golden age.

Poetry, pottery, and scroll painting flourished under the new regime. Academies were set up to promote the arts, and an exam system encouraged scholars to join the government. After the Tang Dynasty's decline, the Song Dynasty ruled and maintained the empire's cultural and economic prosperity. This period of peace and growth saw China's population rise to more than 100 million.

618–626
Governor Li Yuan ended the brief reign of the Sui Dynasty and proclaimed himself Emperor Gaozu, the first ruler of the Tang Dynasty.

626–649
Emperor Taizong, the son of Gaozu, encouraged learning and the arts, and expanded the empire's borders.

690–705
The Tang Dynasty was briefly interrupted by the Zhou Dynasty, led by Empress Wu Zetian, a former mistress of Emperor Taizong.

712–756
Emperor Xuanzong established academies for musicians and poets. He was overthrown by a rebellion led by the warlord An Lushan.

820–907
Assassinations and corruption weakened the Tang Dynasty, leading to rival armies clashing throughout the fragmented empire.

960–1126
The Song Dynasty rose to power and encouraged classic Chinese traditions, improved living conditions, and organized an increase in rice and iron production.

1127–1279
After losing territory in the north to the Jin Dynasty, the Song Dynasty continued to reign in the south, but eventually fell to the Mongol Empire.

Scroll painting
Painted by Zhang Zeduan during the Song Dynasty, *Along the River* was more than 16½ ft (5 m) long. This color version of the scroll was created during the Qing Dynasty (1644–1911).

78 the medieval world ○ **THE CRUSADES**

c. 50,000 The number of Crusaders that fought in the Second Crusade.

Multiple battles

The first four Crusades involved thousands of soldiers fighting in violent battles across the Middle East, with power and land shifting between Muslim and Christian forces. As the battles raged on, the Middle East endured five more "Minor Crusades," as well as other smaller campaigns and internal conflicts.

The First Crusade

Since 638, Muslim rulers had controlled the Holy Land. In 1095, Pope Urban II called for the First Crusade, and a year later armies marched east to take back the city of Jerusalem from the Muslims. Within three years of fighting, they regained control of the city and established four Crusader states.

THE SIEGE OF JERUSALEM

The Second Crusade

After defeat in the First Crusade, the Muslim Seljuk Empire declared *jihad*, or holy war, against the Crusader states. German and French soldiers marched east, but they were defeated by Seljuk forces at Damascus in present-day Syria.

The Third Crusade

Forty years later, the Muslim sultan of Egypt, Saladin, captured the city of Jerusalem from the Crusaders. A third Crusade, led by many kings such as King Richard the Lionheart of England, reestablished Christian rule in the region, but was unable to take back Jerusalem. Instead, Richard and Saladin agreed a treaty that allowed Christian pilgrims safe passage into the city.

KING RICHARD I

The Fourth Crusade

Called for by Pope Innocent III, the Fourth Crusade set out to once again recapture Jerusalem. However, the armies were diverted to Constantinople, and the Crusaders sacked the city for its wealth.

Crusades Five to Nine

For the next 90 years, the Crusaders fought five more holy campaigns that saw their grip on the Middle East weaken. Their presence in the Holy Land ended in the late 13th century, when a new Muslim dynasty, the Mamluks, led by Sultan Baybars, forced the Christian Crusaders to retreat and head home.

SULTAN BAYBARS

Timeline

1095–1099

1147–1149

1189–1192

1202–1204

1217–1291

The Crusades

From the end of the 11th century, European Christian armies embarked on a series of military campaigns called the Crusades. They invaded Muslim empires in an effort to gain control of cities in the Holy Land, a region in the Middle East sacred to both Christians and Muslims.

For the next 200 years, these campaigns were led by European kings and nobles, and involved thousands of knights who traveled east to battle Muslim forces. At first, the Crusaders were victorious and captured several key cities across the Middle East as they took advantage of divisions between the Muslim empires. The Crusaders established small kingdoms and built huge castles throughout the region to defend their newly conquered lands. However, the Muslim forces defended their land, and eventually defeated the Crusaders, forcing 0them to return home to Europe.

Arrow loops
Openings along the walls and the towers allowed archers to fire on the enemy below.

Krak des Chevaliers

The Crusaders captured, built, and adapted many castles to defend their newly established states. Krak des Chevaliers in present-day Syria was built by Muslims in 1031, but was captured in 1110 by Christian armies, who expanded it from 1142–1170. With thick stone walls and towers, this castle proved to be a formidable fortress.

A long journey east

In heavy armor and carrying their equipment and supplies, most of the Crusaders marched east for months across dangerous terrain. They traveled more than 2,000 miles (3,220 km) from western Europe to Jerusalem. In later Crusades, they sailed across the Mediterranean Sea—a voyage that was faster and safer than the journey across land.

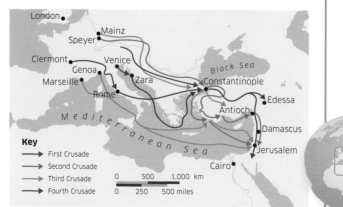

London
Mainz
Speyer
Clermont
Venice
Genoa
Zara
Marseille
Rome
Black Sea
Constantinople
Antioch
Edessa
Mediterranean Sea
Damascus
Jerusalem
Cairo

Key
→ First Crusade
→ Second Crusade
→ Third Crusade
→ Fourth Crusade

0   500   1,000 km
0   250   500 miles

Climbing the walls
The invading forces used long ladders to climb the castle's outer walls.

Machicolations
Holes in the floor at the edge of battlements, called machicolations, allowed the defending army to drop rocks and boiling oil on the invaders below.

During the Crusades, **several religious orders of knights** were formed, including the **Knights Templar** and the **Knights Hospitaller**.

2,000 The **maximum number of knights Krak des Chevaliers** could hold.

79

Order of knights
The Knights Hospitaller, who controlled Krak des Chevaliers, were an order of knights that wore distinctive black clothing with white crosses.

Inner citadel
The middle part of the castle had a chapel and main hall, and was entered through a second, heavily guarded gateway.

Catapult defense
The Crusaders used catapults, known as trebuchets, to launch huge rocks from the top of large towers. They were used to target siege towers and machines, as well as break up attacking lines of enemy soldiers.

Battering ram
Many armies favored this type of siege machine, which was used to break open castle walls and doors. To protect the soldiers operating the ram, sloping roofs were built to deflect arrows and boiling oil.

Moat
Between the outer walls and the inner citadel was a moat of water, a further barrier for invaders.

Turrets
The castle's outer wall contained several round towers that allowed soldiers to defend in every direction.

KINGDOM OF AKSUM
Date: 100–900 CE

Located on the Red Sea coast in what is modern-day north Ethiopia and Eritrea, Aksum grew rich on trade. The kingdom converted to Christianity c. 340 CE. Legend says that the kings of Aksum were descended from King Solomon and the Queen of Sheba, prominent figures in the Bible.

AKSUMITE COIN

KANEM-BORNU EMPIRE
Date: c. 700–c. 1840

This empire emerged around Lake Chad. It formed at the southern end of the trade route that crossed the Sahara Desert to other settlements on the Mediterranean coast. Traders exchanged salt, ostrich feathers, and ivory for horses and guns. The empire reached its peak in the 17th century.

PART OF A KANEM-BORNU HORSE HARNESS

> "Among the gold mines of the plains … is a fortress **made of stones** of marvellous size."

Vicente Pegado, a Portuguese captain, after visiting Great Zimbabwe, 1531

KINGDOM OF ZIMBABWE
Date: From the 12th century to 1450

The city of Great Zimbabwe was once the center of the powerful Kingdom of Zimbabwe in southeast Africa. Its rulers controlled the gold trade between inland regions and the Indian Ocean coast. The modern-day country of Zimbabwe is named after this kingdom. The Great Enclosure, the most impressive part of the city, may have been the royal palace.

Narrow passageway
Historians think a narrow passage that ran for 180 ft (55 m) between the outer and inner walls may have been used as a secret escape route if the city was invaded.

Clay house
A group of clay-walled thatched huts within a circular walled enclosure may have been home to the king and his family.

Inner wall
A maze of inner walls within the Great Enclosure divided public and private spaces.

Outer wall
The outer wall, made of cut blocks of granite, was 32 ft (9.7 m) high in some places.

Sub-Saharan kingdoms

About 3,000 years ago, groups of farmers began migrating out of the rain forests of West Africa into much of sub-Saharan Africa—the vast region of Africa south of the Sahara Desert.

These farmers, who spoke many different forms of Bantu languages, taught the hunter-gatherers and cattle-herders living in the grasslands how to use iron. Around 100 BCE, people from Asia brought tame camels into North Africa. North African traders could now cross the Sahara Desert to bring back gold from sub-Saharan Africa. These changes led to organized kingdoms emerging in different parts of the region.

KINGDOM OF BENIN
Date: 1200–1897

The wealthy Kingdom of Benin, in what is modern-day Nigeria, was ruled by a powerful king called an Oba. The kingdom's people, the Edo, made many kinds of art, including fine metalwork. In 1897, British soldiers stormed the Oba's palace and looted all their treasures.

BRONZE BENIN SCULPTURE

1 million The approximate number of **stones** used to **build** the **Great Enclosure** at **Great Zimbabwe**.

100,000 The **population of Timbuktu**, capital of the Mali Empire, in **1500**.

81

Soapstone bird
At least eight sculptures of an eaglelike bird, carved from soapstone, were found in the ruins of Great Zimbabwe.

Conical tower
A tall tower at the end of the passage probably had religious or symbolic meaning.

Patterns
Part of the outer wall was decorated with a pattern of chevrons (V-shapes).

Courtyard
A large courtyard near the main entrance may have been used for ceremonies.

MALI EMPIRE
Date: From 1230 to the 16th century

The vast empire of Mali lay on the southwestern edge of the Sahara Desert. Its most famous ruler, Mansa Musa I, was a Muslim and the richest person in the world at the time. He ordered the building of the Great Mosque in Timbuktu, a city famous for its artists and scientists.

MALIAN POTTERY

KINGDOM OF KONGO
Date: 1390–1914

The Kingdom of Kongo, in what is modern-day Angola, was the most powerful state in Central Africa. The kingdom traded in cloth and pottery. Its rulers converted to Christianity after the arrival of Portuguese traders in 1483. It became a Portuguese colony in 1914.

KONGOLESE SWORD

SONGHAI EMPIRE
Date: c. 1335–1591

Sonni Ali was the first ruler of the Songhai Empire. He took control of gold trade routes across the Sahara Desert from the Mali Empire, which was by then in decline. Songhai's capital was Gao on the Niger River in modern-day Mali.

TOMB OF SONGHAI EMPEROR ASKIA MOHAMMED

82 the medieval world • POLYNESIAN EXPANSION

Statues on Easter Island once had eyes made from coral and a volcanic glass known as obsidian.

Polynesian expansion

Around 1400 BCE, people living in Southeast Asia sailed east from New Guinea to find new homes. They began to settle on thousands of islands in the Pacific Ocean known as Polynesia (meaning "many islands").

Polynesia stretches from New Zealand in the south to Hawaii in the north and Easter Island in the east. The earliest Polynesians sailed eastwards. They continued to explore and settle the Pacific until Polynesian cultures spread across the whole region east of Fiji. Polynesians shared similar languages and beliefs, but developed their own identities and ways of life.

WAVES OF MIGRATIONS

The Lapita people from the Bismarck Archipelago, off New Guinea, sailed to Fiji, Samoa, and Tonga in c. 1400 BCE. More than a thousand years later, they settled on the eastern Polynesian islands. A few centuries later, they discovered and settled Hawaii and Easter Island. The final migration occurred around 1,000 years ago, when Polynesian seafarers landed in New Zealand.

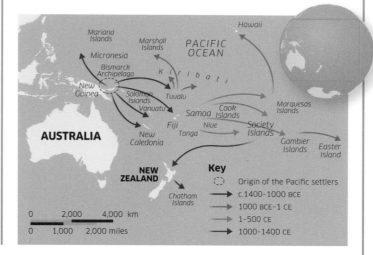

Key
- ◌ Origin of the Pacific settlers
- → c.1400–1000 BCE
- → 1000 BCE–1 CE
- → 1–500 CE
- → 1000–1400 CE

OUTRIGGER CANOE

Polynesians were expert sailors and built canoes called outriggers. These boats were made from two hulls attached to each other with logs and rope. Outriggers varied in size and were fast, robust, and could withstand voyages of up to 3,000 miles (4,800 km). Polynesians are thought to have been the first people to navigate across open ocean, using the stars, sea currents, weather patterns, and migrating birds to chart their course.

Rope
Polynesians made rope out of coconut fibers to hold their masts upright.

Prow
The prow (front end) of the canoe cut through choppy water.

THE SPREAD OF ANIMALS

Polynesian explorers brought animals such as pigs, chickens, and dogs with them as they settled new islands. Dogs were used to hunt, while pigs and chickens were sources of food. Stowaway rats, attracted by food on the boats, also spread from island to island. The newly introduced animals and the settlers' overhunting caused many native mammals and birds to become extinct.

PIG

RAT

CHICKEN

SAUDELEUR DYNASTY

The Saudeleur Dynasty (c. 1100–1628) was one of the first organized governments in the region and ruled the island of Pohnpei in Micronesia for more than 500 years. It was established by twins, Olisihpa and Olosohpa, who arrived in a canoe.

Nan Madol
The capital of the Saudeleur Dynasty, Nan Madol was built on man-made islands and canals. Historians call it the "Venice of the Pacific."

HAWAII

Made up of volcanic islands, Hawaii was settled by Polynesian explorers in about 400 CE. Over several centuries, more migrations from Tahiti and the Society Islands brought new religions and ideas to the islands. When the migrations ended, Hawaii started to develop its own culture, art, and spiritualism, including Ho'omana (which means "to make life force"). Followers of Ho'omana meditated while visualizing special symbols to focus their minds and bodies.

Kahanu
A symbol of energy.

Ke-Ao Lanihuli
A symbol of purity.

Uli-Nana-Pono
A symbol of calm.

Kahanuala
A symbol of breath.

MAORI CULTURE

In the 13th century, the Maori were the first people to settle in what is now called New Zealand. They called the islands Aotearoa, meaning "land of the long white cloud." The settlers lived in large groups that were ruled by chiefs. Their beliefs were passed on through songs and dance, and they worshipped more than 70 gods.

Maori mask
Traditionally, Maori masks were intricately carved from wood. The masks honored their ancestors.

10 million sq miles (25 million sq km)—the **total area** that **Polynesia** covers in the **Pacific Ocean**.

6,500 miles (10,500 km)—the **distance Polynesians traveled over several generations** from **New Guinea to Easter Island**.

83

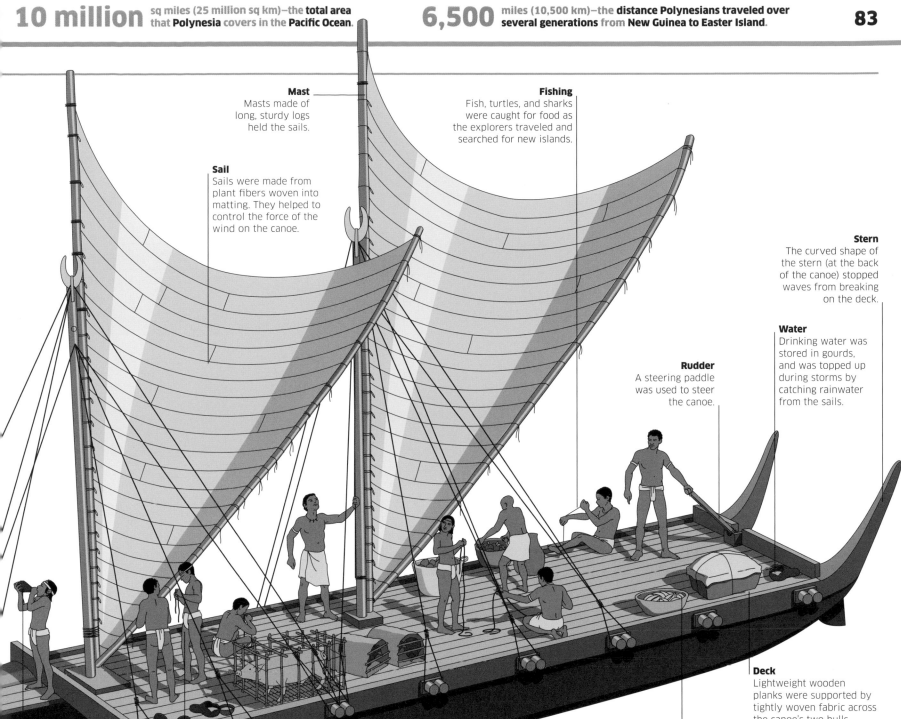

Mast
Masts made of long, sturdy logs held the sails.

Fishing
Fish, turtles, and sharks were caught for food as the explorers traveled and searched for new islands.

Sail
Sails were made from plant fibers woven into matting. They helped to control the force of the wind on the canoe.

Stern
The curved shape of the stern (at the back of the canoe) stopped waves from breaking on the deck.

Water
Drinking water was stored in gourds, and was topped up during storms by catching rainwater from the sails.

Rudder
A steering paddle was used to steer the canoe.

Deck
Lightweight wooden planks were supported by tightly woven fabric across the canoe's two hulls.

Storage
The hollow hulls provided space to store supplies, which also weighed down the canoe to keep it stable at sea.

Food
As well as food for the journey, plants, seeds, and animals were transported to help start new settlements.

Polynesian explorer
Several families would travel on the canoe as they searched for new islands to settle.

Conch
Conch shell horns, known as *Pu*, were used to communicate across the water between the canoe and people on shore.

Hull
Large tree trunks were carved and hollowed out to create the main hulls of the canoe.

EASTER ISLAND

Polynesians colonized Rapa Nui (known today as Easter Island) between 800 and 1200 CE. They built large stone statues called moai, which represented their ancestors and were worshipped as gods. As the population grew, it split into tribes, which fought for resources such as wood and food that were becomig scarce. After c. 1500, the people of Rapa Nui toppled the moai statues and adopted a new belief system with new gods. They organized annual rituals, which saw them compete against each other every year to select the island's ruling tribe.

Polynesian navigators
used shells, sticks, and coconut fibers to make simple maps of the islands and sea currents they experienced on their journeys.

Moai statues
All of the Moai statues faced outwards from the island and were placed on ceremonial platforms.

The Mongol Empire

In the late 12th and early 13th centuries, the Mongol tribes were nomads living in the grasslands of Central Asia. Temüjin, a chieftain who later took the name Genghis Khan ("universal ruler"), united them in 1206. From then until 1368, the Mongols conquered large areas of Asia, the Middle East, and Europe, forming one of the largest empires in history.

Genghis Khan and his descendants commanded large armies of warriors skilled at fighting on horseback, and used this military might to overwhelm their enemies and expand their territory. The Mongol Empire eventually covered an area of more than 9 million sq miles (23 million sq km). Though the empire was created through warfare, Mongol rule brought peace and stability, and people were able to travel between Asia and Europe in relative safety.

1185–1206
Genghis Khan united the nomadic tribes living in Central Asia.

1219–1221
The Mongols defeated the Khwarazmian Dynasty in Central Asia, claiming their lands and their trade routes from Europe to Asia.

1229–1241
After Genghis Khan's death, his son Ögodei became the Great Khan and expanded the empire, conquering northern China.

1241–1251
After Ogedei's death, a power struggle lasted for several years. Eventually Genghis Khan's grandson, Mongke Khan, defeated his rivals to claim power.

1258
The Mongol Empire conquered parts of the Middle East, plundering Baghdad, and ending the rule of the Muslim Abbasid Dynasty.

1260–1294
After a period of civil war, Kublai Khan took control of the Mongol Empire. He defeated the Song Dynasty and started the Yuan Dynasty. He was the first non-Chinese ruler of the whole of China.

1330–1368
The Mongol Empire fragmented after Kublai Khan's death and was weakened further by the spread of the bubonic plague. In China, the Yuan Dynasty was defeated by the Ming Dynasty.

The Siege of Baghdad
The Mongol Empire attacked Baghdad in modern-day Iraq in 1258, which led to the fall of the Muslim Abbasid Caliphate. The Mongol forces, led by Hulagu Khan, went on to conquer most of western Asia.

Ancient Americas

Between about 3000 BCE and 1697 CE, several mighty civilizations and empires flourished in what is now present-day Mexico, Central America, and the western regions of South America.

One of the first civilizations to form in the Americas was that of the Norte Chico (from c.3200 BCE), who farmed cotton on the coastal regions of present-day Peru. The later Olmec of Mexico (1200–400 BCE) built impressive buildings and crafted monuments and sculptures. From these two early cultures grew three great civilizations—the Maya and Aztecs in Mexico, and the Incas in Peru. These four great empires built settlements in hot deserts, dense jungles, and on mountainsides. They constructed large pyramids, immense road networks, and thought of unique ways to farm in challenging landscapes. They were extremely religious and held lavish ceremonies, and performed human sacrifices to appease their many gods. They used gold, a resource the civilizations had in abundance, to decorate their temples and religious buildings, and to make jewelry and ornaments.

The Incas

The Inca Empire was established in 1438 on the Pacific coast of South America. The Incas were master stonemasons who constructed around 25,000 miles (40,000km) of roads as well as large mountainside cities. The city of Machu Picchu (meaning "old mountain") was 7,972ft (2,430m) above sea level and sat on the side of Huayna Picchu, a peak in the Andes mountains. Abandoned around the time of the Spanish conquest in the 16th century, the city remained undiscovered by Western explorers until 1911.

Temple of the Sun
The Incas visited this semi-circular building to worship the sun god, Inti. An altar in the temple lined up perfectly with a window and the sun during the summer solstice, and is thought to have been used for religious ceremonies.

Solar heating
The Incas positioned their buildings so that they were heated by the sun throughout the day, which kept the residents warm at night.

Royal palace
The Incas used the best stone to build a palace that may have been for Emperor Pachacuti in 1450.

Social areas
Across the city were large, square areas, known as plazas, for locals to meet and watch religious ceremonies and festivals.

Intihuatana
Standing at the top of a large terraced pyramid, this ritual stone was used as an astronomical clock or calendar to plan when to farm and when to hold festivals of sun worship.

200,000 The approximate number of people who lived in Tenochtitlán, the Aztec capital, during its peak.

87

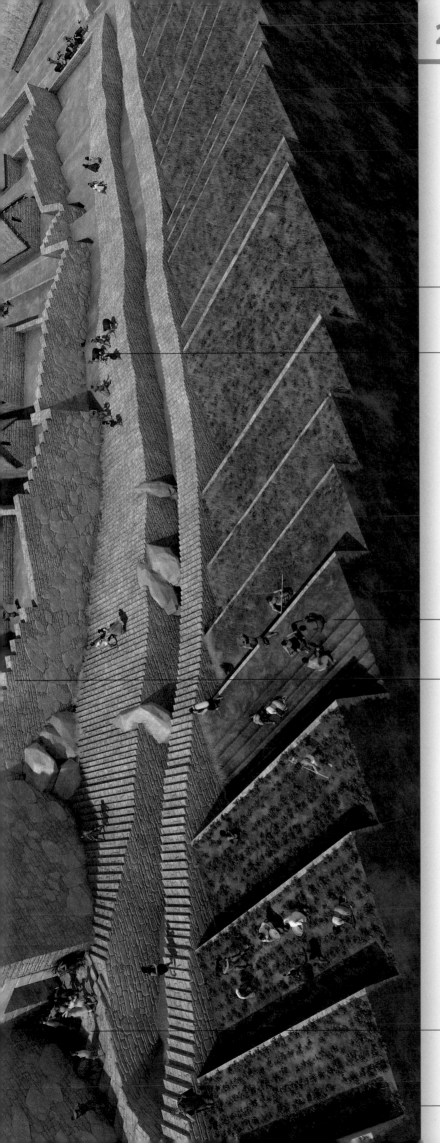

Roads

The Incas built roads made out of stone that cleaved through mountainous landscape. This vast road system connected cities to each other. Messengers ran to and from way-stations between cities, carrying messages to one another.

Bricks

Builders carved each brick to fit perfectly into place so they did not need mortar to glue bricks together.

Andenes

Stepped terraces called *andenes* were cut into the steep mountainside to grow crops, such as maize, cocoa, and potatoes. Stone walls helped to prevent landslides caused by torrential rain.

Llamas

Domestic animals such as llamas were used to transport goods between towns.

Farming tools

The Incas used multipurpose tools such as the *raucana* (a rudimentary gardening tool) to prepare soil, harvest potatoes, and remove weeds.

THE OLMECS
Dates: c.1200–c.400 BCE

The Olmec civilization emerged along the southern coast of the Gulf of Mexico. They lived in large settlements and farmed crops such as corn and beans. The Olmecs traded goods made from jade and obsidian, and carved large stone heads that were up to 3 m (10 ft) tall. They worshipped many gods and believed some animals were sacred. Many of their beliefs were adopted by later civilizations, such as the Aztecs and Mayans. The Olmecs may have developed the first writing in the Americas.

OLMEC HEAD SCULPTURE

THE MAYA
Dates: 1000 BCE–1697 CE

Ranging from the Yucatan Peninsula in present-day Mexico to parts of Central America, the Maya civilization was made up of self-ruling city-states, such as Palenque. The Maya had their own written language, and were master mathematicians and builders. With no central capital to overthrow, the Maya did not fall easily when the Spanish invaded in the 16th century. It took the Europeans nearly 200 years to conquer them.

JADE MAYA MASK

THE AZTECS
Dates: 1325–1521

Ruling over most of what is now present-day Mexico, the Aztec emperors had millions of subjects who they controlled with threats of war, violence, and ritual sacrifice. The Aztec capital, Tenochtitlán, was built on a marshy island in Lake Texcoco, where Mexico City stands today. It had a pyramid at its center and many temples, as well as man-made islands that were used to grow crops.

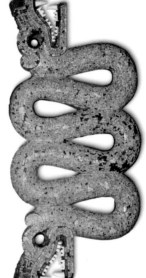

AZTEC DOUBLE-HEADED SERPENT SCULPTURE

88 the medieval world ○ MING CHINA

24 emperors **resided at the Forbidden City** between the Ming and Qing dynasties.

Ming China

The Ming Dynasty seized power from the Mongol Yuan Dynasty in 1368 and went on to rule China for 276 years. The Ming period was an era of change for China, and was known for its porcelain and great buildings.

The early Ming emperors fortified the northern borders, protecting China from Mongol invaders. Trade and exploration were encouraged, and new types of food arrived from around the world. This led to an increase in crop production, and the population more than doubled. But in the last century of the dynasty, years of money problems and poor harvests led to rebellion, and the Ming Dynasty eventually collapsed in 1644.

THE HONGWU EMPEROR

In 1368, Zhu Yuanzhang became the first emperor of the Ming Dynasty, and became known as the Hongwu Emperor. He brought all parts of the government under his own authority, and established a new law code, known as the Grand Pronouncements. A commanding leader, Hongwu was also fearful of betrayal. He set up a secret police force to protect his power.

Peasant warrior
Born into poverty, Zhu Yuanzhang led the forces fighting against the Yuan Dynasty, and eventually became emperor.

VOYAGES OF ZHENG HE

Zheng He (1371–1433) was one of China's greatest explorers. As an admiral of the imperial fleet, he commanded a treasure fleet of several hundred ships on seven voyages to India, the Persian Gulf, and the east coast of Africa. He contacted new cultures, expanded China's influence, and returned with spices, gems, and trade representatives from foreign nations.

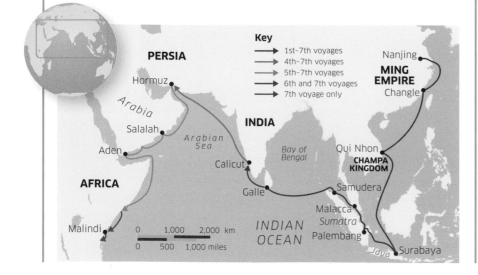

Key
→ 1st–7th voyages
→ 4th–7th voyages
→ 5th–7th voyages
→ 6th and 7th voyages
→ 7th voyage only

PERSIA
Hormuz
Arabia
Salalah
Aden
Arabian Sea
AFRICA
Malindi
INDIA
Calicut
Bay of Bengal
Galle
INDIAN OCEAN
Nanjing
MING EMPIRE
Changle
Qui Nhon
CHAMPA KINGDOM
Samudera
Malacca
Sumatra
Palembang
Java
Surabaya

0   1,000   2,000 km
0   500   1,000 miles

THE GREAT WALL

During the era of the Ming Dynasty, the Great Wall of China was rebuilt and expanded to protect the empire from the Mongol tribes invading from the north. New building techniques allowed the wall to be reinforced with battlements, watchtowers, and military fortresses.

Northern vantage point
New watchtowers allowed the Chinese military to watch the border and react quickly to any attacks by enemies.

THE FORBIDDEN CITY

The third emperor of the Ming Dynasty, Yongle (who ruled from 1402 to 1424), moved the capital to Beijing. In 1406, he ordered the construction of a new palace complex. It housed the imperial family, court officials, and important foreign visitors, as well as many servants. The palace was heavily guarded and access into the complex was restricted, so it became known as the Forbidden City. It was one of the largest palaces in the world, with 980 buildings and around 9,000 rooms. Its many buildings were topped with golden yellow tiles, which was the emperor's official color.

Gateway
On each side of the outer wall was a guarded gateway into the complex.

Outer wall
The outer wall of the city was 26 ft (8 m) high and 26 ft (8 m) wide at its base.

Layout of the city
The city was planned using ancient Chinese rules of design. Important buildings faced south, to honor the sun, and the ceremonial palaces were arranged in groups of three, symbolizing heaven and holiness.

Meridian Gate
The great main gate into the complex was on the south wall.

c. 27,800 sailors **crewed** Zheng He's fleet on his **first voyage**.

In 2014, a **porcelain vase** from the Ming Dynasty sold for **$21.6 million**.

89

MING PORCELAIN

In 1368, the Hongwu Emperor re-established the Imperial Porcelain factory, which had been founded by the previous Song Dynasty, in Jingdezhen. The factory perfected old techniques created by the Tang Dynasty to produce porcelain wares for the imperial palace. The distinctive blue-and-white Ming porcelain became popular and was exported around the world.

PILGRIM FLASK   **GLOBULAR VASE**   **SLEEVE VASE**

The Sacred Way
Leading to the Yongle Emperor's tomb, a 4-mile (7-km) path was lined with statues of generals, imperial officials, and animals.

THE MING TOMBS

At the foot of Tianshou Mountain, north of Beijing, the emperors of the Ming Dynasty built a complex of mausoleums, known as the Thirteen Tombs of the Ming Dynasty. The whole complex covered an area of 46 sq miles (120 sq km).

Inner Court
The emperor and his family lived in the northern part of the complex.

Imperial garden
The imperial gardens were used for relaxation, exercise, and ceremonies.

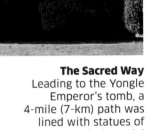

Hall of Supreme Harmony
The grandest building in the Ming Empire, this hall housed the throne room and hosted major ceremonies.

Watchtower
Guards kept watch for enemy soldiers and assassins from the corner watchtowers.

Moat
The city was protected by a 170 ft- (50 m-) wide moat around its perimeter.

Central platform
The main halls in the outer court were built on a 26 ft- (8 m-) high platform.

Outer court
The southern part of the palace was where the emperor held official ceremonies.

It took 14 years and around 100,000 craftsmen to build the Forbidden City.

THE AGE OF EXPLORATION

Between the 14th and 17th centuries, new discoveries and voyages of exploration transformed people's knowledge of the world. In Asia, the Middle East, and Europe, scientists made revolutionary breakthroughs, while artists used new methods to portray the world in a realistic way. Europeans also explored and colonized the Americas, at the expense of native populations.

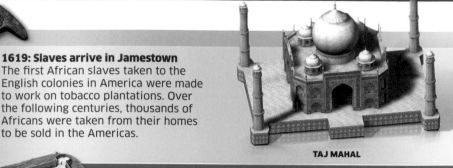

SLAVE ANKLETS

1619: Slaves arrive in Jamestown
The first African slaves taken to the English colonies in America were made to work on tobacco plantations. Over the following centuries, thousands of Africans were taken from their homes to be sold in the Americas.

1632–1653: The Taj Mahal
The fifth Mughal emperor, Shah Jahan, ordered the construction of many palaces and mosques. The Taj Mahal was a tomb built for his wife, Mumtaz Mahal. Shah Jahan himself was also buried here after his death.

TAJ MAHAL

JAMESTOWN

1607: Jamestown
A group of English colonists built a settlement called Jamestown on the banks of the James River in modern-day Virginia. It was the first successful English colony in North America.

1603: Edo Japan
Tokugawa Ieyasu united Japan under his rule and moved the capital to Edo (modern-day Tokyo). This began an era of peace in Japan that saw the arts flourish. A new form of theater, kabuki, entertained the public.

KABUKI ACTOR

KOREAN TURTLE SHIP

Timeline of the age of exploration

From the 15th century, a new curiosity about the world led to many daring voyages, the questioning of established beliefs, and the beginnings of modern science.

When the Italian explorer Christopher Columbus first landed in the Americas in 1492, he opened up new continents for European exploration, and the nations of Europe began to create empires to rival those of East Asia, India, and the Islamic Middle East. In Europe itself, the rediscovery of ancient knowledge led to the Renaissance ("rebirth"), a period of great artistic and cultural achievement. It was followed by the Scientific Revolution, a time of new discoveries and inventions, many of which challenged previously accepted views of the universe.

1520–1566: Suleiman the Magnificent
The longest-ruling emperor of the Ottoman Empire, Suleiman the Magnificent, oversaw a golden age of Islamic arts, crafts, science, and architecture.

DECORATED OTTOMAN PLATE

16TH-CENTURY GLOBE

1519–1522: Voyage of Magellan
The Portuguese explorer Ferdinand Magellan led an expedition to circumnavigate (sail all the way around) the Earth. Magellan died on the voyage, but the crew of one of his five ships made it home.

HERNÁN CORTÉS

GUTENBERG PRESS

1450s: The Gutenberg Bible
Johannes Gutenberg invented a printing press that revolutionized the production of books. One of the first books he mass-produced was a version of the Bible, bringing its words to a wider audience.

OTTOMAN SHIELD

1453: The fall of Constantinople
The Islamic Ottomans conquered Constantinople (modern-day Istanbul), the capital of the Byzantine Empire. Christian scholars and scientists fled from the city to Europe, bringing with them new ideas and ancient texts that helped to kick-start the Renaissance.

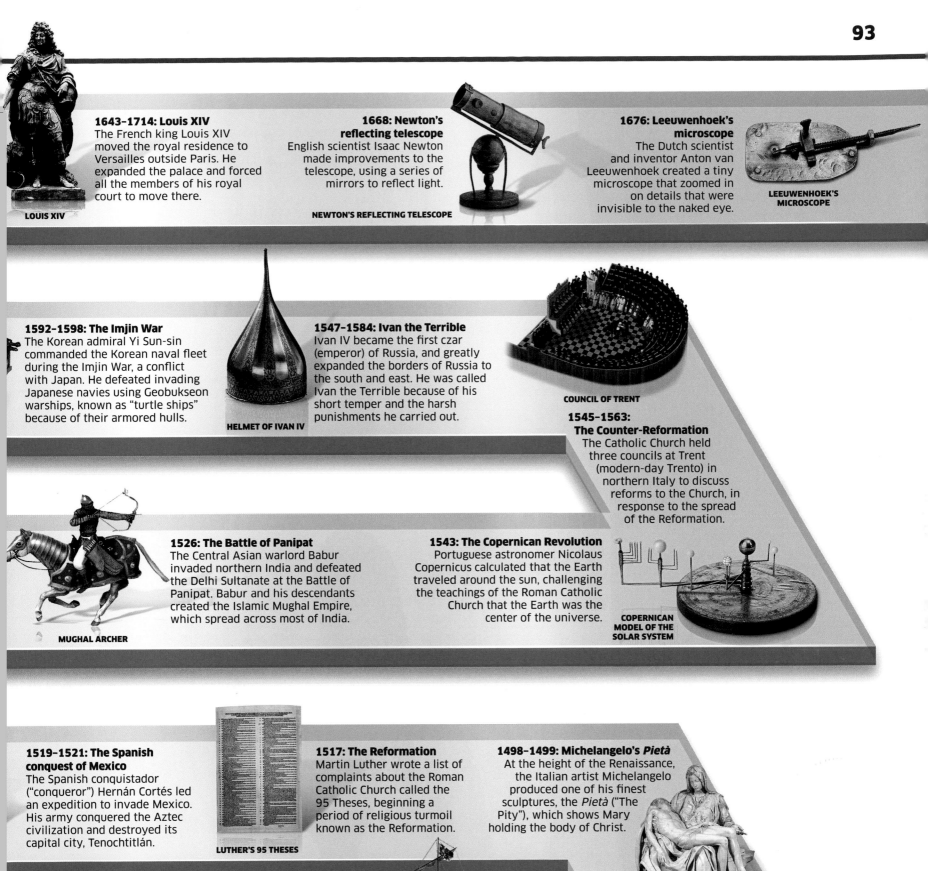

1643–1714: Louis XIV
The French king Louis XIV moved the royal residence to Versailles outside Paris. He expanded the palace and forced all the members of his royal court to move there.

LOUIS XIV

1668: Newton's reflecting telescope
English scientist Isaac Newton made improvements to the telescope, using a series of mirrors to reflect light.

NEWTON'S REFLECTING TELESCOPE

1676: Leeuwenhoek's microscope
The Dutch scientist and inventor Anton van Leeuwenhoek created a tiny microscope that zoomed in on details that were invisible to the naked eye.

LEEUWENHOEK'S MICROSCOPE

1592–1598: The Imjin War
The Korean admiral Yi Sun-sin commanded the Korean naval fleet during the Imjin War, a conflict with Japan. He defeated invading Japanese navies using Geobukseon warships, known as "turtle ships" because of their armored hulls.

HELMET OF IVAN IV

1547–1584: Ivan the Terrible
Ivan IV became the first czar (emperor) of Russia, and greatly expanded the borders of Russia to the south and east. He was called Ivan the Terrible because of his short temper and the harsh punishments he carried out.

COUNCIL OF TRENT

1545–1563: The Counter-Reformation
The Catholic Church held three councils at Trent (modern-day Trento) in northern Italy to discuss reforms to the Church, in response to the spread of the Reformation.

1526: The Battle of Panipat
The Central Asian warlord Babur invaded northern India and defeated the Delhi Sultanate at the Battle of Panipat. Babur and his descendants created the Islamic Mughal Empire, which spread across most of India.

MUGHAL ARCHER

1543: The Copernican Revolution
Portuguese astronomer Nicolaus Copernicus calculated that the Earth traveled around the sun, challenging the teachings of the Roman Catholic Church that the Earth was the center of the universe.

COPERNICAN MODEL OF THE SOLAR SYSTEM

1519–1521: The Spanish conquest of Mexico
The Spanish conquistador ("conqueror") Hernán Cortés led an expedition to invade Mexico. His army conquered the Aztec civilization and destroyed its capital city, Tenochtitlán.

LUTHER'S 95 THESES

1517: The Reformation
Martin Luther wrote a list of complaints about the Roman Catholic Church called the 95 Theses, beginning a period of religious turmoil known as the Reformation.

1498–1499: Michelangelo's *Pietà*
At the height of the Renaissance, the Italian artist Michelangelo produced one of his finest sculptures, the *Pietà* ("The Pity"), which shows Mary holding the body of Christ.

PIETÀ

1449–1492: Lorenzo de Medici
The politician Lorenzo de Medici, known as Lorenzo the Magnificent, came to power in Florence in Italy. Lorenzo was a great patron of the arts, and under his rule, the city became the heart of the Renaissance.

LORENZO DE MEDICI

SPANISH CARAVEL

1492: Voyage of Columbus
Christopher Columbus landed in the West Indies in the Caribbean in his search for a new sea route to Asia. He brought back news of the lands he visited to his patrons in Spain, inspiring many explorers to make voyages to the Americas.

The Renaissance

Much of the knowledge gathered during ancient times was lost to Europeans in the medieval era due to wars, disease, and famine, and the Church and its teachings dominated society. However, from the 14th century, Europe experienced what became known as the Renaissance, meaning "rebirth" in French.

Scholars and artists revisited scientific ideas and art styles from ancient Rome and Greece, and were also influenced by Islamic cultures from the east. New ideas and outlooks developed across Europe and challenged the traditional views of the Church. This led to new advances in art, literature, science, and theater. Painters and sculptors, formerly regarded as artisans (craft workers), were praised for their artistic achievements.

⦿ ELEMENTS OF THE RENAISSANCE

During the Renaissance, Europeans rediscovered ancient thought and culture. However, new and original ideas and techniques also developed and spread across the continent.

The revival of ancient ideas

Philosophers and scientists studied the works of the great thinkers and writers of ancient civilizations, such as Socrates, Plato, Aristotle, and Cicero. They inspired Renaissance philosophers to look beyond the teachings of the Church and question all aspects of European society.

Learning from the ancients
Plato and Aristotle are at the center of Renaissance artist Raphael's painting *The School of Athens*.

⦿ FLORENCE

The Renaissance started in the city-state of Florence, in modern-day Italy. In the late 14th century, Florence was a wealthy city and its businessmen and merchants used their money to support artists, craftsmen, and thinkers, such as the painter and architect Giotto di Bondone and the writer Dante Alighieri.

Sculpture

Renaissance sculptors, such as Donatello and Michelangelo, used new techniques to make their art look realistic. They studied the human body and its expressions and movements to make their sculptures more natural.

Sculpture of David
Between 1501 and 1504, the sculptor Michelangelo carved the biblical hero David out of marble.

Portraits
Renaissance artists painted people in as much detail as possible.

Architecture

Renaissance architects were influenced by the buildings of ancient Rome and Greece with their domes, arches, and columns. Renaissance designs in turn influenced engineers to think of new ways to build.

Florence Cathedral
Filippo Brunelleschi designed the massive dome of Florence's cathedral. It was constructed without the use of scaffolding.

Lorenzo de Medici

The Medici family were influential merchants, bankers, and politicians in Florence for more than 200 years. Lorenzo de Medici ruled Florence from 1449 to 1492 and was known as Lorenzo the Magnificent. He was a patron of the arts and sponsored many artists, including Sandro Botticelli and Michelangelo.

14 The **number of years it took artist** Leonardo da Vinci to paint the *Mona Lisa*.

4 members of the **Medici family**, at separate times, were **elected as Pope**.

95

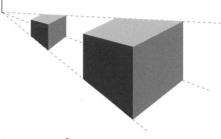

Vanishing point

Perspective

Renaissance artists developed new methods to make their works look more realistic. They started to use perspective to add depth to scenes, making objects painted on a flat surface look closer or further away. The use of light and shade also helped Renaissance art to look more three-dimensional.

Renaissance humanism

Humanists believed that a study of mankind, rather than God, should be at the center of learning. They looked to texts from ancient times, especially in the art of persuasion, grammar, and history to help them become useful members of society.

Humanist literature
In Praise of Folly, by Erasmus, questioned the values of medieval society and the teachings of the Church.

Patron
Wealthy patrons financially supported the master and helped build the artist's reputation.

Master
A creative mentor, the master guided the artistic styles of the studio and workroom.

THE NORTHERN RENAISSANCE

The Renaissance spread out of Italy and into northern Europe during a period known as the Northern Renaissance. Italian masters inspired artists from across Europe and were invited by kings and queens to attend their royal courts. In the mid-15th century, the printing press, a machine that could quickly produce books, was invented. This helped spread the new ideas of the Renaissance.

A Renaissance workshop
Flemish artist Jan van der Straet illustrated the busy studio of Dutch painter Jan van Eyck in his painting *The Invention of Oil Paint*, c. 1590.

Apprentice
Young apprentices performed basic tasks before learning from the master.

Mixing colors
Experienced apprentices ground and mixed the materials for making different colors.

Sketchers
Apprentices often sketched the main painting in the workshop to practice their skills.

Sculpture
Sculptures and paintings were often produced in the same workshop.

Platform
The master sometimes stood on a platform to be at the best angle to paint.

"Painting is poetry which is **seen and not heard.**"

Leonardo da Vinci, *A Treatise of Painting*, 1651

Early Korea

Before the rise of the Joseon Dynasty in 1392, the history of the Korean peninsula was influenced by its ever-changing relationship with the powerful Chinese dynasties to its north. Local kingdoms also competed for land and power. Buddhism, introduced from China in 372 CE, flourished during the period of the early kingdoms but was later suppressed during the Joseon era.

Timeline

The Three Kingdoms

During the period of "The Three Kingdoms," Korea was split between three rival powers: Silla and Baekje in the south, and Goguryeo in the north. Toward the end of the era, the Silla Kingdom, allied with the Tang Dynasty of China, defeated its rivals and unified the peninsula under Korean rule for the first time.

670–935

BUDDHA SILLA

Goryeo Dynasty

As the ruling Silla Kingdom broke apart with a series of uprisings and rebellions, a new kingdom, Goryeo, formed under Wang Geon. After years of war, Silla and the rebelling Baekje surrendered to Goryeo, unifying Korea once more. A long period of peace and prosperity followed, though the country suffered civil wars in the 12th century.

935–1392

Mongol occupation

The rule of the Goryeo Dynasty was interrupted in 1270 by the Mongol Empire. After nearly 40 years of Mongol attacks, the Goryeo surrendered and were controlled by the Mongol Yuan Dynasty for around 80 years. The Goryeo royal family remained as puppet rulers until the 1350s, when King Gongmin drove the Mongols out. By now, however, the dynasty was in decline.

1270–1356

Cannon fire
Crewed by about 50 marines, a Geobukseon was armed on all four sides with about 26 small cannon. In the naval battles of the Imjin War, the warships' firepower overwhelmed the Japanese fleet, which was armed only with bows and arrows and primitive long guns known as arquebuses.

Extra power
Two sails were used during windy weather, boosting the warship's speed.

Sharp protection
To stop enemy marines attempting to board the ship, the roof was covered with metal spikes.

Oar power
The Geobukseon didn't rely on wind power like other vessels of the time. It was powered by a crew of about 70 oarsmen. The oars increased the warship's ability to maneuver during battle, meaning it could turn very quickly and surprise enemy ships.

Rest and recovery
The lower deck was home to the kitchen and housed the sleeping quarters.

13 of **Yi Sun-sin's ships** defeated **133 Japanese warships** in the **Battle of Myeongnyang**.

Sejong the Great's reforms allowed people of **any class** to work in the **government**.

97

Joseon Korea

Lasting for more than 500 years, the rule of the Joseon Dynasty (1392–1897) shaped many of modern-day Korea's social and cultural traditions.

After the fall of the Goryeo Dynasty in 1392, the Kingdom of Great Joseon was established by General Yi Seong-gye, who became the first king, taking the title Taejo ("Great Ancestor"). The new dynasty expanded its boundaries north and moved its capital city to the city of Hanyang, known today as Seoul. The kings of Joseon oversaw massive advancements in government, science, and technology, as well as a golden age of culture and education. However, after several invasion attempts from Japan and China in the 16th and 17th centuries, the Joseon Dynasty entered a period of isolation from the outside world, when it became known as the "Hermit Kingdom."

The turtle ship

One of the famous technological achievements of the Joseon Dynasty was its warship, the Geobukseon. Known as the "turtle ship" because of its turtle-shell shape, it had a protective roof and was armed with many cannon. It was a formidable force at sea and helped Admiral Yi Sun-sin defeat the Japanese during the Imjin War.

Hidden surprise
A layer of straw was placed over the protective roof to lure enemy boarders onto the sharp spikes.

Fire-breathing dragon
At the front of the ship was a wooden dragon head. This hid a cannon or a burner that released fire and smoke, striking fear into the enemy and also helping conceal the ship's movements.

Admiral Yi Sun-sin

After a brilliant career as an army officer, Yi Sun-sin was promoted to admiral in the Joseon navy during the Imjin War (1592–1598). He heroically commanded the Joseon fleet and didn't lose a single naval battle against the invading Japanese.

"I CAN BE APPROACHED, BUT NEVER PUSHED; BEFRIENDED BUT NEVER COERCED; KILLED BUT NEVER SHAMED"
Yi Sun-sin, in a letter to fellow admiral Son Ko-i

Sejong the Great

During his 32-year reign (1418–1450), the fourth king of the Joseon Dynasty, Sejong, revolutionized how the government ruled the kingdom, improving the lives of ordinary people. He realized it was important for everyone to have access to education and knowledge, and personally created the Korean alphabet. He also encouraged scientific research, which led to developments in agriculture, astronomy, and medicine.

Progressive king Sejong's rule emphasized the importance of education.

Hangul script

Before Sejong the Great's reign, the kingdoms of Korea had used classical Chinese as their writing system. It was complex, which meant that only the educated could read and write. In 1446, a new alphabet was created, called Hangul, which used 28 simple vowels and consonants in blocks of syllables.

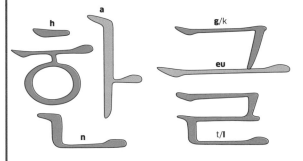

h a g/k

eu

n t/l

A new way to write
The new script of Hangul was originally read from top to bottom, though today it is read from left to right. Consonants were based on the shapes the mouth made when speaking them.

Great sultans

The Ottoman Empire was ruled by a leader known as a sultan. The sultan had complete control over the empire. The role of the sultan normally passed from father to son. Toward the later years of the empire, most of the sultan's responsibilities were given to key government officials.

Murad I
Murad I conquered Adrianople, a city in the Byzantine Empire, and made it the capital of the Ottoman Empire. Murad expanded the empire north into Europe and large areas of the Balkans.

Bayezid I
The son of Murad I, Bayezid I continued his father's conquest of Europe. He also defeated and united rival states in Anatolia. In 1402, Bayezid I clashed with the Mongol Timurid Dynasty, suffering a major defeat at Ankara.

Mehmed II
In 1444, after his father gave up the throne, a 12-year-old Mehmed II briefly ruled for two years. His father was persuaded to return. After his father died, Mehmed II conquered the Byzantine capital of Constantinople (modern-day Istanbul).

Timeline   1362–1389   1389–1402   1444–1446 / 1451–1481

The Ottoman Empire

In the late 13th century, Osman I, a tribal warlord, conquered lands in Anatolia (in modern-day Turkey) that belonged to the Byzantine Empire. With these regions under his control, he established the Ottoman Empire.

The Ottomans raised large armies, and with their military might, they quickly expanded their empire into eastern Europe, North Africa, and the Middle East. The capital of the empire was eventually moved to the city of Constantinople, which the Ottomans also called Istanbul. By the 16th century, the Ottoman Empire had entered a golden age under the rulership of several inspiring leaders, who encouraged military discipline, science, art, and architecture. However, poor leadership and competition with other powers in Europe and Asia eventually contributed to the empire's decline. The empire was dismantled in 1922 and its central region became the Republic of Turkey.

◎ GROWTH OF THE EMPIRE

The Ottoman Empire grew rapidly over a period of 200 years. It claimed land from the Muslim empires in North Africa and the Byzantine Empire in eastern Europe.

EUROPE

Adrianople • Istanbul

Cairo •

AFRICA

Key
- The empire in 1512
- The empire in 1520
- The empire in 1566
- The empire in 1639

◎ WARFARE

The Ottoman army played an important role in the rise of the empire. Cavalry units and elite troops known as the Janissaries helped the empire win many carefully planned battles. In the 15th century, the Ottomans became skilled gunsmiths and built huge cannons that were used to besiege cities during conflicts.

BOOTS

ZIRH GOMLEK (MAIL AND PLATE COAT)

CHICHAK (HELMET)

KILIJ (SWORD)

KALKAN (SMALL SHIELD)

◎ ARCHITECTURE

The Ottoman Empire had creative architects who designed many buildings, such as mosques, palaces, and public baths, that were built in the many regions they conquered. Ottoman buildings were decorated with geometric designs and were made from lavish materials, such as exotic woods, mother of pearl, and gold.

Exquisite patterns
The Blue Mosque in Istanbul was built in the 17th century. Its interior is decorated with patterned tiles and stained-glass windows.

30 million The population of the Ottoman Empire at its peak in 1683.

20,000 The approximate **number of tiles** that were **used** to decorate the interior of the **Blue Mosque**.

99

Selim the Grim
Leading aggressive military campaigns, Selim the Grim expanded the Ottoman Empire greatly. In 1517, he defeated the Muslim empire of the Mamluk Dynasty, taking control of North Africa and the Middle East.

1512–1520

Suleiman the Magnificent
Of all the Ottoman sultans, Suleiman the Magnificent ruled the longest. His reign marked the height of the empire's golden age. He also expanded Ottoman borders, encouraged trade, and improved the navy.

1520–1566

Selim II
The son of Suleiman the Magnificent, Selim II did not inherit his father's skill for governance. He was distracted by the luxuries of royal life and relied on his chief minister, Mehmed Sokollu, to govern the empire.

1566–1574

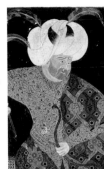

Mehmed IV
After his mentally ill father lost power, Mehmed became the sultan at the age of six. He was too young to rule, so the role of the sultan changed. Most of its powers were given to a new position, the chief minister.

1648–1687

ARTS OF THE GOLDEN AGE

Many forms of art, such as pottery and embroidery, flourished in the Ottoman Empire during the 16th and 17th centuries. An imperial painting school was established and the art of handwriting, known as calligraphy, was practiced. The Ottoman Empire was well known for its beautiful pottery, known as Iznik ware, as well as elaborately designed rugs and carpets, and intricately decorated tiles.

ASIA

Baghdad

17TH-CENTURY DECORATED OTTOMAN PLATE

16TH-CENTURY DECORATED OTTOMAN TILES

OTTOMAN SCIENCE

Scholars in the Ottoman Empire learned from the classical scientists of the previous Muslim empires. They wrote new encyclopedias of medicine and drew maps of the world. The empire also contributed to advances in astronomy and mechanical engineering.

Astronomers
At the observatory in Constantinople (modern-day Istanbul), mathematician and astronomer Taqi al-Din used the first astronomical clocks to study the stars.

"Like a new star, it will scatter the darkness of ignorance"

Johannes Gutenberg, on his new printing press, c.1450

Ink pads
Before each press, oil-based ink was added to the metal blocks of type held in place inside the forme. Workers known as "beaters" used round ink pads to dab the sticky ink evenly across the type.

The printing workshop
Johannes Gutenberg developed a more efficient printing press, easy-to-make movable metal type, and a new reliable and versatile oil-based ink. He also divided the printing process into parts, with specialized workers responsible for each stage.

Movable metal type
Gutenberg, a goldsmith, used his knowledge of metals to create hard-wearing metal blocks, known as movable type. Every block had a back-to-front letter on one side. It was placed into a frame, known as a "forme," to spell out a word or sentence for printing. The movable type could then easily be reordered, ready for printing the next page.

Pulling the lever
The worker who operated the press was called a "puller." He pulled the lever across to press the damp paper against the inked forme, one page at a time.

Forming the words
About 300 different kinds of type were needed to produce the Gutenberg Bible, from punctuation marks to upper- and lowercase letters.

Damp paper
The stiff paper had to be softened with water before printing, to help the ink stick to it.

The printing press
Gutenberg based the design of his printing press on screw presses used at the time to make wine.

Quality control
Each page was read and checked to make sure the print was accurate.

2,500 The approximate number of **type blocks used per page in the Gutenberg Bible**.

48 The number of **original Gutenberg Bibles** that are **known still to survive today**.

101

The Printing Revolution

In around 1450, German goldsmith Johannes Gutenberg perfected a new printing process. His innovation transformed how people shared ideas and information across the world.

Until the 15th century, books were rare and expensive. They were usually written and copied by hand and could take years to complete. Johannes Gutenberg invented an efficient printing press that allowed him to produce quality prints over and over again. By 1500, there were more than a thousand of Gutenberg's presses across western Europe, manufacturing millions of books. For years, reading had been the privilege of nobles, scribes, and priests, but as books became more affordable for all parts of society, a new educated class began to emerge.

The Gutenberg Bible

In the mid-1450s, Gutenberg used his printing press to produce a 1,286-page, two-volume Bible. Although his printing press was much faster than writing by hand, it still took him several years to print around 180 copies – 45 on calfskin and 135 on paper. Once printed, each Bible was decorated with hand-drawn illustrations, at the request of its owner – usually a prominent and wealthy church leader.

Timeline

The evolution of printing

Gutenberg didn't invent movable type– wooden and ceramic type were invented in China in the 11th century, and metal type was first used in Korea during the 13th century. But Gutenberg's printing process was so efficient that it hardly changed until the 19th century, when advances in steam power meant that presses could operate at higher speeds.

Steam power
1811

In Germany, inventor Friedrich Koenig and engineer Andreas Friedrich Bauer designed a steam-powered press. It used cylinder rollers to print on both sides of the paper.

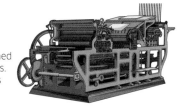

Linotype machine
1886

German inventor Ottmar Mergenthaler's machine allowed workers to assemble lines of metal type, known as "slugs," using a keyboard. This was much quicker than ordering type by hand and greatly sped up the process.

Photocopying
1960s

The photocopier machine transformed how documents and pages were copied in offices around the world. Its dry printing process, known as xerography, used powdered ink and heat to create copies.

Digital technology
Today

Large-scale modern printing presses can print thousands of color pages per minute, while computers and wireless printers let people print easily at home, too.

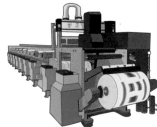

Drying line
The newly printed damp pages were hung up so the paper and ink could dry.

Finishing touches
An artist or "illuminator" added elaborate decorations known as illuminations to the printed pages.

The Gutenberg Bible
The completed Bibles were all sold, with some selling for the price of 30 florins, an enormous amount of money at the time.

Early Russia

In the 7th century, Slavic tribes started to settle in the northwest of modern-day Russia. From these small beginnings grew one of the world's mightiest empires.

The tribes unified in the 9th century and began to expand their territory. Important trade routes between Europe and Asia helped early Russian principalities—small states governed by a prince in the name of a Grand Prince—to grow wealthy. The Russians adopted Christianity, and under different forms of government, early Russia continued to expand its borders, finally becoming the Russian Empire in 1721.

○ KIEVAN RUS

Established in the 9th century, Kievan Rus was the first state to occupy what is now Russian territory. Over the next four centuries, it grew to become one of the largest and wealthiest powers in Europe. At its peak it stretched from the Baltic Sea in the north to the Black Sea in the south, before being invaded by Mongol warriors in 1237.

The Rurik Dynasty

The Rurik Dynasty was established by the Viking chieftain Rurik, who united the warring Slavic tribes of the region. The Rurik Dynasty survived the Mongol invasion of Kievan Rus, ruling Russia for more than 700 years.

Invitation to rule
Rurik, along with his two brothers, were invited by the Slavs to rule over them.

○ THE DUCHY OF MUSCOVY

After the fall of Kiev to the Mongols, Russia split into many small principalities. The Duchy of Muscovy, centered around Moscow, slowly grew more powerful and became the center of the Russian Orthodox Church. Chosen by the Mongol rulers to collect taxes from all the other principalities, Muscovy eventually gained enough power, wealth, and influence to unify Russia and raise an army to defeat their Mongol overlords.

Russia expands

The monarchs of Moscow used their wealth to purchase land, gaining control over most of the Moscow basin. In 1380, Grand Prince Dmitry Donskoy expanded Moscow's control further and conquered the surrounding states of Rostov and Ryazan. Further gains under Dmitry's successors, Vasily I and Vasily II, strengthened Moscow's power in the region.

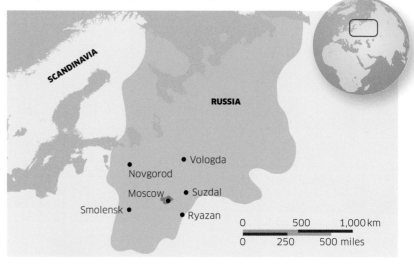

Expansion of Russian territory

| ■ 1300 | ■ Muscovy territories acquired by 1533 |

IVAN THE GREAT

Ivan the Great

In 1462, Ivan III (known as Ivan the Great) came to power. He continued to extend the realms of Moscow, expanding north into Novgorod, as well as south into modern-day Ukraine. He also drove out the Mongols and installed himself as supreme ruler in 1485. By the end of his reign, he had tripled the size of the Duchy of Muscovy and had started to take land away from the state princes and give it to his loyal nobles.

Timeline

Early Russia

From its formation as Kievan Rus, through the rise of Moscow, to the rule of the czars, Russia continued to expand. By the time that Peter the Great became the first emperor of the Russian Empire, it had become the largest country in the world.

c.650–862

Slavs and Vikings
In the 7th century, Slavic tribes began to migrate beyond their homelands in central and eastern Europe. Some moved east, settling in what is now northwest Russia. In the 9th century, Viking traders from across the Baltic Sea began to sail down the region's rivers, and opened up trading links with the Slavs. Rurik, a Viking chieftain, united the warring tribes of the region. He set up a new capital at Novgorod in 862.

880–972

Expansion of Kievan Rus
Rurik was succeeded by Prince Oleg, who expanded his lands to the south. Oleg captured the Slavic city of Kiev, which he made his capital in 882, and founded Kievan Rus. The new state controlled the river trade routes between Scandinavia and the Byzantine Empire, growing rich by trading fur, wax, and honey, as well as slaves. The state expanded quickly in the 10th century under Grand Prince Sviatoslav, who took Balkan lands to the south.

988

The Russian Orthodox Church
Seeking closer ties with the Byzantine Empire, Grand Prince Vladimir, now known as Vladimir the Great, made the Eastern Orthodox Church the official religion of Kievan Rus, forcing mass baptism on his subjects. He also married a daughter of the Byzantine emperor, and oversaw the beginning of a golden age in art, architecture, and learning.

1019–1054

Yaroslav the Wise
Kievan Rus flourished under Yaroslav, who created new laws and strengthened the state through military campaigns and foreign diplomacy. He also continued the spread of Christianity.

SEAL OF GRAND PRINCE YAROSLAV THE WISE

Moscow's famous **St. Basil's Cathedral** was built under the orders of **Ivan the Terrible** in 1552.

97% of people in the **Russian Empire** were **peasants** at its formation in 1721.

103

THE CZARDOM OF RUSSIA

In 1547, Ivan the Terrible was crowned the first czar ("supreme ruler") of all Russia. During the period of czardom, Russia transformed into a major European power, expanding its territory east into Siberia and gaining land on its western borders. Though czars held political power, their authority was limited by the Church and nobles. From 1682, Czar Peter I (later known as Peter the Great) reduced the influence of the nobles, and proclaimed himself emperor of the Russian Empire in 1721.

Serfdom

The noble class created a system called serfdom to control the poorest peasants, known as serfs. They were forced to work on the land owned by their noble masters, and–like slaves–could be bought or sold. They were also conscripted into the army at times of war. Catherine the Great massively expanded serfdom in the late 18th century to feed Russia's growing empire. The system was finally abolished in 1861, under Czar Alexander II.

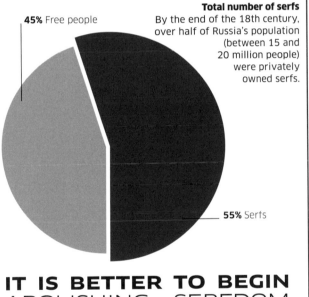

45% Free people

Total number of serfs
By the end of the 18th century, over half of Russia's population (between 15 and 20 million people) were privately owned serfs.

55% Serfs

IT IS BETTER TO BEGIN ABOLISHING SERFDOM FROM ABOVE THAN WAIT FOR IT TO BEGIN ABOLISHING ITSELF FROM BELOW
Alexander II, in a speech to Moscow nobles, 1856

Cossacks

The Cossack peoples originated around the Black and Caspian seas. Fiercely independent, they formed warrior bands of light cavalry, who often rebelled against the Russians. Later, they allied with the Czardom of Russia, helping defend it against Mongol attacks and extend its borders to the east. In the 18th century, the Cossacks lost their independence, and males were forced into Russian military service. Their bravery and skill were much feared by their enemies.

Yermak Timofeyevich
In 1581, Cossack leader Yermak Timofeyevich successfully invaded western Siberia with 840 soldiers and conquered the tribes living there. He helped expand Russia's borders.

BE PATIENT, COSSACK, AND YOU WILL ONE DAY BE A CHIEFTAIN
Russian proverb

The first parliament

The czars used councils of advisers to discuss issues that affected the state. Early councils, called dumas, were made up of boyars (noblemen). As the Czardom of Russia expanded in the 16th century, the Zemsky Sobor ("Assembly of the Land") was formed. Regarded as Russia's first parliament, it was made up of religious and military leaders, boyars, landowners, and merchants.

The first Romanov czar
The Zemsky Sobor elected the first czar of the Romanov Dynasty, Mikhail I. Here he is shown at the front of the steps, receiving news of his election from the Zemsky Sobor.

1237–1253	1283–1380	1547–1584	1598–1613	1613–1676
Mongol invasion After Yaroslav's death, Kievan Rus split into separate, warring principalities, and became vulnerable to attack. In 1237, Batu Khan led an invasion by a group of Mongol warriors known as the Tatars. Each prince was made to pay tribute to their Mongol overlords, who ruled the region for more than 200 years.	**Rise of the Duchy of Muscovy** In the late 13th century, Daniel I, son of Rurik Prince Alexander Nevsky, helped to establish the Duchy of Muscovy in the city-state of Moscow. In 1380, an army led by Prince Dmitry Donskoy defeated the Tatars in battle, giving birth to the idea of a Russian nation.	**Ivan the Terrible** A brutal leader, Ivan IV was known as Ivan the Terrible because of his short temper and the harsh punishments he handed out. He even murdered his own son. However, during the early part of his reign he was a reformer, and established the first Zemsky Sobor (parliament).	**The Time of Troubles** The Rurik Dynasty came to an end in 1598 when Fyodor, Ivan IV's son, died childless. There followed a period of crisis as conflict sprang up between the boyars (nobles), landowners, and merchants, and foreign states tried to lay claim to the throne. In 1607, Poland claimed the throne and invaded Moscow. After five years of civil war, a Cossack army threw out the Polish invaders.	**Early Romanov rulers** To restore order after the Time of Troubles, Mikhail Romanov, brother of Ivan the Terrible's first wife, was selected as czar. Mikhail's rule saw the biggest territorial expansion in Russian history as most of Siberia was conquered. The reign of his successor, Alexis I, saw many wars and rebellions. Alexis also produced a new code of law that officially defined serfdom.

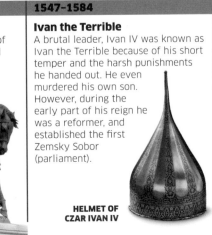

GRAND PRINCE OF MOSCOW DMITRY DONSKOY

HELMET OF CZAR IVAN IV

Voyages of exploration

European merchants traveling to Asia over land were often heavily taxed or attacked by marauders. In the 15th and 16th centuries, European nations funded naval voyages to search for new trade routes to Asia.

European powers led many expeditions across the Atlantic, as well as around Africa, to find these new routes. As new lands and civilizations became known to Europe, the world became more connected than ever before. Goods, religions, and ideas were traded and exchanged across huge distances for the first time. However, European powers also exploited these new lands, draining their natural resources and sometimes enslaving the native populations.

1415–1460
Portuguese Prince Henry the Navigator financed many naval expeditions down the west coast of Africa.

1492
In search of a western trade route to Asia, Italian explorer Christopher Columbus became the first European to discover the Americas.

1497
England financed a search for a northwestern trade route to Asia, which saw Italian explorer John Cabot land in Newfoundland, in modern-day Canada.

1498
Vasco da Gama became the first European to sail around Africa and arrive in India, establishing new maritime trade routes for Portugal.

1507
German mapmaker Martin Waldseemuller drew a map of the "new world," naming it "America" after Italian explorer Amerigo Vespucci.

1519–1522
Portuguese explorer Ferdinand Magellan led a five-ship expedition to sail around the world. He died before completing the journey, and only one of his ships made the journey home.

1541–1542
In an eight-month journey, Spanish explorer Francisco de Orellana sailed along the whole of the Amazon River.

1577–1580
English explorer Sir Francis Drake became the first captain to lead a successful voyage around the world.

The Strait of Magellan
Ferdinand Magellan sailed through the channel between the South American mainland and the islands of Tierra del Fuego. He discovered that it was the safest route from the Atlantic to the Pacific Ocean. The channel was later named after him—the Strait of Magellan.

Conquest of the Americas

After Christopher Columbus landed in the Americas in 1492, Spanish explorers and soldiers crossed the Atlantic in search of fortune and new lands to conquer.

Throughout the 16th and 17th centuries, the Spanish invaders, known as conquistadors (conquerors), plundered gold and silver and seized land, bringing to an end the great Aztec, Inca, and Maya civilizations. Equipped with armor, guns, and horses, they destroyed cities, killing thousands of people. They brought with them European diseases such as measles, flu, and smallpox, against which the native people had no natural resistance. After the Spanish conquered the Americas, they forced the people to convert to Christianity, destroying their old way of life.

⊙ EARLY EXPLORERS

Hispaniola, the large Caribbean island explored by Christopher Columbus in 1492, became the center of Spanish operations in the Americas, which they called the New World. Rumors of gold and the search for a route to Asia led the first conquistadors to explore more widely. Within 20 years, they had mapped the whole of the Caribbean, and began to explore the American mainland.

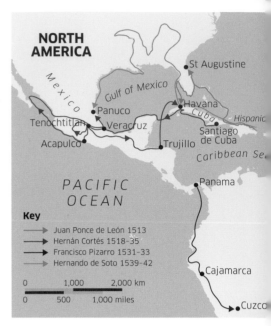

Key
→ Juan Ponce de León 1513
→ Hernán Cortés 1518–35
→ Francisco Pizarro 1531–33
→ Hernando de Soto 1539–42

⊙ SPANISH SUCCESS

The Spanish found it easy to defeat the native people—Cortés only had an army of about 600 men, while Pizarro conquered the vast Inca Empire with 180 men. The Spanish invaders fought with steel swords, guns, and cannons, and had horses (then unknown in the Americas). The native warriors fought with more basic weapons—clubs, javelins, and arrows, which could not pierce European armor.

The end of the Aztec Empire

When Hernán Cortés landed in Mexico in 1519, he headed for Tenochtitlán, capital of the vast Aztec Empire. The Aztec ruler Montezuma II thought the Spaniards were messengers from their Aztec god Quetzalcoatl and welcomed them into the city. Two years later, Cortés returned to the Aztec capital with his army and destroyed Tenochtitlán, ending nearly 200 years of Aztec rule.

Montezuma II greets Cortés
In Tenochtitlán, Cortés was given gifts of gold and silver by Montezuma, fueling the conquistador's greed for the precious metals.

The conquest of the Incas

When Francisco Pizarro reached Peru with his small army in 1532, the Inca Empire had been weakened by internal rivalries. Pizarro tricked the emperor Atahualpa into a meeting, ordered his men to open fire on the Incas, and took the emperor prisoner. Pizarro demanded and received a huge ransom in gold and silver, before having Atahualpa treacherously killed. Pizarro marched his men to Cuzco, the Inca capital, which fell without a struggle. Inca resistance to Spanish rule had ended by 1572.

Skilled craftspeople
This Inca drinking vessel was carved from wood. The Incas were skilled craftspeople, but after the Spanish conquest many were forced to abandon their crafts and work in the silver and gold mines.

Defeating the Maya

By the time the Spanish arrived in the 16th century, the great cities of the Maya civilization had long been abandoned. The Maya lived in scattered towns and villages in the northern Yucatan Peninsula of Mexico. In 1521, the king of Spain granted the conquistador Francisco de Montejo the right to take over the Yucatan, but it proved difficult because of the scattered Maya strongholds. De Montejo's son eventually completed the conquest in 1546, although the last remote Maya stronghold didn't fall until 1697.

These bars and dots represented numbers.

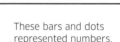

Painted codex
This Maya codex (a folding book) was sent to Europe during the Spanish conquest. It is one of the few books that were not destroyed by the conquistadors.

When the Spanish explorer **Hernán Cortés** landed in Mexico in 1519, **he burned his ships** so that his crew could not desert him.

1521 The year the **Aztec capital Tenochtitlán**—home to 300,000 people—was **destroyed by the conquistadors**.

107

ATLANTIC
OCEAN

**SOUTH
AMERICA**

Seeking new worlds

The conquistadors were often soldiers or the sons of minor noble families. The conquest of the Americas offered them a chance to become rich. When they arrived in the Americas, they found food plants such as potatoes and tomatoes as well as animals such as guinea pigs and llamas, previously unknown in Europe. Although many of the conquistadors were Spanish, some European adventurers joined the conquest, helping to lay the foundations of a vast Spanish Empire in the Americas.

Juan Ponce de León
In 1513, Juan Ponce de León landed on the southeast coast of North America. He named the area Florida (Spanish for "land of flowers"). When he couldn't find gold, he took slaves instead.

Hernán Cortés
After hearing stories about the treasures of the Aztec rulers, Cortés abandoned his law studies in Spain to make his fortune in the Americas. In 1519, he led an expedition to invade Mexico.

Francisco Pizarro
A ruthlessly ambitious man, Francisco Pizarro went on several expeditions to the Americas. In 1532, backed by the Spanish king, he led his own expedition to conquer the Inca Empire of Peru.

Hernando de Soto
In 1539, Hernando de Soto set sail from Cuba for North America. He landed in Florida and three years later reached the banks of the Mississippi River—the first European to do so.

SEARCHING FOR GOLD AND SILVER

Many of the conquistadors were lured to the Americas by rumors of a fabulously rich city ruled by a king covered in gold, called El Dorado (meaning "The Golden One"). It was never found, but huge quantities of gold and silver plundered from the great civilizations were loaded into the treasure ships bound for the Spanish port of Seville. By the end of the 16th century, Spain had become the wealthiest nation in Europe.

Gold from Peru
This gold ceremonial knife survived the plunder. Most of the gold seized by the conquistadors was melted to make gold coins.

"We Spaniards know a sickness of the heart that only **gold can cure.**"

Hernán Cortés, when greeted by Montezuma's messenger, 1521

Silver mine

In 1545, the Spanish invaders found the world's greatest source of silver in Potosí (in present-day Bolivia). They transported more than 30,000 African slaves to work in the Potosí mines. By the end of the 16th century, about 60 percent of the world's silver came from Potosí.

Rich mountain
A mining town sprang up around the source of the silver—Cerro Potosí (Spanish for "Rich Mountain").

BANNING RELIGION

The Catholic religion was important to the Spanish, and the conquistadors banned the native religions. Their expeditions to the Americas were always accompanied by a priest, who was responsible for converting the native people. The conquistadors also destroyed temples, burned books, and executed local priests.

Aztec gods
The Aztecs worshipped many gods. The feathered snake god Quetzalcoatl was the god of creation. He is shown here (left) in combat with his brother Tezcatlipoca, the destructive god.

108 the age of exploration ∘ **THE REFORMATION**

282 The number of **printing presses in Europe** by 1500.

The Reformation

For 1,000 years, the Roman Catholic Church was the only branch of Christianity in western Europe and it was a powerful force in people's lives. Even rulers were subject to the laws laid down by its leader, the Pope. But by the 16th century, the Roman Catholic Church had become deeply unpopular.

At this time, members of the clergy—bishops, priests, and monks—were believed by many people to be greedy and corrupt. In 1517, a monk named Martin Luther nailed his 95 Theses, a list of protests against the practices of the Catholic Church, to the door of a church in Wittenberg in Germany. This started a religious revolution that has come to be known as the Reformation. The upheaval it caused spread quickly through Europe, leaving a lasting division between Roman Catholics and Protestants—people who followed new branches of Christianity that sprang from the Reformation.

EARLY REFORMERS

Although Martin Luther is seen as the person who started the Reformation, he was not the first to criticize the Church's teachings—Jan Hus in Bohemia (in modern-day Czech Republic) and John Wycliffe in England held similar views 100 years earlier. But other reformers quickly followed Luther's lead. By the 1530s, Protestantism had split into two main branches: Lutheranism and Calvinism.

Martin Luther
Luther was angry that the Church was selling "indulgences," allowing rich people to buy pardons for their sins. After continuing his attacks against this practice, Luther was excommunicated (excluded from the Church) in 1521.

THE SPREAD OF PROTESTANTISM

By 1600, Protestantism was widely spread throughout northern Germany, Switzerland, the Dutch Republic, England, Scotland, and Scandinavia. France was predominantly Catholic, though significant numbers of Protestants lived in parts of the south and west. Spain, Portugal, and Italy remained Catholic.

Key
- Mainly Protestant areas
- Mainly Catholic areas

BRITAIN
GERMANY
FRANCE
SPAIN
ITALY

COUNTER-REFORMATION

Alarmed by the spread of Protestantism, the Catholic Church launched the Counter-Reformation. Its aim was to strengthen the loyalty of Church members and prevent people leaving. The Jesuits, a new teaching order of priests backed by the Pope, established schools and colleges to improve the quality of religious education. To make worship more attractive, churches were built in a beautiful and ornate style, and church music was encouraged. The Roman Inquisition, a church court, was created to judge heretics (people accused of denying Catholic beliefs).

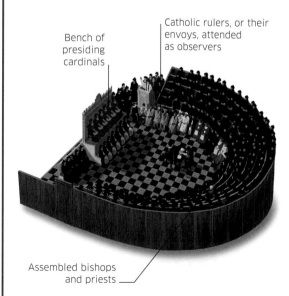

Bench of presiding cardinals

Catholic rulers, or their envoys, attended as observers

Assembled bishops and priests

The Council of Trent
An assembly of Catholic Church leaders, called the Council of Trent, met three times between 1545 and 1563 to discuss ways of reforming the Church.

The power of the press
First developed in Germany in around 1450, the printing press was still a relatively new technology when Luther wrote his 95 Theses. Printed copies of his text, translated from Latin into German, were widely circulated. Luther was one of the first people to realize the power of the printed word to reach a wider audience. The stream of pamphlets and books put out by him and other reformers helped Protestantism spread more rapidly.

War of words
This German propaganda sheet attacked the Catholic practice of selling indulgences to fill the money chests of the Catholic Church.

Ulrich Zwingli
A priest and friend of Luther, Zwingli led the Reformation in Switzerland. He wanted to simplify worship and believed that what was written in the Bible was more important than the Church's laws.

John Calvin
Frenchman John Calvin fled from Catholic France to Switzerland in 1535, where he established a stricter version of Luther's Protestantism, known as Calvinism.

THE CHURCH OF ENGLAND
When the Pope would not allow King Henry VIII to divorce his first wife, he made himself supreme head of the Church in England. The country became Protestant under Edward VI, then Catholic again under Mary I. Elizabeth I restored Protestantism in England in 1558.

The Tudors
This painting of the Tudors shows each of the family at the height of their reign. Henry VIII is in the center, with Mary I on his right. To his left are a nine-year-old Edward VI, and Elizabeth I.

THE WARS OF RELIGION
Arguments over religion plunged Europe into a series of violent wars. In the Spanish-ruled Netherlands, Protestants rebelled against the harsh policies of Philip II of Spain, leading to the Dutch Wars of Independence (1568– 1648). Thousands of French Protestants (Huguenots) were massacred in Paris on a single day in 1572 during the French Wars of Religion (1562–1598). The deep divide between Catholics and Protestants was the immediate cause of the Thirty Years' War, which brought most of Europe into conflict from 1618 to 1648.

Battle of White Mountain
Fought near Prague in Bohemia (in modern-day Czech Republic) in 1620, the Battle of White Mountain was the first major conflict of the Thirty Years' War. The Bohemian Protestants were defeated by the Catholic troops of the Holy Roman Empire.

IN SOME PARTS OF GERMANY, THE POPULATION FELL BY **UP TO 40%** DURING THE **THIRTY YEARS' WAR**

KABUL

Tomb of Babur
Babur conquered the Afghan city of Kabul in 1504. He was a lover of gardens, and asked to be buried in the garden he had created in Kabul.

PANIPAT

SHAHJAHANABAD

Battle of Panipat
Babur's army won a great victory at Panipat in 1526, defeating the Delhi Sultanate, which ruled this part of India.

AGRA

Jama Masjid
Shah Jahan moved the Mughal capital from Agra in 1639 to the walled city of Shahjahanabad (known as Old Delhi today), where he built the Jama Masjid, one of the world's largest mosques.

Taj Mahal
Shah Jahan built the famous Taj Mahal in Agra as a tomb for his beloved wife, Mumtaz Mahal. Shah Jahan himself was also buried here.

Key

■ The Mughal Empire in 1606

■ Territory gained by the Mughals by 1707

Trade in Surat
The port of Surat was a meeting place for European, Arab, and Indian traders. It prospered under the Mughals before being sacked by the Maratha king Shivaji in 1664.

Baji Rao
The greatest general of the Maratha Empire, Baji Rao (1700–1740) never lost a battle. He contributed to the rapid expansion of the Marathas over the entire Indian subcontinent.

SURAT

PUNE

The Maratha Empire
The Marathas were a Hindu warrior people living around the city of Pune in the west of India. In the mid-17th century, the Marathas began to conquer the surrounding lands. By 1797, the Maratha Empire stretched from Peshawar in the north to Tanjore (modern-day Thanjavur) in the south.

Peshawar

0   500   1,000 km
0   250   500 miles

MARATHA EMPIRE

Pune

Arabian Sea

Bay of Bengal

INDIAN OCEAN

Tanjore

Key

■ Maratha Empire at its greatest extent in 1797

The Mughal Empire

In the 16th century, Babur, a warlord from Central Asia, invaded a small region of northern India. His descendants built a great empire that, by the end of the 17th century, extended over most of modern-day India, Pakistan, and Bangladesh.

The Mughal emperors were descended from the Mongol people of Central Asia. Like the north Indian rulers Babur defeated, they were Muslims, following the religion of Islam. Under Mughal rule, Islamic art and culture, especially miniature painting and architecture, flourished. Babur's grandson, Akbar, expanded the Mughal Empire south into regions that he won from Hindu princes. Muslims and Hindus initially lived side by side in relative peace, as Akbar allowed the Hindus to worship their own gods. But relations worsened as the rule of the Mughals became more intolerant in the late 18th century. Many local Hindu rulers, such as the Maratha of southwest India, began to revolt, weakening Mughal power.

150 million The **population** of the Mughal Empire in around 1700.

1 million The **number of soldiers** in the Mughal army during the reign of **Aurangzeb**.

111

ALLAHABAD

CALCUTTA

The British take control

From 1696, the British East India Company was based at Fort William near Calcutta (modern-day Kolkata). In 1757, the Company, which had its own armed forces, attempted to seize control of the region. At the Battle of Plassey, its forces defeated the Nawab of Bengal, a prince who ruled the area in the name of the Mughals. It was a decisive victory. The Mughal Empire had all but collapsed at this time, and the way was open for the British to take control of India.

Fort of Allahabad

Akbar's great fort at Allahabad was the center of Mughal control in northeast India. It was built at the meeting place of the Ganges and Jamuna rivers, a sacred site for Hindus.

BIJAPUR

Gol Gumbaz

Bijapur was the capital of a Muslim sultanate (state) in central India. The sultans of Bijapur built great tombs for themselves, the most famous of which is the Gol Gumbaz mausoleum of Sultan Mohammad Adil Shah. Bijapur became part of the Mughal Empire in 1686. It briefly gained independence in 1724, but was later conquered by the first Maratha emperor, Rajaram II, in 1760.

Sivaganga Fort

King Shivaji's half-brother Venkoji captured Tanjore (modern-day Thanjavur) in 1674, where he established a Maratha kingdom, ruling from Sivaganga Fort (now called Thanjavur Palace).

TANJORE

The expansion of Mughal rule

The spread of the Mughal Empire beyond its initial northern territories was mainly due to two emperors: Akbar, who imposed Mughal power right across India from the Arabian Sea to the Bay of Bengal, and Aurangzeb, who conquered all but the far south. The Marathas' power base was around Pune in the west.

Mughal and Maratha rulers

The Mughal Dynasty ruled India from 1526 to 1857 under 18 emperors. The greatest of these rulers lived during the 16th and 17th centuries, the golden age of the Mughal Empire. The empire's rapid decline after 1700 was due in part to the growing success of the Marathas, who formed their own kingdom based in western India.

Timeline

Babur

1526–1530

The founder of the Mughal dynasty of emperors, Babur was born in Fergana (now in Uzbekistan) in Central Asia. A soldier from the age of 15, he conquered Herat and Kabul in Afghanistan before invading in India in 1526. Babur was a poet and wrote a book of memoirs, the Baburnama. His name means "tiger" in Persian.

Akbar the Great

1556–1605

The grandson of Babur, Akbar was the third Mughal emperor. By the time of his death, he ruled over most of India. He was tolerant of other religions and gave Hindu princes positions at his court. Like all the Mughal emperors, he was a great patron of the arts, blending Islamic, Persian, and Indian traditions. His reign coincided with that of Elizabeth I of England.

Shah Jahan

1628–1658

The fifth Mughal emperor, Shah Jahan, is best known for building many beautiful palaces, mosques, and tombs, including the Taj Mahal in Agra, the Shalimar Gardens in Lahore, and the Jama Masjid and Red Fort in Delhi. When false rumors of his death spread in 1657, war broke out among Shah Jahan's four sons. His third son, Aurangzeb, took control and threw him in prison, where he died eight years later.

Aurangzeb

1658–1707

Aurangzeb's conquests in the south of India expanded Mughal territory to its greatest extent. Aurangzeb ruled his subjects strictly, introducing laws to ban music and dancing, and destroying hundreds of Hindu temples. He forced his Hindu and other non-Muslim subjects to pay high taxes to fund his constant wars. After his death, the Mughal Empire fell quickly apart under a succession of weak rulers.

Shivaji

1674–1680

Shivaji came from the Bhonsle clan of Maratha warriors in the west of India. He led a Hindu campaign of resistance against the Muslim rulers of Bijapur before beginning to push back against the Mughals. Regarded as the founder of the Maratha Empire, he named himself king in 1674 in a traditional Hindu ceremony.

The Scientific Revolution

In the 16th and 17th centuries, pioneering thinkers made major scientific discoveries that changed the way people looked at the world. This period of progress is known as the Scientific Revolution.

Instead of relying on the accepted teachings of the Church and philosophers, scientists tested new ideas and theories through observation, investigation, and experimentation. Helped by new inventions, their discoveries laid the foundations of modern science.

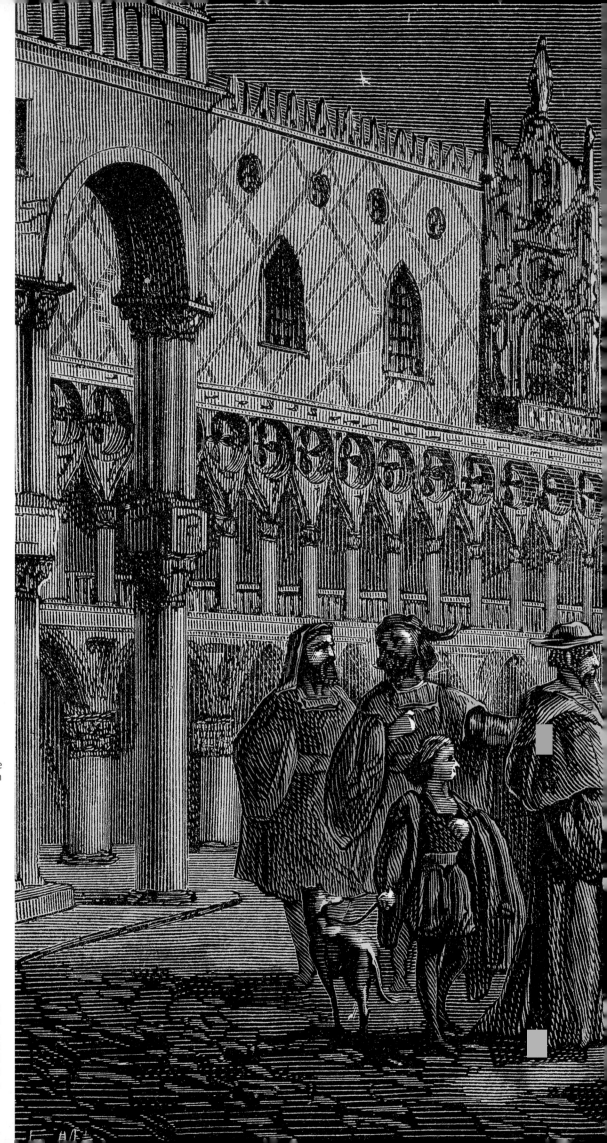

1543
Polish astronomer Nicolaus Copernicus calculated that Earth and other planets orbit the sun, challenging the Church's teaching that the sun circled the Earth.

1628
English physician William Harvey proved that the heart pumps blood around the body.

1656
Dutch inventor Christiaan Huygens built the first pendulum clock, which was more accurate than previous clocks.

1672
English physicist Isaac Newton carried out an experiment that proved that white light is made up of different colors.

1687
Isaac Newton was the first scientist to explain how the movement of the planets is governed by gravity (an invisible force that pulls all matter together).

1610
Italian scientist Galileo Galilei observed four moons in orbit around Jupiter, and supported Copernicus' idea of Earth orbiting the sun. He also discovered mountains on the moon and sunspots.

1637
French philosopher René Descartes published his influential book titled *Discourse on Method*. In it he argued that all ideas should be questioned.

1665
English scientist Robert Hooke published *Micrographia*—a book about his study of minute objects observed through a microscope. He was also the first person to describe plant cells.

1676
Anton van Leeuwenhoek, a Dutch scientist, made powerful microscopes that magnified objects up to 270 times. This allowed him to observe bacteria swimming in a drop of water.

Galileo and his telescope
Galileo built a telescope that allowed him to see further than previous models had, and in 1609 he demonstrated his device to the ruler of Venice, who helped fund Galileo's research. Here, he is shown standing to the right of his telescope.

Colonial life

When the first Europeans arrived in North America in the 16th century, the land was inhabited by groups of Native American farmers. By the 18th century, the number of European settlers numbered about 250,000. The colonies established their own schools and churches, and the country of origin of the settlers—English, French, Dutch, and Spanish—influenced the lifestyle of each region.

St. Augustine

Founded by the Spanish, St. Augustine in Florida was the first permanent European settlement in North America. It was constructed as a fort to prevent Florida, part of the Spanish Empire, from being colonized by French settlers.

Roanoke Island

English settlers founded a colony on Roanoke Island off the coast of what is now North Carolina. But the settlement failed. When a ship returned in 1590 with much needed supplies for the settlers, there was no sign of any of the inhabitants. Their fate has remained a mystery.

Québec

French explorer Samuel Champlain founded Québec on the St. Lawrence River in modern-day Canada. It became the capital of New France, which included all French colonial territory in North America.

The slave trade

About 20 African slaves arrived at Jamestown, Virginia, on board two English armed ships, which had seized a Spanish ship carrying slaves to Mexico. Purchased by English tobacco growers, they were the first of thousands of Africans to endure slavery in colonial North America.

Timeline	1565	1587	1608	1619

Jamestown

In 1607, a party of 104 English men arrived on the eastern shores of North America to start a settlement. The site chosen was near the James River, which was deep enough to allow large ships from England to anchor nearby. The settlement was named Jamestown, and after a difficult few years, it became the first successful English colony in North America. The early settlement consisted of timber-framed houses protected by a triangular palisade (fence).

Women settlers
The first women arrived in 1608. In addition to working in the home, they undertook much of the farm labour.

Church
Every settler was expected to attend the prayer services held in the church.

Storehouse
A large timber-framed storehouse stood in the centre of the fort.

River
Some of the first settlers may have died from drinking brackish water (a mixture of salt and fresh water) from the river.

More than half
of the Jamestown settlers died from disease or starvation during the terrible winter of 1609–1610.

Trading with Powhatans
The local Native American Powhatans traded food with the settlers in exchange for tools, copper, and trinkets.

Canoe
The Powhatans travelled on the river in canoes they made by hollowing out trees with fire and oyster-shell tools.

Timber building
The walls of the single-room, timber-framed houses were made of daub, a sticky mixture of clay, grass, and animal dung.

1621 The date the **Pilgrim Fathers and local Wampanoag people** held the first **Thanksgiving** to celebrate Plymouth colony's first harvest.

13 The number of **British colonies** founded between **1607 and 1733.**

115

English settlers
A group of religious English settlers known as the Pilgrim Fathers reached the eastern coast of North America on a ship called the *Mayflower*. They started a settlement in Plymouth, Massachusetts, where they could practise their religious beliefs without being persecuted. They only just survived their first winter.

1620

New Amsterdam
Dutch traders bought the island of Manhattan from local Native Americans. They named it New Amsterdam, part of the Dutch colony of the New Netherlands that lay along the fertile Hudson River. The English seized the prosperous settlement in 1664, renaming it New York.

1626

Harvard College
The first college in North America was founded by British colonists in Cambridge, Massachusetts. It was named Harvard after Reverend John Harvard, who donated his library of books and part of his wealth to the college upon his death. Today, Harvard is the oldest university in the US.

1636

First newspaper
Printer Benjamin Harris of Boston, Massachusetts, published the first newspaper in Britain's North American colonies. It was called *Publick Occurrences*. Harris, however, failed to obtain permission from the governor of Massachusetts, who ordered every copy to be seized and destroyed.

1690

Reaching the Pacific
Travelling by canoe along the rivers of northwest Canada, Scottish fur trader and explorer Alexander Mackenzie reached the coast of the Pacific Ocean. He was the first European to complete the gruelling east-west overland crossing of North America. His party included six fur trappers and two Native American guides.

1793

Early colonial America

Europeans first began arriving in North America in the 16th century to set up colonies. Many were lured by stories of gold or fertile soil for farming. Others wanted to escape religious persecution.

In the 16th century, French settlers established forts on the St. Lawrence River in what is now Canada. They traded with the Native Americans, exchanging guns and tools for animal furs. Further south, British settlers established colonies along the east coast of what is now the US, while the Spanish focused on New Spain. The European powers fought each other for control over these territories, and there were often conflicts with the Native American people, who originally occupied the lands.

Marshy site
Jamestown was built on low-lying marshy land riddled with mosquitoes that caused malaria and other illnesses.

Defences
Projecting defence structures called bulwarks were built at each corner of the triangular settlement.

Cannon
Cannons were used to defend the settlement from attack.

The Powhatans
Jamestown lay in territory belonging to the Native American Powhatan people. During the first winter, the Powhatans supplied the settlers with maize (corn) and showed them how to grow crops in their new environment. But later on relations between the two groups grew more hostile, and conflicts were frequent.

Pocahontas
Pocahontas, the daughter of Chief Powhatan, married a settler, John Rolfe, in 1614.

King Philip's War
Disputes over land between Europeans and Native Americans often exploded into war. In 1675, a leader who took the name King Philip led an uprising against the colonies of New England (Massachusetts, Rhode Island, and Connecticut). Many towns were attacked before King Philip was hunted down and executed in 1676. Thousands of Native Americans were killed or made slaves.

Colonial territories
This map shows European possession of land in North America in 1750. France and Britain had claimed most of the eastern areas of North America. Florida, Mexico, and California were under Spanish control. European countries also colonized the Caribbean islands. Large parts of North America, however, remained unexplored and unsettled by Europeans at this time.

Key
- British territory
- Spanish territory
- French territory
- Unclaimed land

0   500   1,000 km
0   250   500 miles

Hudson Bay
RUPERT'S LAND
St. Lawrence River
Québec
Hudson River
Plymouth
New York
Jamestown
Roanoke Island
NEW FRANCE
BRITISH COLONIES
VICEROYALTY OF NEW SPAIN
St. Augustine
PACIFIC OCEAN
ATLANTIC OCEAN
Gulf of Mexico

116 the age of exploration ◦ **THE DUTCH GOLDEN AGE**

8 The number of **months** it took to sail from **Amsterdam to Batavia** in the 17th century.

The Dutch Golden Age

In the 17th century, the Dutch Republic (present-day Netherlands) became one of the wealthiest countries in the world. Its growing prosperity created a golden age in which Dutch science, art, and architecture flourished.

The Dutch Republic came into being in 1581 when the seven northern provinces of what was then the Spanish Netherlands formed a union to free themselves from Spanish control. After a long war, they gained their independence in 1609. Despite being the smallest of the European powers, in less than a century, the new Dutch Republic had successfully created a vast overseas trading empire through a combination of seagoing expertise, a strong navy, and clever business practices.

THE DUTCH EAST INDIA COMPANY

In 1602, the Dutch government gave the Dutch East India Company the sole right to trade in Asia. By 1611, it was controlling the profitable spice trade into Europe and soon became the world's largest trading company. It had the power to start wars, make treaties with other countries, and create new colonies. The company's headquarters were at Batavia (modern-day Jakarta) on the Indonesian island of Java. For nearly 200 years, the Dutch East India Company dominated overseas trade.

East Indiaman
Large sailing ships known as East Indiamen sailed regularly between Amsterdam and Batavia.

THE STOCK EXCHANGE

The Dutch economy boomed as a result of its overseas trade. Goods from all around the world were brought to Amsterdam and stored in the city's warehouses before being sold on. In 1611, a group of Amsterdam merchants built the Stock Exchange as a place to meet with traders and exchange information. The main trading activity took place in a large open courtyard surrounded by pillars. Each pillar was numbered, to indicate where people could find traders and make their deals.

Pillars of trade
The Amsterdam Stock Exchange could hold up to 5,000 people. No shouting was allowed, and children and beggars were kept out.

THE DUTCH EAST INDIA COMPANY WAS THE FIRST COMMERCIAL COMPANY TO SELL SHARES ON THE STOCK EXCHANGE.

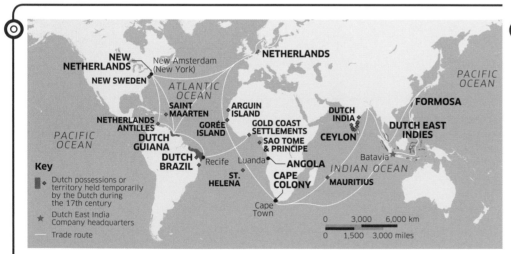

Key
- Dutch possessions or territory held temporarily by the Dutch during the 17th century
- ★ Dutch East India Company headquarters
- — Trade route

THE DUTCH EMPIRE

The Dutch became the leading trading nation by capturing Portuguese forts in the East Indies (present-day Indonesia) and Ceylon (present-day Sri Lanka). They founded Cape Colony (now in modern-day South Africa) and seized territories from Spain and Portugal in South America. While the Dutch East India Company dominated trade in Asia, the Dutch West India Company was set up in 1621 to control trade in the Americas and West Africa.

KEY DISCOVERIES

Dutch scientists and inventors made important discoveries in the 17th century. Glasses-maker Hans Lippershey built the first telescope in 1608. Christiaan Huygens, an astronomer, discovered Saturn's largest moon in 1655. The following year, he built the first pendulum clock. Self-taught scientist Anton von Leeuwenhoek made incredibly accurate microscopes in the 1670s and was the first person to describe bacteria.

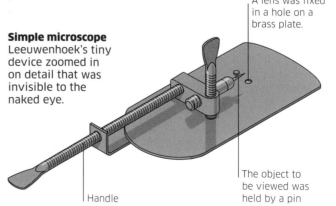

A lens was fixed in a hole on a brass plate.

Simple microscope
Leeuwenhoek's tiny device zoomed in on detail that was invisible to the naked eye.

Handle

The object to be viewed was held by a pin

At the height of its power, the **Dutch East India Company** **owned more than half** of the world's seagoing ships.

1.3 million The **estimated number of paintings** produced by **Dutch artists** between **1640 and 1660**.

117

DUTCH ART

There was a great demand for paintings among wealthy merchants during this period. Instead of producing religious paintings, Dutch painters such as Rembrandt, Johannes Vermeer, and Frans Hals developed new styles. They painted portraits and scenes of everyday life that showed people working or enjoying themselves.

Making lace
Vermeer specialized in painting domestic scenes such as this incredibly detailed work called *The Lacemaker* (1669).

A GROWING CITY

Amsterdam was the leading city in Holland (the largest of the Dutch Republic's seven provinces). In the early 17th century, three major canals were built around the medieval city center. Amsterdam's wealthiest inhabitants lived in splendid houses overlooking these canals, while new neighborhoods were built around the outskirts of the city to provide housing for a growing population.

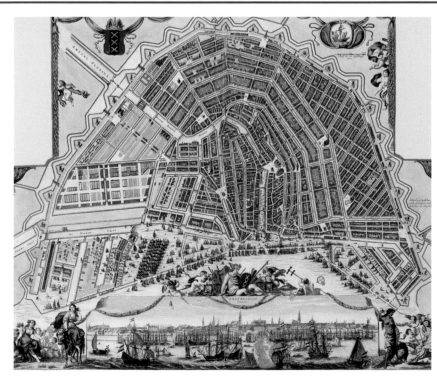

Ring of canals
This map from 1690 shows the city's distinctive half-moon shape with its network of canals, which has remained largely the same to this day.

Population explosion

Amsterdam's growing prosperity and atmosphere of tolerance attracted large numbers of immigrants. Many arrived in the Dutch city to escape from religious persecution in their own country. As a result, Amsterdam's population soared in the 17th century.

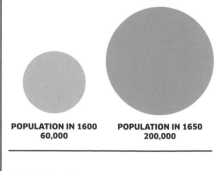

POPULATION IN 1600
60,000

POPULATION IN 1650
200,000

ABOUT 60 PERCENT OF THE
DUTCH POPULATION
LIVED IN SMALL
TOWNS OR CITIES.

118 the age of exploration ○ EDO JAPAN

90 The number of battles fought by Tokugawa Ieyasu to unify Japan under his rule.

Edo Japan

In 1603, Tokugawa Ieyasu, head of the powerful Tokugawa clan, became shogun—the supreme military ruler of Japan. He brought an end to Japan's internal wars and moved the capital to Edo, a remote fishing village that later became the city of Tokyo.

The Tokugawa shoguns ruled Japan in the name of the emperor for more than 250 years. The third shogun, Tokugawa Iemitsu, did not trust Europeans and their Christian religion. He expelled them from Japan, with the exception of a small Dutch trading post, and in 1639, he banned Japanese people from traveling abroad. The country was cut off from the outside world until 1868. This period of isolation was a time of peace and stability, in which the power of the warrior class known as the samurai declined. Closed to the outside world, Japan began a golden age of prosperity and great cultural activity.

Kabuki theater
One of the most popular entertainments of Edo Japan was kabuki theater, a new style of comic dance-drama, often depicting scenes from daily life. Kabuki was livelier than Noh, Japan's older, more graceful form of theater. The colorful, exciting kabuki performances attracted large crowds of people.

Extra seating
The area above the stage was only used to seat audience members when the rest of the theater was full.

Lighting
Theaters were often open all day, with performances of historical plays, everyday stories, and dance interludes happening one after the other. When night fell, performances continued with torches and lanterns to light the stage.

Noisy fans
Spectators clapped loudly and shouted the names of their favorite actors.

Top boxes
The wealthiest audience members occupied the boxes (*masu-seki*) at the top of the theater, which gave the best view of the stage.

Costumes
The actors' brightly patterned costumes were not always easy to wear. They could weigh as much as 44 lb (20 kg).

Raised walkway
Actors entered or exited the stage along a raised walkway called a *hanamichi*, meaning "flower path." The walkway was also used to play out important scenes.

The audience pit
The cheapest seats were in the pit, which was divided into separate square boxes.

15 Tokugawa shoguns ruled over Japan during the Edo period.

The first kabuki play was performed in **1603** in the city of **Kyoto**.

1868 The year the city of **Edo** was renamed **Tokyo**.

119

Roofed stage
The stage was covered by a roof to make it seem as if the play was being performed outside. Kabuki was based on earlier dance-dramas performed in front of temples or shrines.

Art and entertainment
The wealthy people living in Edo and other urban centers referred to the cultural entertainments of the city as *ukiyo*, meaning "floating world." Poets, painters, and craftspeople created works of great elegance and detail. Art and entertainment became more affordable and reached a wider audience. Many of the important pastimes and practices recognized today as part of traditional Japanese culture emerged during the Edo period.

Woodblock printing
Artists created simple but beautiful pictures by applying ink to carved wooden blocks and pressing sheets of paper onto them. This early 19th-century print shows Mount Fuji, Japan's most sacred mountain.

Geisha
In Edo Japan, geisha were women entertainers who danced, sang, and played the *shamisen*, a traditional stringed instrument. They wore colorful kimonos (robes) and elaborate makeup.

Sumo wrestlers
Sumo, a form of wrestling, became a popular entertainment in the Edo period. The first professional sumo wrestlers were often former samurai warriors who needed a new source of income.

Stage scenery
The portable scenery (*kakiwari*) was hand-drawn.

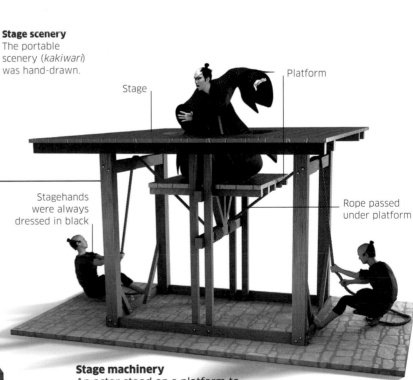

Stage

Platform

Stagehands were always dressed in black

Rope passed under platform

Stage machinery
An actor stood on a platform to make a dramatic entrance onto, or disappearance from, the stage. The platform was raised or lowered by stagehands working below.

Revolving stage
The stage had a revolving mechanism for rapid scene changes.

Kabuki actors
Male actors played both male and female parts. This tradition has been maintained to the present day.

The Atlantic slave trade

Between the 16th and 19th centuries, about 12 million Africans were bought as goods, packed into ships, and sent across the Atlantic to the Americas, where they were sold as slaves.

The settlement of the Americas in the 16th century by Europeans led to the growth of the African slave trade. The purpose of this trade was to give settlers an endless supply of free labor by forcibly uprooting men, women, and children from their homes and resettling them on the other side of the world. The vast majority of the slaves were taken from western Africa. Many died on the terrible journey across the Atlantic, and those that survived were sold at auction houses. Slaves were the legal property of their owners, and the majority of the slaves were forced to work on plantations (large estates growing crops such as cotton). It was not until the end of the 19th century that the slave trade was abolished.

⊙ THE SLAVE TRIANGLE

The slave trade involved Europe, Africa, and the Americas. European traders shipped goods such as cotton cloth to West Africa in exchange for slaves. The ships then crossed the Atlantic, where merchants sold their human cargo at a profit before returning to Europe laden with goods such as sugar and coffee to sell.

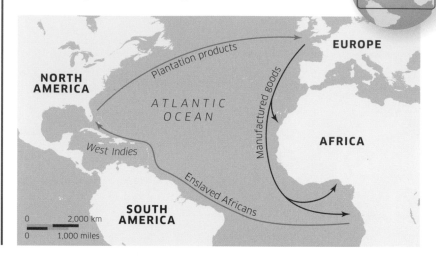

⊙ FOR SALE

On reaching the Americas, the slaves were immediately sold in auctions. Families and friends who had managed to stay together on the long journey from Africa were often separated, never to see each other again—the highest bidder did not always want to buy the entire family. In a system known as a "scramble," some buyers paid the captain a fixed sum beforehand. As soon as the gates were opened, they rushed in to grab the slaves they wanted. Once purchased, the slaves were given new names and had to learn a new language. Forced to work long hours, a third of all slaves died within three years of their arrival, fueling the demand for more.

A slave auction
Plantation owners preferred young, healthy men who could work long hours. They fetched a higher price than women and children.

IN 1860, ON THE EVE OF THE US CIVIL WAR, THERE WERE 4 MILLION AFRICAN AMERICANS IN SLAVERY.

18 The estimated **number of hours** a slave was made to work during the harvest period.

100,000 The number of slaves shipped from Africa to the Americas each year in the late 18th century.

121

Slave forts

Some African rulers became wealthy from the trade in slaves. They sent raiding parties far inland to seize people, marching them to slave forts built by European trading companies on the West African coast. The captives were held in cells until the arrival of the next slave ship.

Cape Coast Castle
This slave fort in Ghana was used by British traders in the 18th century. Its cells held up to 1,500 slaves.

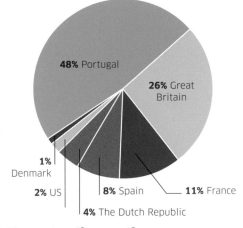

48% Portugal
26% Great Britain
1% Denmark
2% US
8% Spain
11% France
4% The Dutch Republic

Slave-trading nations

By the mid-16th century, Portugal and Spain were sending slaves across the Atlantic to their colonies in Brazil and the Caribbean. In 1713, Britain won a 30-year contract to supply slaves to Spain's colonies, and by the mid-18th century nearly 75 percent of all slaves sent across the Atlantic were carried in Portuguese or British ships.

The Middle Passage

The voyage from Africa to the West Indies and North America was known as the Middle Passage. To maximize profits, up to 600 slaves were crammed into tiny spaces below deck. The men were chained to prevent them from rebelling. Food and water were scarce, and there was no sanitation on a voyage that lasted up to 10 weeks. Many slaves died on the voyage.

The lack of space meant that slaves had to lie on their backs.

A slave ship
This illustration shows the interior of the 18th-century British slave ship *Brookes*.

ANKLE SHACKLES

BRANDING IRON

WHIP

LIFE IN CHAINS

Most of the Africans shipped to the West Indies or North America ended up working on plantations. White overseers (supervisors) hired by the plantation owners would whip them if they did not work hard enough, or shackle them if they tried to escape. Slaves had no legal rights, and many were branded with their owner's mark. Any child born to an enslaved mother was legally a slave for life, and even old people were expected to work.

ABOLITION

The Quakers (members of a Christian group) led the first protests against slavery in North America and Britain. After a 20-year campaign, William Wilberforce, a British politician, helped bring about the end of British involvement in the Atlantic slave trade in 1807, but slave ownership remained legal in British colonies until 1834. The publication of the anti-slavery novel *Uncle Tom's Cabin* by Harriet Beecher Stowe in 1852 boosted calls for the abolition of slavery in the US. This came about in 1865 when the US government passed the 13th Amendment—a law making the practice of slavery illegal.

Road to freedom
Harriet Tubman, a former slave (seen here on the far left), led more than 300 slaves to freedom along the Underground Railroad. This was a network of secret escape routes and safe houses organized by abolitionists in the early 19th century.

Absolute monarchs

In 17th- and 18th-century Europe, many nations' rulers were absolute monarchs. This meant they were in total control of their states and empires, making the laws and deciding when to go to war.

These rulers believed that their authority came from God, not from their subjects, and therefore they had a divine right to rule. As absolute monarchs, they were free to act as they wished, and didn't have to obey their own laws—everyone else had to obey their decisions. The rulers lived in splendid palaces and filled their royal courts with nobility.

1682
King Louis XIV of France made the Palace of Versailles outside Paris his principal residence. Louis had ordered the original chateau to be enlarged and expanded over the previous two decades into a complex that could accommodate his entire government.

1740
Frederick II, later known as Frederick the Great, became king of Prussia, a German state. His wars with Austria and several Polish states doubled the size of Prussia, but he also reformed the government and was a great patron of the arts.

1772
The rulers of Russia, Austria, and Prussia divided a third of Poland's land between themselves in the First Partition of Poland.

1789
Poor people in France, resentful of the luxuries enjoyed by the royalty and nobility, began a revolution that brought an end to the monarchy. The French Revolution triggered the decline of absolute monarchy in Europe.

1703
Czar Peter I of Russia, known as Peter the Great, created a new capital city, which he named St. Petersburg after his patron saint.

1721
Peter the Great of Russia won the Great Northern War against Sweden. This victory made the Russian Empire a major power in Europe.

1764
Catherine II of Russia, known as Catherine the Great, had a new wing built in the Winter Palace in St. Petersburg to house her vast collection of paintings and porcelain. Today it forms part of the Hermitage Museum.

1783
Catherine the Great expanded the Russian Empire southward to Crimea, a peninsula in eastern Europe, to give Russia a port on the Black Sea.

At the court of King Louis XIV of France
King Louis XIV moved his entire court to the Palace of Versailles, insisting that his nobles live there, too. The vast palace contained more than 700 rooms, 1,200 fireplaces, and 67 staircases.

THE AGE OF REVOLUTION

In the mid-18th century, new technological innovations and revolutionary ideas began to transform the world. The Industrial Revolution spread from Britain, changing how people lived and worked. Struggles for independence in North and South America inspired revolutions in Europe. New ideas about nationhood led to European expansion across Africa, South Asia, and the Pacific.

ZULU SHIELD

1879: The Anglo-Zulu War
Fought between the British and the Zulu Kingdom, the six-month Anglo-Zulu War ended in a British victory. The British made the Zulu lands into a colony.

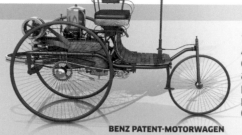

BENZ PATENT-MOTORWAGEN

1888: The Benz Patent Motorwagen
After German inventor Karl Benz designed his gasoline-powered automobile, his wife and business partner Bertha Benz generated publicity for the car by driving it 66 miles (106 km) across Germany.

1871: The Unification of Germany
King William I of Prussia became the first emperor of a united Germany. In the same year, the states of Italy also united into a single nation.

CIVIL WAR NAPOLEON GUN

1861–1865: The US Civil War
The US was torn apart by a bitter civil war in which states in the North and South fought each other over the enslavement of African Americans and the rights of individual states.

Timeline of the age of revolution

After the American Revolution, ideals of freedom and equality were taken up by groups all over the world. At the same time, the Industrial Revolution transformed everyday life, as people moved from the countryside to work in factories.

The people of South America liberated their continent from Spanish and Portuguese rule. In Europe, the French monarchy was abolished, the Greeks won independence, and Germany and Italy both unified into single nations. But countries old and new still looked to increase their territory, using new technology to achieve their aims. The US spread westward, causing conflict with American Indians. Most of Africa, India, Southeast Asia, Australia, and the Pacific Islands were colonized by European powers.

1821–1830: The Greek War of Independence
The Greeks fought to free themselves from the rule of the Ottoman Empire. With the assistance of Britain, France, and Russia, Greece won the war in 1830, and became an independent state in 1832.

GREEK GENERAL THEODOROS KOLOKOTRONIS

SIMÓN BOLÍVAR

1810–1825: South American Wars
The struggle to end 300 years of Spanish and Portuguese rule in South America was led by revolutionaries such as Simón Bolívar. By 1825, all of Spain's colonies except Cuba and Puerto Rico had been liberated, while Portugal lost control of Brazil.

PRUSSIAN KING FREDERICK II'S MILITARY COAT

1756–1763: The Seven Years' War
Fought across five continents, the Seven Years' War was the first wide-scale global conflict. Britain and France struggled for colonial supremacy in North America and India, while the ongoing tensions between Prussia (in modern-day Germany) and Russia drew in allies on both sides.

JAMES WATT'S STEAM ENGINE

1765: Steam power
Scottish engineer James Watt developed a steam engine that was more efficient than previous models. Watt's steam engine provided the power needed to run factory machines on a massive scale, beginning the Industrial Revolution.

AMERICAN INDIAN GHOST DANCE SHIRT

1890: The Battle of Wounded Knee
The Battle of Wounded Knee was the last major conflict between US soldiers and American Indians. It ended in the massacre of up to 200 Sioux–members of the largest American Indian group living on the northern plains.

STATUE OF LIBERTY

1892–1954: Ellis Island
With millions of people from around the world traveling to the US to live, Ellis Island in Upper New York Bay served as a center for processing and managing new arrivals.

THE 1903 WRIGHT FLYER

1903: The first powered flight
In North Carolina, aviation pioneers the Wright Brothers designed the first successful powered aircraft, flying it four times in a single day.

SURGICAL TOOLS

1865: Lister's antiseptics
British surgeon Joseph Lister began to use antiseptic substances on surgical instruments, open wounds, and dressings. The antiseptics destroyed germs and prevented infection from spreading. The death rate at his hospital fell by two-thirds.

BRITISH-BUILT INDIAN TRAIN

1858–1947: British Raj
Britain took control of India in a period known as the British Raj. The British built railroads and schools, but they also denied local rulers and people a share in political power.

1829: Revolutionary engine
In England, trials were held to decide which steam engines would be used on the Liverpool and Manchester Railway–the world's first inter-city line. Reaching a record speed of 29 mph (47 km/h), Robert Stephenson's *Rocket* won the trials.

STEPHENSON'S *ROCKET*

1836: The Oregon Trail
In the 19th century, thousands of US settlers headed west in search of new land to farm. They set out in wagons along the Oregon Trail, with the first settlers arriving in Oregon in 1836.

COVERED WAGON

NAPOLEONIC PISTOL

1803–1815: The Napoleonic Wars
For more than a decade, the newly created republic of France was at war with much of the rest of Europe. Under the leadership of the ambitious French emperor Napoleon Bonaparte, a series of victories brought much of Europe under French control.

1789–1799: The French Revolution
Anger against the monarchy and nobility boiled over into revolution in France. The king, and later many nobles and anyone labeled as an "enemy of the revolution" were executed by guillotine.

GUILLOTINE

COLONIAL ARMY KNAPSACK

1775–1783: The American Revolution
Angered by rising taxes, the 13 British colonies of North America rebelled against British rule. The war ended with a victory for the colonists, creating the United States of America.

HMS *SIRIUS* OF THE FIRST FLEET

1788: The First Fleet
The first British colonists arrived in Australia on the ships of the First Fleet. They were mostly convicts–sent to Australia to serve out their sentences–and their guards. They established the first colony at Sydney.

The Seven Years' War

Fought between 1756 and 1763, the Seven Years' War was the first global conflict. It involved every major European power of the time, with the fighting taking place in the Americas, Africa, and Asia as well as Europe.

In the early 18th century, France and Britain were constantly trying to seize each other's colonial territories in North America, the Caribbean, and India. When, in 1756, growing tensions between the major powers in Europe erupted into war, Britain supported the north German kingdom of Prussia, while France (previously an ally of Prussia) switched its allegiance to Austria. The stage was set for the fighting to spread to different parts of the world. In some countries the war is known by different names—in the US, the colonial conflict is known as the French and Indian War.

THE WAR IN EUROPE

In 1740, Frederick II of Prussia invaded Silesia (then part of Austria). Backed by France and Russia, Austria wanted to regain control of Silesia, and when the Prussian king marched his troops into Saxony (an Austrian ally) in 1756, it signaled the start of the Seven Years' War. During the conflict, both sides experienced triumphs as well as heavy losses.

Battle of Rossbach
At the Battle of Rossbach (1757), Frederick II led his troops to his greatest tactical victory, defeating the much larger French-Austrian force.

WAR IN NORTH AMERICA

France and Britain had already been fighting each other for two years before the main war began in Europe in 1756. Both sides had allies from native tribes, and most of the fighting took place in New France (the name given to France's North American territories).

George Washington

The commander of the British colonial army in Virginia was George Washington (who later became the first president of the US). In 1754, he led an ambush against the French at Fort Duquesne, triggering the French and Indian War.

Key battles

In 1759, British General James Wolfe sailed his army down the St. Lawrence River to seize the French fortress of Québec. The following year, Britain defeated the French at Montreal. Nearly all of France's North American territories were now in the hands of British forces.

Battle for Québec
A small British force crossed the St. Lawrence River to take the defenders of Québec by surprise.

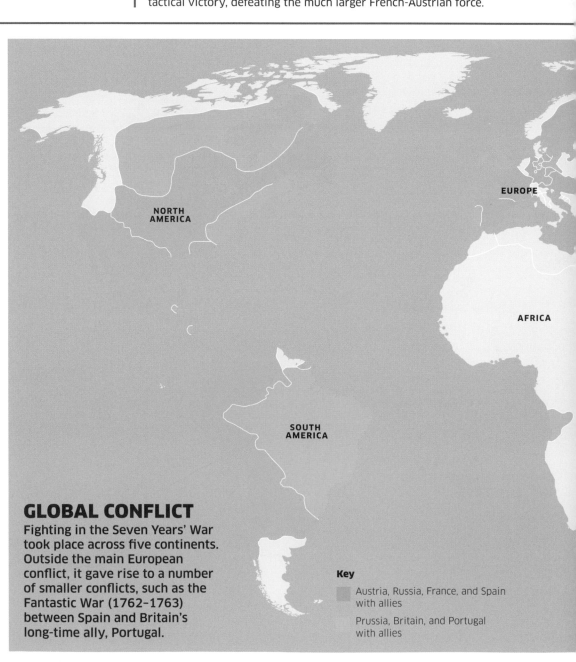

GLOBAL CONFLICT

Fighting in the Seven Years' War took place across five continents. Outside the main European conflict, it gave rise to a number of smaller conflicts, such as the Fantastic War (1762–1763) between Spain and Britain's long-time ally, Portugal.

Key

Austria, Russia, France, and Spain with allies

Prussia, Britain, and Portugal with allies

186 The **number of troops** led by George Washington on his expedition to **Fort Duquesne** in 1754.

The **end of French power in India** marked the rise of British **influence in India**, which lasted for nearly **200 years**.

129

Warring monarchs

The war in Europe was shaped by the ruling monarchs of the time. A brilliant military leader, Frederick II was crowned king of Prussia in 1740, the same year that Maria Theresa became ruler of Austria, while Peter III succeeded as czar (emperor) of Russia in 1762.

Frederick II

Within months of becoming king, Frederick II set about transforming his small kingdom into a major military power. He reformed his army, and often led his troops into battle.

Maria Theresa

Austria's Maria Theresa was only 23 when she came to the throne. Although she made her husband Emperor Francis I co-ruler, she guided Austria's foreign policy.

Peter and Catherine

On becoming czar, Peter III made peace with Prussia, bringing the war to an end. His wife, Catherine the Great, led a plot to get rid of him and ruled Russia alone for the next 34 years.

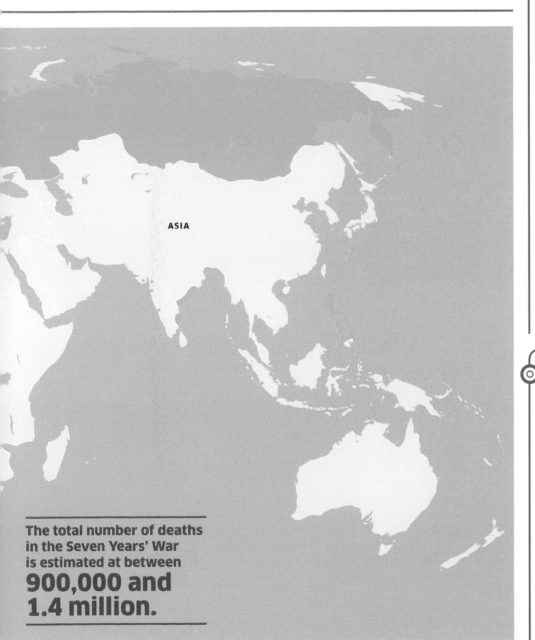

ASIA

The total number of deaths in the Seven Years' War is estimated at between

900,000 and 1.4 million.

EUROPEAN ARMIES

The sizes of the armies involved in the conflict are shown here. Helped by British forces, Frederick II battled against the combined forces of Russia, Austria, and France.

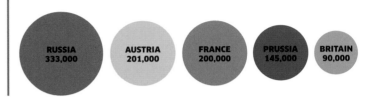

| RUSSIA 333,000 | AUSTRIA 201,000 | FRANCE 200,000 | PRUSSIA 145,000 | BRITAIN 90,000 |

COLONIAL RIVALS

The colonial rivalry between Britain and France spread the war around the world. In India, Britain won the battle of Plassey in 1757 against the ruler of Bengal (a French ally) and, in 1761, seized the key French port of Pondicherry. Britain also captured French bases in West Africa and the Caribbean islands of Guadeloupe and Martinique. With Spain's entry into the war on the French side in 1761, fighting spread to the Spanish colonies in the Philippines, Cuba, and South America.

Battle of Plassey
Despite being outnumbered six to one, the British force defeated a French-backed Indian army at the Battle of Plassey.

PEACE TREATIES

By 1763, all sides wanted to stop fighting. The Treaty of Paris made peace between Britain and France and their allies, while the Treaty of Hubertusburg ended the war between Prussia and Austria. In Europe, Prussia was left in possession of Silesia. Britain took control of French North America and gained colonies in India and the Caribbean, making Britain the world's leading colonial empire.

The Treaty of Paris
France, Britain, and Spain signed the Treaty of Paris in 1763.

The Industrial Revolution

The Industrial Revolution was a period of rapid economic and social change, beginning in Britain in the mid-18th century and spreading to Europe and the US. The process of industrialization saw people move from farming jobs in the countryside to find work in new factories, mines, and mills.

A number of technological inventions brought about the revolution. Improvements in agriculture made it possible to produce more food to feed a growing population, but they also meant that fewer farm workers were needed to work on the land. New industrial technologies also allowed items such as cloth, pottery, and tools to be mass-produced in factories. The wealthy were eager to buy machine-made goods and to invest in new industrial businesses, and their money drove the revolution forward.

Changing landscape

The industrial age changed the landscape forever as mills and factories were built, and coal was mined on a much larger scale. Cramped streets of houses sprang up around the new workplaces, while tall factory chimneys pumped filthy smoke into the atmosphere. A network of canals and locks linked the industrial centers to trading ports and cities.

Pollution
Burning coal to power the steam engines created pollution in the new industrial towns.

Wheel power
The winding wheel hoisted the basket that carried miners and coal carts up and down the shaft.

Steam engine
In 1712, Thomas Newcomen designed a steam engine to pump floodwater out of mines. James Watt's design of 1765 (shown above) transformed the jerky up-and-down action of Newcomen's engine into a smooth, efficient motion that turned a wheel. Watt's improved steam engine was quickly put to use, driving machines in factories and mills.

Wooden carts
Coal was loaded onto shallow wooden carts with iron wheels.

Upcast shaft
Coal was hoisted to the surface through upcast shafts.

Furnace
The furnace ventilated the mine and removed poisonous gases.

Child labor
Poor families could not afford to send their children to school, so children as young as five worked in mines and factories. Their small fingers made them good at detailed jobs and they could squeeze their bodies into tight spaces. But accidents were frequent, causing terrible injuries and even death.

Pit props
Wooden pit props stopped the mine from collapsing.

Downcast shaft
A second shaft was used to winch workers down in a large wicker basket called a corf.

Horses
Horses and pit ponies were used to pull small wooden carts underground.

500 The estimated number of **steam engines** in use in British **mines and factories** by 1800.

60,000 miles (100,000 km) of thread could be **produced in a 12-hour shift** using a single **100-horsepower engine.**

131

Canal barge
New networks of canals allowed goods to be transported from mills and factories straight to large towns, where they were sold in stores.

Textile mill
New machines that increased the production rate of cloth in the 1770s led to the creation of large textile mills.

Working in the mills
Mill owners tended to employ women and children because they could be paid less than men. It was hard work keeping the fast-moving machines running. A moment's carelessness, and a mill worker might easily lose a finger—or worse.

Railroad bridge
The development of the railroads led to great feats of engineering as tracks were laid and viaducts, bridges, and tunnels were built.

Steam train
By the 1850s, railroads had replaced canals as the principal means of transportation in England, with steam locomotives hauling long lines of trucks.

Workers' cottages
Factory and mine owners housed their workers in rows of cheaply built homes. Many were not provided with clean water or proper sewage systems, so disease was rampant.

Coalface
Miners dug their way horizontally along a coal seam, hacking away at the coalface with pickaxes.

Shallow coal seam
Smaller seams did not have tracks or horses so women and children, crawling on all fours, hauled the coal.

Trappers
Trapdoors kept air flowing through the mine. They were opened and shut by young children called trappers.

Railroads

By the early 19th century, locomotives—steam engines that moved—were being used to pull heavy loads in mines and quarries. One of the pioneers of steam locomotion was George Stephenson. In 1825, he oversaw construction of the world's first public railroad, which ran between the towns of Stockton and Darlington in the north of England.

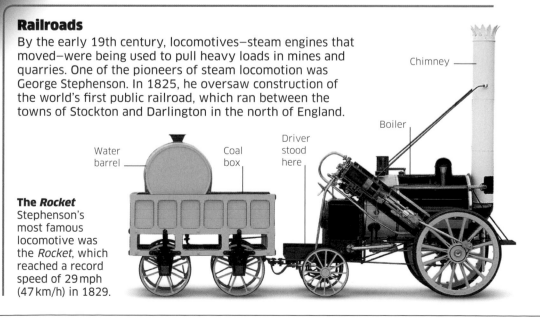

Chimney

Boiler

Water barrel

Coal box

Driver stood here

The *Rocket*
Stephenson's most famous locomotive was the *Rocket*, which reached a record speed of 29 mph (47 km/h) in 1829.

American independence

In the late 18th century, people living in the British colonies on the east coast of North America demanded an end to British rule, and set about creating their own independent nation.

The colonists were angered by the taxes imposed on them by the distant governing body—the British parliament—without their consent. Riots turned to war as the Americans fought for independence. Eventually, the British were defeated and forced to withdraw, leading to the establishment of a new nation—the United States of America.

1764
The British enforce a tax on sugar coming into the colonies.

1765
The Stamp Act was passed by the British parliament. This imposed a tax on all legal documents, books, and newspaper used by the colonists.

1770
During a protest in Boston, Massachusetts, British soldiers fired on rioters, killing five of them.

1773
Colonists protesting against favorable taxation treatment for British-imported tea, threw a shipment of tea into Boston Harbor, an event known as the Boston Tea Party.

1775
Colonial armies defeated British forces at the battles of Lexington and Concord, Massachusetts, starting the American Revolution.

1776
On July 4, representatives of the 13 colonies in Congress adopted the Declaration of Independence, which set out the reasons for ending British rule.

1778
France declared war on Britain in support of the Americans. Soon afterward, Spain joined the alliance against Britain.

1781
The surrender by the British at Yorktown, Virginia, brought the American Revolution to an end.

1783
Britain signed the Treaty of Paris, confirming the independence of the United States of America.

The Declaration of Independence
Thomas Jefferson, a lawyer who later became the third US president, was responsible for writing most of the Declaration of Independence. He is shown here presenting the first draft to Congress in June 1776.

Forced removal

To make room for settlers, the Indian Removal Act of 1830 forced the Cherokee and other Native American nations to leave their lands in the southeast and relocate in Indian Territory west of the Mississippi River.

Trail of Tears
The march west was so terrible, the Cherokee named it the Trail of Tears. Thousands of Cherokees died of disease or starvation.

California Gold Rush

In 1848, news spread that gold had been discovered in California, a remote, unpopulated area on the west coast. Within five years, 250,000 immigrants arrived there from all over the world in the hope of finding gold.

Come to California!
Posters and advertisements encouraged settlers to try their luck in the goldfields of California.

Land incentive

In 1862, to help push the westward expansion, the US government offered Americans a free plot of land in the west if they lived on it for at least five years.

A new life
For some freed slaves the offer of a plot of land was one of the few ways they could make a new life for themselves.

Wagon train
For safety, settlers traveled together in long lines, or trains, each with about 30 wagons. Sometimes there were as many as 200 wagons.

Families on the trail
Whole families of pioneers made the journey. Young children, the sick, and the very old rode on the wagon.

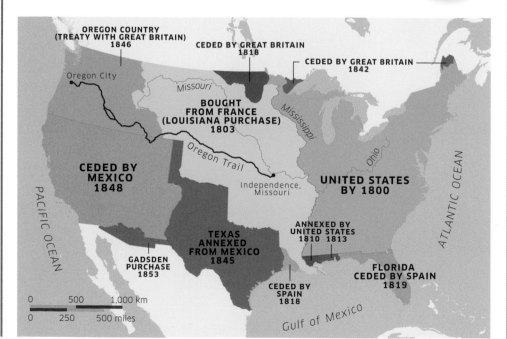

Wooden wheels
Wheels were made of wood with a thin rim of iron to prevent wear. Even today, their tracks are evident along parts of the trail.

Iron axles
The axles were made of iron to withstand the heavy jolting over rough terrain.

Expanding the frontier

Between 1780 and 1850, the US frontier was pushed west across the continent from the original 13 colonies on the east coast. Territory was acquired through various purchases, treaties, and wars. In 1803, France sold its vast territory in the Midwest, known as the Louisiana Purchase. Other territories were gained from Spain, Great Britain, and Mexico.

OREGON COUNTRY
(TREATY WITH GREAT BRITAIN)
1846
CEDED BY GREAT BRITAIN
1818
CEDED BY GREAT BRITAIN
1842
Oregon City
Missouri
BOUGHT
FROM FRANCE
(LOUISIANA PURCHASE)
1803
Mississippi
Oregon Trail
CEDED BY
MEXICO
1848
Ohio
UNITED STATES
BY 1800
Independence,
Missouri
PACIFIC OCEAN
ATLANTIC OCEAN
ANNEXED BY
UNITED STATES
1810 1813
TEXAS
ANNEXED
FROM MEXICO
1845
GADSDEN
PURCHASE
1853
FLORIDA
CEDED BY SPAIN
1819
CEDED BY
SPAIN
1818
0   500   1,000 km
0   250   500 miles
Gulf of Mexico

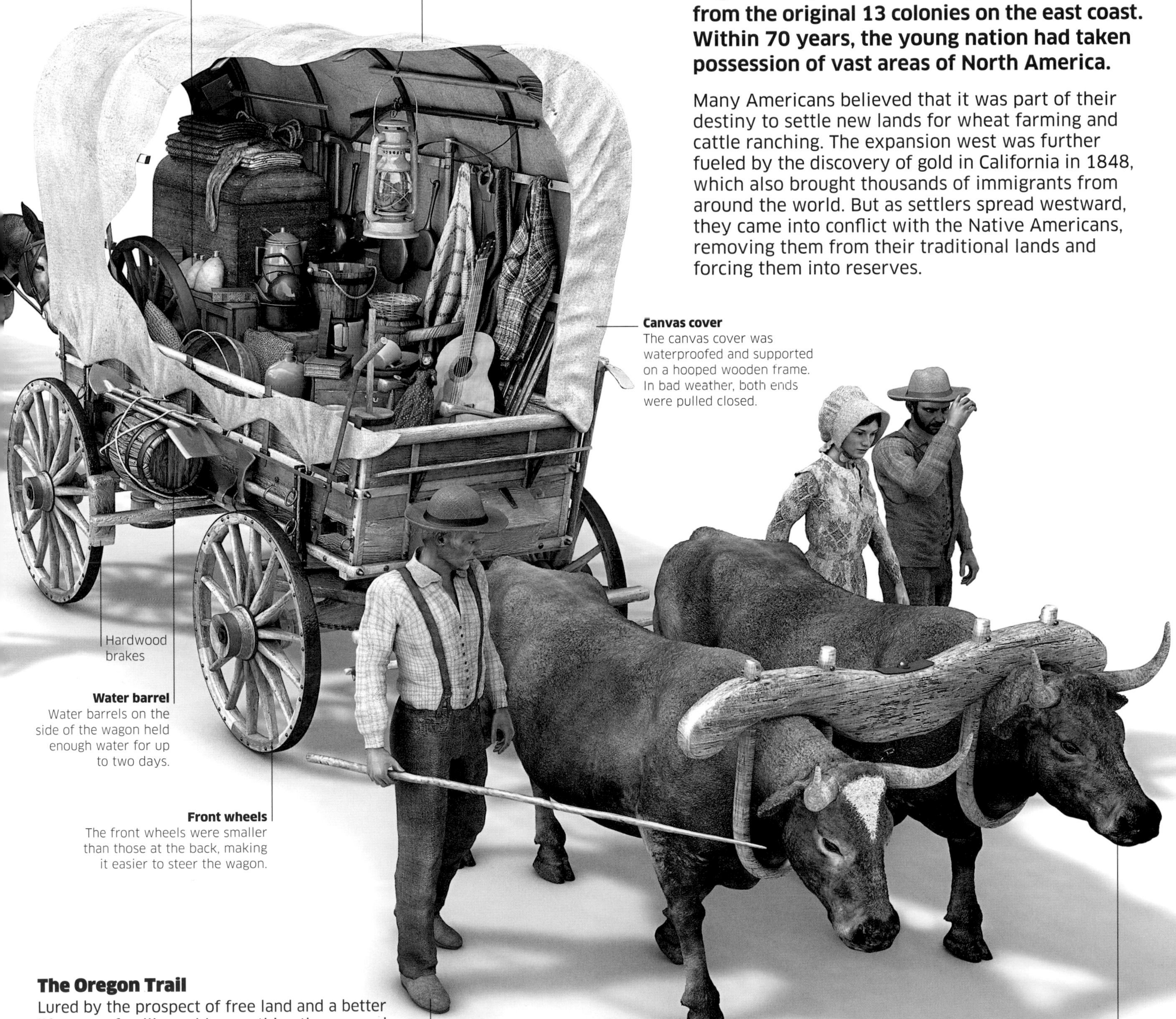

Food and supplies
The wagons were packed with food to last the journey, as well as guns and tools, and a few treasured items from home.

Prairie schooner
The covered wagons were known as prairie schooners because their shape resembled a sailing ship (schooner) in full sail.

The expansion of the US

After gaining independence in 1783, the US began to expand its territory west and south from the original 13 colonies on the east coast. Within 70 years, the young nation had taken possession of vast areas of North America.

Many Americans believed that it was part of their destiny to settle new lands for wheat farming and cattle ranching. The expansion west was further fueled by the discovery of gold in California in 1848, which also brought thousands of immigrants from around the world. But as settlers spread westward, they came into conflict with the Native Americans, removing them from their traditional lands and forcing them into reserves.

Canvas cover
The canvas cover was waterproofed and supported on a hooped wooden frame. In bad weather, both ends were pulled closed.

Hardwood brakes

Water barrel
Water barrels on the side of the wagon held enough water for up to two days.

Front wheels
The front wheels were smaller than those at the back, making it easier to steer the wagon.

The Oregon Trail
Lured by the prospect of free land and a better life, many families sold everything they owned in search of new opportunities in Oregon Country (the present-day states of Oregon, Washington, and Idaho). They made the perilous journey along the Oregon Trail in covered wagons—a journey that stretched 2,000 miles (3,200 km) from Missouri to Oregon.

Traveling on foot
To reduce the weight of the wagons, most men and women walked the trail.

Oxen team
Oxen usually pulled the wagons as they were cheaper, stronger, and easier to work than horses.

Colonizing Australia and the Pacific

From the 17th century to the 19th century, European nations expanded their presence in the Pacific Ocean.

Explorers, mapmakers, and merchants set sail to look for new trading opportunities and build new seaports. They explored and charted Australia, New Zealand, and the many Pacific islands. Throughout the region, governments, merchants, and missionaries set up colonies. Early colonists came into contact with indigenous people and claimed their land. European diseases spread throughout the local populations, and violent conflicts broke out over land ownership and local tribal rights.

◎ EUROPEAN EXPLORERS

Willem Janszoon, a Dutch explorer, was the first recorded European to land in Australia with his crew in 1606. Spanish and Portuguese explorers soon followed. Another Dutch explorer, Abel Tasman, sailed to, and charted, the island that is now called Tasmania. Over a century later, British explorer and mapmaker Captain James Cook embarked on a voyage that took him along the eastern coasts of Australia and New Zealand. On later expeditions, he charted the Hawaiian coasts and areas of the Pacific Ocean and Antarctica.

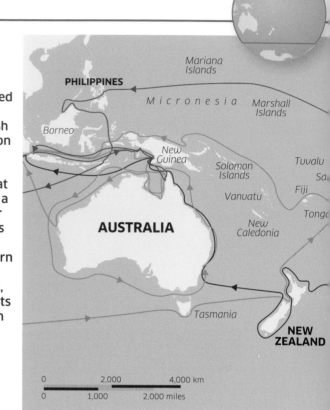

◎ AUSTRALIA

The Aborigine people had lived in Australia for more than 50,000 years before the British started colonizing the coastline in the late 18th century. At first, the local Aborigines were welcoming. However, as more land was taken away from them, fighting broke out, and tens of thousands of Aborigines died in the clashes. By the early 19th century, British settlements had spread all along the coast. In 1827, Britain laid claim to all of Australia.

Unfamiliar animals

Many Australian animals, especially marsupials such as kangaroos and wallabies, were unknown to Europeans. Explorers described them as combinations of cats, apes, meerkats, snakes, rats, and squirrels. Some of the first explorers, curious about how they tasted, hunted the local wildlife.

Kangaroo
British artist George Stubbs was one of the first people to paint a kangaroo in 1772. He based his artwork on sketches brought back by explorers.

Gold rush

In 1851, gold was discovered in New South Wales (southeastern Australia), leading to a gold rush. Ships arrived from Britain, Europe, the US, and China, loaded with passengers hoping to mine and sell the gold to become rich. Within 10 years, gold had also been discovered in neighbouring states Victoria and Queensland, and the number of colonists there doubled from 450,000 to more than 1 million.

Prisoner colonies

Most of the early colonists sent to Australia against their will were convicted criminals. They worked the land, built roads and settlements, and prepared the new colonies for future settlers. The convicts became skilled in many trades, from farming and shepherding to shoemaking and tailoring. Many finished their prison sentences in Australia and received Certificates of Freedom, allowing them to marry and buy land.

Sydney settlement, 1788

The first British colony was established in Port Jackson in 1788 and was named Sydney, after the British Home Secretary Lord Sydney.

Latrobe gold nugget
Discovered in 1853, the Latrobe Nugget was one of the largest clusters of cubic gold ever found, weighing 25 oz (717 g).

1803 The year British navigator **Matthew Flinders** became the **first European** to sail **all the way around Australia**.

c. 160,000 The **number of criminals** that were **sent to Australia** during **British colonization**.

137

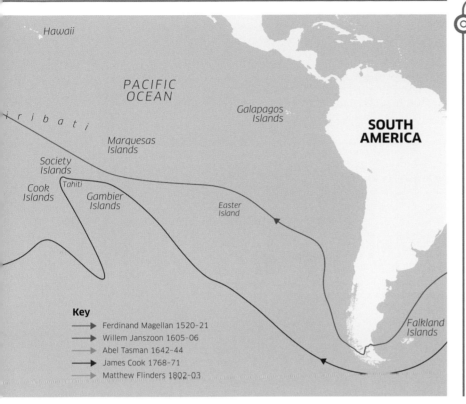

PACIFIC OCEAN

Hawaii

Kiribati

Marquesas Islands

Galapagos Islands

SOUTH AMERICA

Society Islands

Tahiti

Cook Islands

Gambier Islands

Easter Island

Falkland Islands

Key
→ Ferdinand Magellan 1520–21
→ Willem Janszoon 1605–06
→ Abel Tasman 1642–44
→ James Cook 1768–71
→ Matthew Flinders 1802–03

⊚ EFFECT ON INDIGENOUS POPULATIONS

The number of British and European colonists that arrived in Australia and New Zealand rose sharply from the early 19th century. As the colonist numbers grew, indigenous populations fell. Colonists unintentionally spread diseases, such as influenza, smallpox, and measles, killing many indigenous peoples. Colonists also claimed land, and this led to violent clashes and further declines in populations.

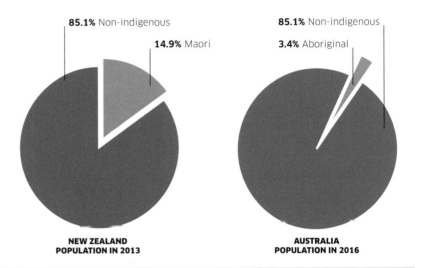

85.1% Non-indigenous

14.9% Maori

NEW ZEALAND POPULATION IN 2013

85.1% Non-indigenous

3.4% Aboriginal

AUSTRALIA POPULATION IN 2016

⊚ NEW ZEALAND AND THE PACIFIC ISLANDS

The indigenous Polynesians were living on the Pacific islands for more than 3,000 years and the Maoris were living on New Zealand since the 13th century before European explorers arrived. After the explorers Tasman and Cook visited New Zealand, European whalers, missionaries, and traders came to the region. British colonists eventually settled on the islands in 1840 after agreements were made with the indigenous Maori population. Over the next 50 years, other islands in the Pacific were claimed by representatives from Britain, France, Germany, and the US.

Missionaries

Christian missionaries played an important role in the relations between colonists and local tribes across the Pacific islands, and they provided education and medical support. In New Zealand, they taught the Maori tribes how to read and helped them create a written Maori language.

Christianity reaches Hawaii
In the 1820s, the people of Hawaii started to convert to Christianity as missionaries arrived from the US.

Maoris and Europeans
Europeans first arrived in New Zealand in the mid-17th century. For the next 200 years, the indigenous Maori tribes fought against—but also sometimes traded with—the European settlers. Maoris traded their potatoes, figs, and flax for European guns.

The Treaty of Waitangi
On February 6, 1840, the British leaders and Maori chiefs signed the Treaty of Waitangi. This gave Britain the right to buy land in New Zealand.

Whaling

In the late 18th century, European whalers hunted many whale species that migrated through New Zealand seas, trading their meat and blubber. Whaling stations and posts were set up throughout the region.

South Sea whaling
Whaling boats needed large crews, and the whaling industry employed many Maoris.

Louis XVI
In 1791, both Louis XVI and Marie Antoinette tried to escape from France but were caught. Taken back to Paris and imprisoned, the king was executed for treason in 1793 by guillotine.

The guillotine
Introduced into France in 1792, the guillotine was designed so that criminals could be executed as painlessly as possible. The device was named after the humane doctor, Joseph-Ignace Guillotin, who proposed its use. Previous methods of execution were far more brutal and horrific.

Guillotine blade
A sharp, heavy, steel blade dropped onto the victim's neck, severing the head from the body.

Basket
The victim's head was caught in a plain woven basket.

Public executioner

Coach
The king was taken to his execution in a coach–other prisoners would have been transported on a cart.

French tricolor flag

Wooden scaffolding

City square
Guillotines were set up in city squares. In Paris, Place de la Révolution (Revolution Square), now named Place de la Concorde, was the scene of many executions.

Women were very active during the revolution and led many of the marches.

The French revolutionaries used the slogan: "liberty, equality, fraternity."

The tricolor French flag was first used during the French Revolution.

139

"The king must die, so that the
"The king must die, so that the country can live."

Maximilien Robespierre, 1792

End of a king

Up to 20,000 people gathered to watch the beheading of the former King Louis XVI on January 21, 1793. Nine months later, Marie Antoinette was executed during the Reign of Terror, a period when people labeled enemies of the revolution were tried and sentenced to death. Between 18,000 and 40,000 people are estimated to have died during the terror campaign.

The French Revolution

Violent riots in Paris in the summer of 1789 marked the start of the French Revolution, and led, three years later, to the execution of King Louis XVI.

Like many European countries in the 18th century, France was an absolute monarchy. The king, who ruled with the aid of a small group of privileged aristocrats, had complete power over his subjects. A series of poor harvests and rising food prices meant that thousands of people were starving throughout the country, especially in Paris. Anger and resentment against the king and his queen, Marie Antoinette, boiled over into revolution, changing France and Europe forever.

Storming of the Bastille

On July 14, 1789, about 600 people attacked the Bastille, a medieval fortress in Paris. It was used as a prison and symbolized royal authority. The rioters freed the seven prisoners held inside, and seized the weapons and gunpowder, marking the start of the revolution. The storming of the Bastille prison on July 14 is still observed as France's national day.

Robespierre

French lawyer Maximilien de Robespierre emerged as a champion of the poor and supporter of human rights. But the extreme measures he took against fellow revolutionaries he regarded as political enemies unleashed the Reign of Terror. Robespierre himself was executed by guillotine in July 1794.

Rights of Man

The Declaration of the Rights of Man and of the Citizen, published in 1789, was an important document that set out the aims of the new revolutionary government. Although there was no mention of the rights of women, the document stated that all men were equal under the law, and that people should be allowed to govern themselves.

Red bonnet
A red cap decorated with a tricolor badge was worn as a symbol of revolution.

Sans-culottes
The Paris revolutionaries were called sans-culottes (without breeches) because they wore loose trousers. Only wealthy men wore silk breeches.

National guardsmen
The National Guard was a citizens' army set up to enforce law and order after the revolution.

Tricoteuses
The market women of Paris took an active part in the riots against the king and queen. During the Reign of Terror, a group would sit and watch the public executions. They were known as the Tricoteuses (knitting women) because they knitted red bonnets for the revolutionaries as they waited to heckle the victims.

140 the age of revolution ∘ THE NAPOLEONIC WARS

At the **height of France's conquests**, more than **44 million subjects** lived under French rule.

The Napoleonic Wars

Napoleon Bonaparte was a brilliant soldier who made himself Emperor of France. From 1803 to 1815, he led France in the Napoleonic Wars, which spread French power throughout Europe.

The Napoleonic Wars were the continuation of the French Revolutionary Wars of 1792–1802. These were fought between the new French Republic, which wanted to revolutionize Europe, and major monarchies (mainly Britain, Austria, Russia, and Prussia), which wanted to end the French Revolution and bring back the king. In 1802, Britain and France signed a treaty to end the conflict. Both sides failed to keep the peace and the Napoleonic Wars began in 1803. Napoleon, who was by this time sole ruler of France, led the French army in a series of triumphant campaigns to conquer much of Europe.

The Battle of Austerlitz

On December 2, 1805, Napoleon's army had one of its greatest victories when it defeated the armies of Austria and Russia at Austerlitz in present-day Czech Republic. Napoleon is seen here (to the right, on the gray horse) after the battle.

Key
- Extent of French Empire in 1812
- French-dependent states in 1812
- French allies in 1812
- ✕ Battle

Europe under Napoleon

Napoleon changed the map of Europe. He joined the Low Countries (modern-day Netherlands and Belgium) and parts of Italy to the French Empire, abolished the Holy Roman Empire that ruled over much of western and central Europe, and placed his brothers and generals on thrones throughout the continent. In 1812, only Britain, Portugal, Russia, and Sweden remained outside Napoleon's control.

Timeline	1795–1802	1804		1805	1806
Napoleon Born on the Mediterranean island of Corsica in 1769, Napoleon began his military education in France at the age of 10. When he became ruler of France, he appointed talented and loyal officers from all backgrounds as his generals. He won his battles because he was a superb strategist.	**Rise to power** As an artillery officer in the revolutionary French army, Napoleon put down a rebellion in Paris and was given command of the army in Italy. Major successes against the Austrians and later in Egypt made Napoleon a national hero. He took part in a successful plot to overthrow the weak revolutionary government, and became First Consul (ruler of France).	**Emperor of France** On December 2, Napoleon crowned himself Emperor of France in Notre Dame Cathedral in Paris before crowning his wife Josephine as empress. The same year he introduced the Napoleonic Code, a system of laws based on the principles of the French Revolution.		**Battle of Trafalgar** A British fleet commanded by Admiral Nelson destroyed the French navy at the Battle of Trafalgar. Nelson was killed just before the British victory. 	**Ruler of Europe** After his crushing defeat of Austria and Russia at the Battle of Austerlitz, Napoleon ruled supreme. He occupied much of Germany and ended the 1,000-year-old Holy Roman Empire by persuading Emperor Francis II to abdicate.

4 million The estimated number of soldiers **recruited by force** to fight in **Napoleon's campaigns**.

Austerlitz is also known as the **Battle of the Three Emperors** because **Napoleon, Alexander I of Russia, and Francis II of Austria** were present on the battlefield.

141

1812	1812	1813	1814	1815

Battle of Salamanca
The Duke of Wellington led British, Portuguese, and Spanish forces to win the Battle of Salamanca, a turning point in the Peninsular War (1808–1814) against Napoleon's army in Spain.

Russian catastrophe
Napoleon invaded Russia. After a narrow victory at Borodino, he marched on Moscow but found the city abandoned. As the cold Russian winter set in, he was forced to retreat. Most of his army perished.

Battle of Leipzig
After his humiliating retreat from Russia, Napoleon met further defeat at the Battle of Leipzig, also known as the Battle of Nations, which was fought from October 16–19, 1813. His vast army of nearly 185,000 men was outnumbered by more than 300,000 troops from Russia, Prussia, Austria, and Sweden. The Battle of Leipzig was the largest land battle in Europe before World War I.

Abdication and exile
Napoleon refused to surrender. His enemies pursued him to France. As the allied army approached Paris, some of his generals persuaded him to abdicate. He was sent into exile on the Italian island of Elba, and Louis XVIII, brother of the last French king Louis XVI, was restored to the French throne. The victorious allies met in Vienna to plan the remaking of Europe.

Battle of Waterloo
Having escaped from Elba in March 1815, Napoleon led his army in the Battle of Waterloo. But his defeat marked the end of the Napoleonic Wars. He was exiled to the remote island of St. Helena in the Atlantic Ocean, where he died in 1821.

The liberation of Latin America

Spanish and Portuguese colonies in the Americas, collectively known as Latin America, were liberated from European control in a series of revolutions from 1810 to 1825.

In the late 18th century, the Spanish set up new laws that limited the power of *Criollos* (people of Spanish blood who were born in the Americas). This angered the people of Latin America, who saw it as an attack on their rights. In the south of the continent, the Argentinian General José de San Martin led a campaign to liberate Argentina, Chile, and southern Peru from Spain. Simón Bolívar, a Venezuelan, was the inspirational leader who freed the northern part of the continent, earning the nickname of *El Libertador* (the Liberator). Meanwhile, Crown Prince Dom Pedro of Portugal declared Brazil's independence after his father, the king, returned to Portugal from Brazil in 1821.

1810
An uprising in Mexico marked the start of the Mexican War of Independence.

1811
A republic was declared in Venezuela, but it collapsed within a year.

1816
Argentina declared its independence from Spain.

1817–1818
José de San Martin crossed the Andes from Argentina to begin the liberation of Chile.

1819–1821
After liberating New Granada (present-day Colombia, Panama, Venezuela, and Ecuador), Simón Bolívar became the first president of the independent state of Gran Colombia.

1821
Spain accepted the independence of Mexico.

1822
Crown Prince of Portugal, Dom Pedro, became the first emperor of Brazil after declaring independence.

1825
Upper Peru, the last Spanish outpost in South America, was liberated and named Bolivia, in honor of Simón Bolívar.

The Battle of Ayacucho
Fought in December 1824 in the Andes Mountains of Peru, the Battle of Ayacucho was the last great battle of the wars of independence. A force of 6,000 soldiers defeated and destroyed a much larger Spanish royalist army, freeing Peru.

39 The number of states in the **German Confederation** at its creation in 1815.

The rise of nations

The Napoleonic Wars of 1803–1815 spread the idea of revolution across Europe. Many people who shared a single language and culture believed that they should be one nation, and have the right to rule themselves.

In the 19th century, some parts of Europe were divided into small states whose people desired a united national identity. In other regions, the people were inspired to rebel against their rulers. These revolutionaries wanted freedom to elect their own governments, and to determine their own futures.

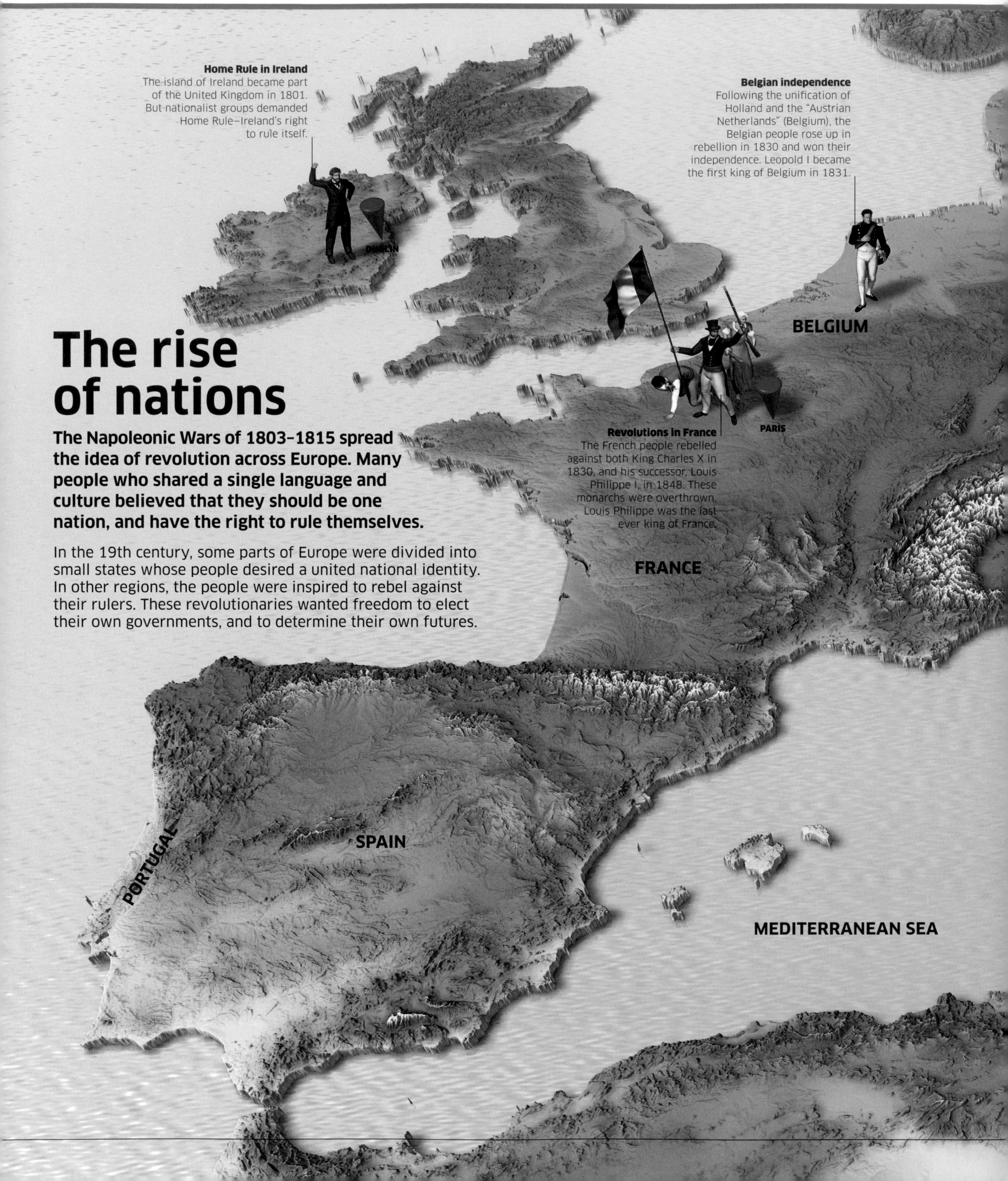
Home Rule in Ireland
The island of Ireland became part of the United Kingdom in 1801. But nationalist groups demanded Home Rule—Ireland's right to rule itself.
DUBLIN
Belgian independence
Following the unification of Holland and the "Austrian Netherlands" (Belgium), the Belgian people rose up in rebellion in 1830 and won their independence. Leopold I became the first king of Belgium in 1831.
BELGIUM
Revolutions in France
The French people rebelled against both King Charles X in 1830, and his successor, Louis Philippe I, in 1848. These monarchs were overthrown. Louis Philippe was the last ever king of France.
PARIS
FRANCE
SPAIN
PORTUGAL
MEDITERRANEAN SEA

Karl Marx's *Communist Manifesto*, which encouraged **working people to rise up in revolution**, was published in 1848.

1,089 The **number of volunteers** who joined Garibaldi's army of liberation in Italy in 1860.

145

A year of revolutions

In 1848, a wave of revolutions spread across Europe, but the revolutionaries did not share the same goals. In France, they wanted more freedom. In Germany, people wanted unification and democratic rule. People in parts of Italy and Hungary fought to leave the Austrian Empire. The revolutions were bloody, but most did not succeed in changing things.

Revolution in Berlin
When people rose up in Berlin in modern-day Germany in 1848, the army was sent in to clear the people from the streets, killing hundreds.

The unification of Germany
Prussia and Austria fought for control of the states in the German Confederation, with Prussia claiming victory. In 1871, King William I of Prussia became the first emperor of a united Germany.

The Congress of Vienna
Held in 1814–1815, the Congress of Vienna created a treaty to reshape Europe after the Napoleonic Wars. It gave power back to many of the old European monarchies, and created the German Confederation.

GERMANY

VIENNA

AUSTRIA

HUNGARY

ITALY

The unification of Italy
The kingdoms of northern Italy were united under King Victor Emmanuel of Sardinia-Piedmont, while General Giuseppe Garibaldi took control of the south. In 1860, when the two met at Teano, Garibaldi gave Victor Emmanuel the south, making him king of a unified Italy.

A century of change
The 19th century was a time of change in Europe. Greece, Serbia, and Bulgaria won their independence from the Ottoman Empire, and Italy and Germany both became single, unified states. Around Europe, ordinary people fought to demand greater political rights.

The Greek War of Independence
In 1821, uprisings against Turkish rule began in Greek-speaking parts of the Ottoman Empire. With Britain, France, and Russia supporting them, the Greeks won independence in 1832.

Until the introduction of **anesthetics** (in the mid-19th century), **patients had to be tied down** during an operation.

The operating theater

In the 19th century, operations often took place in public in a central space surrounded by rows of raised seats, as in a Roman or Greek theater, hence the term "operating theater."

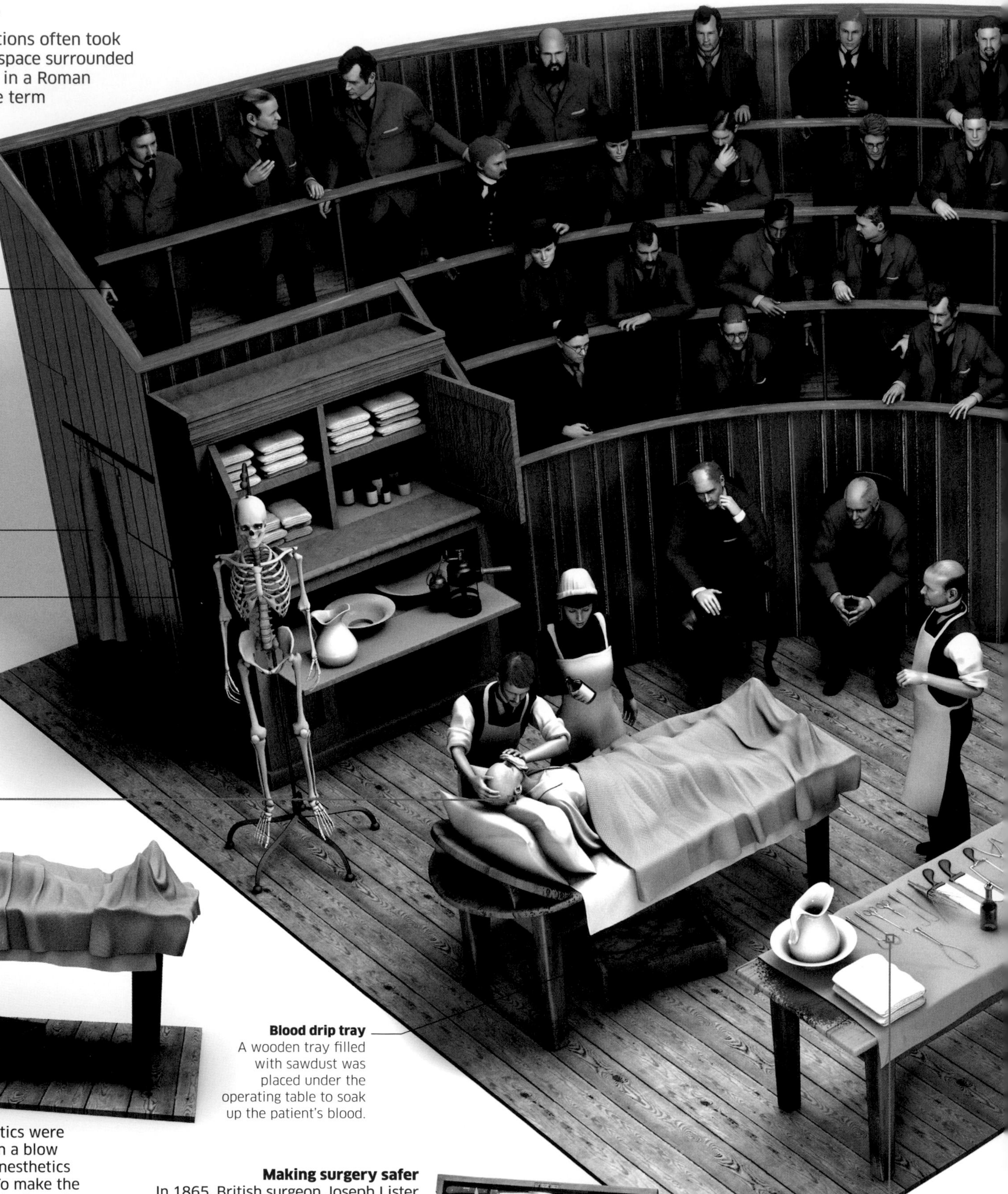

The public
Early theaters were open to the public, with both men and women watching operations.

Work uniform
Surgeons covered themselves in long aprons but wore their everyday street clothes underneath.

Teaching aid
Human skeletons, which were often obtained from workhouses, were used to teach anatomy to medical students.

Blood drip tray
A wooden tray filled with sawdust was placed under the operating table to soak up the patient's blood.

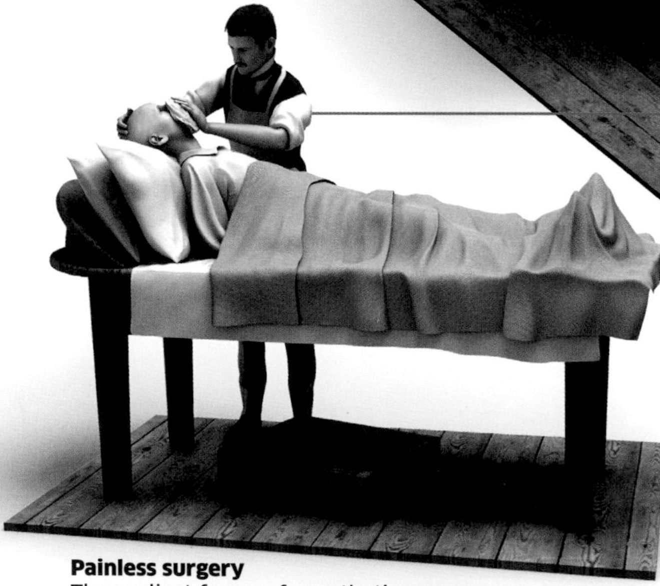

Painless surgery
The earliest forms of anesthetics were alcohol, herbal brews, or even a blow to the head. Sleep-inducing anesthetics came into use in the 1840s. To make the patient unconscious, an anesthetic such as ether or chloroform was inhaled from a damp cloth or mask.

> **"The very first requirement in a hospital is that it should do the sick no harm."**
>
> **Florence Nightingale**, *Notes on Nursing*, 1859

Making surgery safer
In 1865, British surgeon Joseph Lister began experiments to improve cleanliness in the operating theater. He sprayed carbolic acid onto surgical instruments, open wounds, and dressings. This antiseptic substance destroyed germs and prevented infection from spreading. By 1866, the death rate among patients at his hospital had fallen by two-thirds.

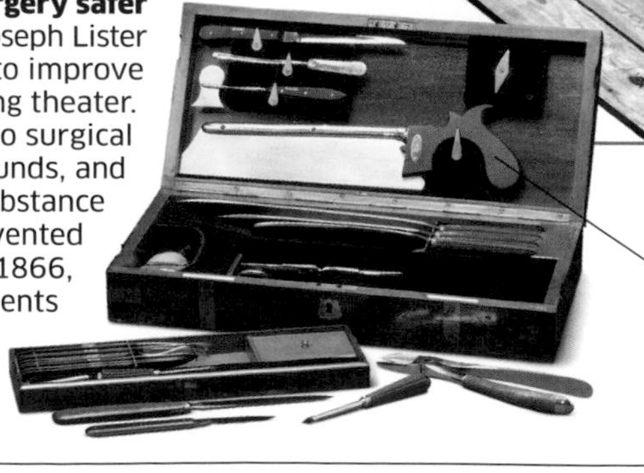

Bone saw
Surgeons used saws to cut through bone as quickly as possible.

In the **mid-19th century**, French scientist **Louis Pasteur** showed that **bacteria cause disease**.

1849 The year British-born **Elizabeth Blackwell** became the **first woman** to qualify as a **doctor** in the US.

1860 The year **Florence Nightingale** set up the **first nursing school**.

147

Medical students
Large numbers of medical students, who were almost all men at this time, crowded the benches.

Washstand
Early surgeons washed their hands but didn't wear rubber gloves until 1898.

Surgical instruments
Saws and other tools for the operation were laid out on a table.

Medical advances

Although scientists in the 17th and 18th centuries revolutionized the medical understanding of the human body, it was not until the 19th century that groundbreaking advances changed the course of medicine.

In the 19th century, the development of effective pain-numbing anesthetics meant that patients no longer suffered from intolerable pain and allowed surgeons to perform more complex operations. Doctors also began to understand the role played by germs in spreading disease. This led to greater cleanliness in the operating theater. By the end of the 19th century, the pioneering work of scientists in improving health care techniques led to a dramatic drop in infection rates throughout the world.

Timeline

Medical science
Five thousand years ago, the ancient Egyptians used herbs to treat all sorts of ailments—from ingrown toenails to crocodile bites. But the ancient Greek physician Hippocrates (460–370 BCE) was the first to reject the commonly held belief that sickness was the will of the gods. Since then, doctors have continued to examine the causes that lead to disease.

1025 CE — Islamic medicine
Persian physician Ibn Sina (also known as Avicenna) compiled *The Canon of Medicine*— a five-volume encyclopedia that contained all the medical knowledge known at that time. His work described how to recognize and treat illnesses, and was the standard medical textbook throughout the Islamic world and medieval Europe.

1543 — Anatomical studies
Flemish anatomist Andreas Vesalius dissected the cadavers (corpses) of executed criminals to make detailed studies of the human body. He published his findings in an illustrated book, *De Humani Corporis Fabrica*.

1628 — Blood circulation
English physician William Harvey showed that the heart's pumping action circulates blood around the body through the arteries before returning it through the veins. Until then, doctors had followed the ideas of ancient Greek surgeon Galen, who believed that blood was made in the liver.

1796 — Vaccination
Edward Jenner, an English physician, developed a smallpox vaccine. He injected a sample of cowpox (a similar but milder disease) into a boy to build up his immunity.

1895 — X-rays
German physicist Wilhelm Röntgen discovered waves of energy that passed through flesh but not bone, creating bone images on photographic plates. He named them X-rays. His discovery allowed doctors to see inside the human body for the first time.

1928 — Penicillin
Alexander Fleming, a Scottish bacteriologist, accidentally discovered a substance in a mold that destroyed bacteria. Fleming called this substance penicillin— it was the first effective antibiotic to be manufactured.

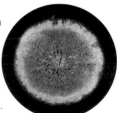

1967 — Heart transplant
In South Africa, surgeon Christiaan Barnard carried out the world's first successful human heart transplant. Although the recipient of the heart died 18 days later of pneumonia, the heart worked until his death, signaling a new era in heart transplant surgery.

148 the age of revolution ∘ **THE US CIVIL WAR**

The **majority of the fighting** in the war took place in the states of **Virginia** and **Tennessee**.

The US Civil War

Between 1861 and 1865, the US was torn apart into North and South by a bitter civil war. The two sides fought over the enslavement of African Americans and the rights of individual states.

The Southern states had always relied on African American slaves to work on plantations of cotton and tobacco—crops that were vital to their economy. The industrial cities of the North, by contrast, had little need for slaves, and public support for the ending of slavery grew in the North in the 1850s. The 1860 election of President Abraham Lincoln, a leading supporter of the abolishment of slavery in the US, kick-started the conflict.

THE UNION AND THE CONFEDERACY

By February 1861, seven southern states—South Carolina, Mississippi, Florida, Alabama, Georgia, Louisiana, and Texas—had broken away from the rest of the US. On February 4, they agreed to form a separate government, the Confederate States of America. The first shots of the war were fired at Fort Sumter in South Carolina on April 12, and within three months, Virginia, Arkansas, North Carolina, and Tennessee had joined the Confederates. Twenty-three states remained in the Union, including the slave-owning "border states."

Division of the states in 1864

- ■ Union states
- ■ Confederate states
- ■ "Border states"
- ■ US Territories

US Territories
Shown as uncolored on the map, the US Territories were regions considered part of the United States but yet to be admitted as states. One, Nevada, became a state in 1864.

NEW TECHNOLOGY

The US Civil War was one of the first industrial wars in history, making use of modern technologies developed during the course of the 19th century. The war was fought across a wide area, so railroads were critically important in carrying troops and supplies to where they were needed on the front lines. Generals were able to communicate with each other by telegraph.

Weapons

Fast-firing repeating rifles, such as the Spencer rifle, were used for the first time in the Civil War. The widely used "Napoleon" field gun could hit a target up to 5,250 ft (1,600 m) away. Also developed at this time was the Gatling gun, an early machine gun.

GATLING GUN

Ironclad battleships

Steam-powered battleships protected by iron or steel plates were known as ironclads. The first-ever battle between ironclads was fought in the Civil War in 1862, on the James River estuary in Virginia.

War photography

The Civil War was one of the first conflicts to be extensively photographed. Dozens of photographers toured the battlefields, and their stark images of soldiers, dead and alive, brought shocking scenes of the war to the public around the world.

Timeline	April 12, 1861	September 17, 1862	December 13, 1862	January 1, 1863
A nation divided When seven US states seceded (broke away) from the Union to form the Confederacy, President Lincoln refused to recognize the new government, and called on them to rejoin the Union. The Confederates refused, and tried to gain control of federal forts in the South. The stage was set for a bloody war that would last for the next four years.	**Fort Sumter attacked** Confederate troops under Brigadier General Beauregard fired on Union soldiers who were guarding Fort Sumter in Charleston, South Carolina. These were the first shots to be fired in the Civil War.  **THE BATTLE AT FORT SUMTER**	**Battle of Antietam** The bloodiest day of fighting in the entire war took place at the Battle of Antietam, in which nearly 23,000 soldiers were wounded or killed. The Union army suffered the most casualties, but managed to halt the advance of General Robert E. Lee's Confederate forces into the Union state of Maryland. The next day Lee was allowed to lead his shattered army back to Virginia.	**Confederate victory** Fortune swung back to the Confederate side at the Battle of Fredericksburg, in Virginia. General Burnside, newly appointed by Lincoln to command the Union army, led 120,000 troops to attack a Confederate force of 80,000—by far the largest number of men to meet in any conflict of the Civil War. Burnside was decisively defeated—a victory that gave fresh hope to the Confederates and led to complaints that the Union's generals were doing a bad job.	**All slaves to be free** President Lincoln gave new purpose and direction to the war by issuing the Emancipation Proclamation. This was an order freeing all slaves in the Confederate states. Of course, this could not happen until the Union had won the war against the Confederates, but his words would eventually lead to the freeing of millions of African American slaves.

THE BATTLE OF GETTYSBURG

The most famous battle of the Civil War was fought over three days, from July 1–3, 1863, around the small town of Gettysburg in Pennsylvania. The Confederates attacked, confident they would win, but the Union army did not give way and eventually won. The battle had the heaviest casualties in the war. Four months after the battle, President Lincoln visited the site and delivered a famous speech known as the Gettysburg Address. In it, he said that the US was "dedicated to the proposition that all men are created equal."

Heavy losses
An estimated 51,000 soldiers were killed, wounded, or listed as missing in the Battle of Gettysburg.

RECONSTRUCTION

The slow process of rebuilding the economy of the South, left in ruins after the war, is known as Reconstruction. Before rejoining the US, each state of the Confederacy had to agree to amendments to the US Constitution—the supreme law of the nation—that ended slavery, granted citizenship to African Americans, and gave the vote to all male citizens.

RECONSTRUCTION ENDED IN 1877, **AND MANY STATE GOVERNMENTS** IMMEDIATELY REVERSED THE **NEW RIGHTS GIVEN TO AFRICAN AMERICANS,** MAKING IT HARD FOR THEM TO VOTE, GO TO SCHOOL, OR FIND PAID WORK.

AFRICAN AMERICANS VOTING IN RICHMOND, VIRGINIA, 1871

March 3, 1863	**July 4, 1863**	**November 15, 1864**	**April 9, 1865**	**April 14, 1865**
First African American regiment The first official regiment of African American soldiers, the 54th Massachusetts Infantry Regiment, was formed to fight in the Union army.  **SERGEANT HENRY F. STEWARD OF THE 54TH MASSACHUSETTS INFANTRY**	**Vicksburg captured** Union troops captured the Confederate fortress of Vicksburg, on the Mississippi River, after a two-month siege. It was a major turning point in the war, coming a day after the Union victory at Gettysburg. The Union now controlled the length of the Mississippi River, dividing Louisiana, Texas, and Arkansas from the rest of the Confederate states, and cutting off supplies.	**March to the Sea** The capture of Atlanta, Georgia, by Union General William T. Sherman in September was a heavy blow to the Confederates. Although deep inside enemy territory, Sherman decided to march his army all the way from Atlanta to the coast at Savannah. He ordered his men to live off the land and destroy farms and factories on their way. This brutal "scorched earth" policy inflicted lasting damage.	**Lee surrenders to Grant** The Confederate capital of Richmond, in Virginia, fell on April 3. The Virginian Confederate army was exhausted. To avoid further losses, Confederate General Robert E. Lee surrendered to General Ulysses S. Grant at Appomattox Court House in Virginia. By May, all the Confederate armies had stopped fighting. The war was finally over.	**Assassination of Lincoln** President Lincoln was shot while attending a play at Ford's Theater in Washington, D.C. He died the next morning. A funeral train took 14 days to transport his body back for burial in his hometown of Springfield, in Illinois. **MEMORIAL TO PRESIDENT LINCOLN IN WASHINGTON, D.C.**

Cattle ranching

In the 19th century, cattle ranching developed on the Great Plains and became an important type of farming in the American West. Cowboys, who included European settlers, Mexicans, and freed African American slaves, worked on the ranches. They rounded up thousands of cattle, taking them to rail towns ready for shipment.

Hard work
Being on a cattle drive was hard, dusty work. Cowboys often spent up to 15 hours a day working.

Frontier towns

Towns with simple wooden buildings and unpaved streets sprang up all over the rugged American West. Land was cheap but life was not easy with the lack of basic food supplies. Some frontier towns were quickly abandoned. Others, such as Dodge City in Kansas, thrived.

DODGE CITY IN 1878

Law and order

The American West was often a dangerous place to live. Organized groups of bandits stole cattle, held up railroad trains, and looted towns. The sheriffs struggled to enforce the law. They put up "Wanted" posters, offering rewards for help in tracking down notorious criminals.

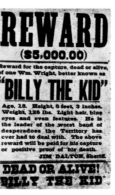

REWARD
($5,000.00)

Reward for the capture, dead or alive, of one Wm. Wright, better known as

"BILLY THE KID"

Age, 18. Height, 5 feet, 3 inches. Weight, 125 lbs. Light hair, blue eyes and even features. He is the leader of the worst band of desperadoes the Territory has ever had to deal with. The above reward will be paid for his capture or positive proof of his death.
JIM DALTON, Sheriff.

DEAD OR ALIVE!
BILLY THE KID

WANTED POSTER

Sioux camp

The largest American Indian group living on the northern plains were the Sioux. They lived a nomadic lifestyle, moving from place to place so that they could follow the migrating bison herds. The Sioux depended on the bison for food but nothing was wasted. They used the hide for making clothes, blankets, and the covering for their portable tepees, while bones and horns were used for making tools and toys.

Framework
Up to 20 long poles were used for the tepee framework. These were tied at the top, forming a cone shape.

Setting camp
Women were responsible for building and dismantling tepees as well as preparing food and making clothes and tools.

Medicine man
The medicine man was an important figure in Sioux life. His chants and rituals protected the tribe from evil spirits.

Life in the Old West

In the 18th and 19th centuries, American Indian tribes inhabited the Great Plains west of the Mississippi River. But their way of life changed with the arrival of the first European settlers in the 1840s.

Known as Plains Indians, these American Indians lived by hunting the huge herds of bison that grazed the grasslands. By the end of the 19th century, thousands of European settlers had taken over their hunting land for farming and cattle ranching. The settlers also built towns and railroads, and hunted the bison to extinction, leading to bitter conflict between the two communities.

600,000 The estimated **population of American Indians in 1800**. By **1900**, the figure had dropped to **250,000**.

151

Dried meat
Thin strips of bison meat were dried on racks in the sun to make a long-lasting food called pemmican.

Painted designs
Some tepees were painted with symbolic shapes and sacred animals.

Bison hide
About 16 bison hides were sewn together to make the tepee cover. Pins made from bone held the hides together.

Smoke flaps
Smoke from the fire inside escaped through flaps that opened at the top of the tepee.

Skilled horse riders
Sioux were excellent horse riders. Many rode bareback, hunting bison at full gallop.

Making leather
To make bison leather, the women stretched a hide, scraped it clean with a bone tool, and then smoked it over a fire to soften it.

Cradleboard
Babies were kept safe in a cradleboard (a lace-up leather bag on a wooden frame). It could be strapped to the carer's back or hung from a saddle.

Fire
A small fire inside the tepee was used both for cooking food and keeping the tepee warm.

Wounded Knee massacre
In 1890, up to 200 Sioux were killed or injured by US soldiers at Wounded Knee Creek in South Dakota. The Sioux belonged to the Ghost Dance religious movement that promised the return of American Indian culture, and many were wearing Ghost Dance shirts. After the massacre, the Sioux were forced to accept life on reservations (small areas of land put aside for them), making it impossible for them to continue their traditional, nomadic way of life.

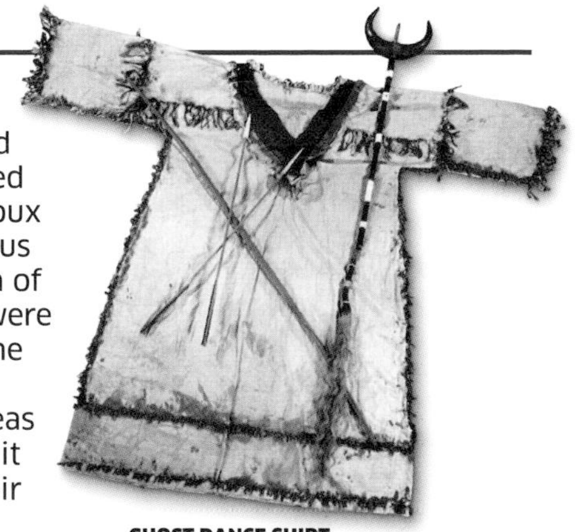

GHOST DANCE SHIRT

13 million bison
roamed the Great Plains in 1840. By 1885, only 200 were left.

Timeline

The history of car design

At first, the automobile was a slow, dangerous, and unreliable way to travel, but throughout the 20th century, it developed into a sophisticated, high-performing machine. Today, safety and environmental concerns have encouraged car manufacturers to design driverless and electric-powered vehicles.

Ford Model T

1908

The first car to be mass-produced, the Model T was cheap and quick to produce. For 12 years, every vehicle sold was black, as this was the fastest-drying paint color at the time.

Volkswagen Beetle

1938

German dictator Adolf Hitler commissioned this reliable, family vehicle as a "people's car" (or "Volkswagen" in German). Designed by Ferdinand Porsche, the five-seater could transport two adults and three children. In 1972, the Volkswagen Beetle became the world's best-selling car, overtaking the Ford Model T's previous record of 15,007,033 vehicles sold.

Willy's Jeep

1940

World War II prompted manufacturers to design the Jeep, a tough, four-wheel drive car that could cope on all sorts of terrain. This military vehicle was light and sturdy enough to be dropped by parachute from a helicopter.

MINI

1959

As cars became cheaper, the world's roads clogged with traffic. Manufacturers started building smaller vehicles for towns and cities, with the MINI becoming a British icon.

Toyota Prius

1997

One of the first hybrid cars, the Toyota Prius was powered by both a gasoline engine and an electric motor, helping to reduce its toxic emissions.

The automobile

Before the car, people traveled long distances using horse-drawn carriages. But in 1888, the first gasoline-powered, horseless vehicle went on sale to the public, kick-starting the age of the automobile.

The automobile evolved little by little throughout the 19th century, with different engineers experimenting in workshops around the world. But it was Karl Benz from Germany, helped by his wife Bertha, whose three-wheeled design became the first automobile available for sale to the public. Powered by an internal combustion engine, the Benz Patent-Motorwagen inspired fear and suspicion at first—it was banned by the German government, and the Catholic Church called it the "devil's carriage."

Spinning flywheel
This horizontal, heavy disk helped keep the engine running smoothly.

Cooling tank
Water stored in the cooling tank prevented the engine from overheating.

Padded seat
Without suspension to aid the automobile's stability, it was a bumpy ride for passengers.

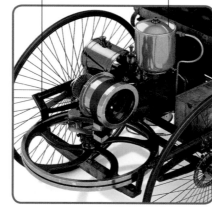

Internal combustion engine

The automobile's engine worked similarly to gasoline-powered car engines today. It burned fuel inside a cylinder to produce gases that pushed tiny pistons up and down. These pistons in turn pushed a crankshaft that made the rear wheels rotate.

Carriage wheels
The steel-lined rear wheels were large, like those of a traditional horse-drawn carriage.

Historic journey

Karl Benz invented the first automobile, but it was his wife Bertha who made it a commercial success. In 1888, she secretly took the car and drove her two sons from Mannheim to Pforzheim in Germany. Although the car broke down several times, Bertha fixed each issue, successfully completing the 66-mile (106-km) journey. News of the achievement hit the press and sales of the Motorwagen took off.

1891 The year **the first car accident took place**, in **Ohio**.

1896 The year the **first speeding ticket** was given to a **reckless driver**.

153

SIDE VIEW

Brake lever
A hand lever was used to slow the vehicle.

Viewing point
Like a horse-drawn carriage, Benz's automobile had a high seat to allow good visibility.

Steering lever
Instead of a steering wheel, the driver changed direction using an upright lever called a tiller.

Hollow frame
The Motorwagen had a tube-shaped, steel framework.

Bicycle tire
The thin-spoked, rubber-lined front wheel was based on the design of a bicycle wheel.

Mass production

In 1913, American businessman Henry Ford introduced a new moving assembly line at his car factory. He separated production of the car, the Model T or "Tin Lizzie," into different stages, with specialized workers adding parts to every vehicle as it rolled along a mechanized moving belt. Ford's moving assembly line sped up car manufacturing, making cars increasingly affordable for the public. By the 1920s, car manufacturers around the world were producing vehicles in the same way.

Moving assembly line
Between 1908 and 1927 the Ford Motor Company built more than 15 million Model Ts. Every 10 seconds a newly finished car rolled off the assembly line, ready to drive.

Racing cars

The dawn of the 20th century saw a huge rise in the popularity of cars. In order to win sales, manufacturers competed with one another to produce the fastest and most powerful car, shown off in the new sport of motor racing. The first official race was held in France in 1895. Since then the sport of motor racing has flourished, from the extreme speeds of Formula 1 to the Le Mans 24-hour race, a yearly endurance test.

PARIS-BORDEAUX 1895   1ᵉʳᵉ VOITURE sur PNEUS MICHELIN

Paris-Bordeaux-Paris
In 1895, French engineer Emile Levassor crossed the finish line of the world's first automobile race. He completed the 732-mile (1,180-km) route from Paris to Bordeaux and back again driving at an average speed of 15 mph (25 km/h).

US immigration

In the 19th century, millions of people left their homes to travel to the US, fleeing natural disasters, religious persecution, and poverty in Asia and Europe.

For those seeking refuge and work, the US was seen as a land of opportunity. People arrived by boat from Asia into San Francisco and from Europe into New York. By the early 1900s, the immigration center at Ellis Island in Upper New York Bay was the country's busiest entry point, processing an estimated 5,000 individuals a day. Some stayed in New York, but many chose to travel further inland, to Chicago, the Midwest, or all the way to California.

1845–1849
In Ireland, a fungus destroyed the country's potato crops, causing widespread famine. To avoid starvation, 500,000 people traveled to the US.

1892
Ellis Island Immigrant Station opened as a US point of entry from Europe. It became the center of immigration into the country.

February 1907
Japan agreed to restrict its people from leaving to settle in the US, amid fears in California that Japanese arrivals were taking jobs from US workers.

1910–1940
A million immigrants, including Chinese, Japanese, Indians, and Mexicans, were processed on Angel Island in the San Francisco Bay.

1924
To control the number of arrivals, a law was passed that required people to register overseas before they traveled to the US.

1881–1924
More than two million Jews from Russia, Austria-Hungary, and Romania arrived in the US, fleeing poverty, violence, and racism.

1900–1910
As sea travel became more affordable, more than two million Italians moved to the US to escape poverty at home.

April 1907
The Port of New York had the busiest month in its history, receiving 197 ships carrying more than 250,000 passengers in total.

1920s
Public opinion turned against immigration, as newcomers were blamed for high unemployment and a lack of housing.

Gateway to America
When immigrants arrived, they were examined by doctors looking for signs of physical illness or mental health problems. In this photograph from 1907, immigrants wait in "pens," having passed the first inspection.

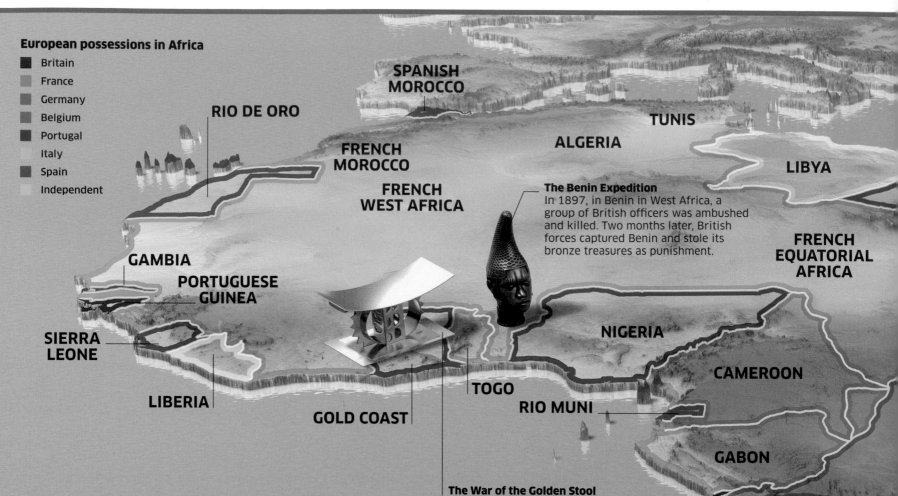

European possessions in Africa

- ■ Britain
- ■ France
- ■ Germany
- ■ Belgium
- ■ Portugal
- ■ Italy
- ■ Spain
- ■ Independent

SPANISH MOROCCO

RIO DE ORO

TUNIS

ALGERIA

LIBYA

FRENCH MOROCCO

FRENCH WEST AFRICA

FRENCH EQUATORIAL AFRICA

GAMBIA

PORTUGUESE GUINEA

SIERRA LEONE

LIBERIA

GOLD COAST

TOGO

RIO MUNI

NIGERIA

CAMEROON

GABON

CABINDA

ANGOLA

GERMAN SOUTHWEST AFRICA

The Benin Expedition
In 1897, in Benin in West Africa, a group of British officers was ambushed and killed. Two months later, British forces captured Benin and stole its bronze treasures as punishment.

The War of the Golden Stool
In 1900, the British governor of Ghana demanded that the Ashanti tribe give him their golden stool, a throne considered by the Ashanti to be sacred. They refused, and war broke out. Although the British won and increased their control in Ghana, the Ashanti successfully guarded the golden stool.

Age of empires

During the 19th century, the desire for wealth, land, and resources led European nations to seek power and influence far beyond their borders.

A wave of colonization took place, in which wealthy, powerful European countries invaded and ruled over territories outside Europe. Britain, France, Germany, Belgium, Portugal, Italy, and Spain divided the continent of Africa between them, claiming large areas of land and taking political and economic control. Of all the European powers, Britain built the largest empire, acquiring the most territory, including India, Australia, New Zealand, and the West Indies.

The British Raj

British rule in India, known as the "British Raj," lasted from 1858 to 1947. India was described as the "jewel in the crown" of the British Empire. The British introduced democracy and railroads to India, but they exploited the country economically and denied local rulers and people a share in resources, crops, and political power.

British train
This British-built train still carries passengers on the Darjeeling Himalayan Railway today.

The "unequal treaties"

After China lost the Opium Wars (1839–1842 and 1856–1860), Britain and France made China sign a series of agreements, later called the "unequal treaties." These treaties forced China to give up control of its ports and give away large areas of territory to other nations.

CANTON (MODERN-DAY GUANGZHOU), A TREATY PORT

Rubber plantation
Before crates of rubber were exported abroad, they were checked by colonial overseers.

Southeast Asia

In Europe, the Industrial Revolution increased demand for rubber, oil, and tin, all of which Southeast Asia could supply. Seeking access to these resources, the British took control on the Malay Peninsula and across Myanmar, and the French took over Vietnam, Cambodia, and French Indochina (modern-day Laos).

10 million The estimated number of **Congolese people killed under King Leopold II of Belgium**.

The **only two African countries** to remain independent were **Abyssinia** (now known as Ethiopia) and **Liberia**.

157

EGYPT

ANGLO-EGYPTIAN SUDAN

BELGIAN CONGO

RHODESIA

BECHUANALAND

UNION OF SOUTH AFRICA

ORANGE FREE STATE

GERMAN EAST AFRICA

BRITISH EAST AFRICA

ABYSSINIA

FRENCH SOMALILAND

BRITISH SOMALILAND

ITALIAN SOMALILAND

MOZAMBIQUE

MADAGASCAR

Suez Canal
Opened in 1869, the French-designed Suez Canal linked the Mediterranean Sea and the Red Sea. This impressive feat of engineering dramatically cut journey times from Asia to Europe, as ships no longer had to sail around Africa.

Belgian Congo
King Leopold II of Belgium made the Congo his personal possession from 1885 to 1908. It was the largest private estate ever possessed by a single person. A brutal leader, he was responsible for millions of deaths, and stripped the country of its natural resources, including elephant ivory.

Abyssinian victory
In 1896, an Abyssinian army led by Emperor Menelik II defeated an invading Italian force, successfully defending its independence.

European exploration
Explorers set out to discover and map new lands. They were often sponsored by governments eager for territorial expansion. It was a dangerous occupation and many paid with their lives.

The Boer Wars
The Boers were descendants of the original white Dutch settlers in southern Africa. Between 1889 and 1902, the Boer states of the Republic of Transvaal and the Orange Free State fought to end British control of South Africa and its gold mines.

The Anglo-Zulu War
In 1879, the British fought a war with the Zulu Kingdom in southeast Africa. The British suffered a humiliating defeat in the Battle of Isandlwana in January, but defeated the Zulu Kingdom in July and turned it into a colony.

Diamond mining
In 1867, diamonds were discovered in South Africa. Mining these diamonds made British businessman Cecil Rhodes one of the world's richest men, but the black laborers working underground in the mines were exploited and underpaid.

Scramble for Africa
By the late 19th century, many European nations were competing for control of Africa. Between 1882 and 1899, Britain seized Egypt, Nigeria, Kenya, the Sudan, and Rhodesia, and established possession of South Africa. From 1884 to 1885, parts of East and West Africa were acquired by Germany. In 1885, King Leopold II of Belgium took over the Congo.

Early flight

Humans have yearned to fly for thousands of years, but it wasn't until 1903, when the Wright brothers' engine-powered aircraft *1903 Wright Flyer* took to the skies, that the dream of human flight became a reality.

The invention of lightweight engines in the late 19th century made powered flight possible, leading the Wright brothers to try out new flying designs. They tried for years to get a plane in the air, and keep it there. In December 1903, they tossed a coin to see who would pilot their latest design. The older brother Wilbur won, but that first test was unsuccessful. In a later trial on December 17, Orville Wright piloted their aircraft for 12 seconds, just skimming above the sands of the North Carolina coast for a distance of 121 ft (37 m). This short flight changed history.

The Wright brothers' first flight

The *1903 Wright Flyer* took off from Kitty Hawk, North Carolina. Orville Wright piloted the plane lying down, steering it with movements of his hips. The *1903 Wright Flyer* was heavier than air, but the engine and propellers drove the plane forward to stop it from crashing back to the ground.

Rudder
A rudder set behind the wings yawed (turned) the aircraft right and left.

Propeller
Two 8-ft (2.4-m) wooden propellers powered by the engine drove the plane forward.

Lightweight structure
The body of the plane was made of wood, covered with finely woven cotton cloth.

Outer wing
The pilot pulled on wires connected to the outer wing to roll (move the left wing down and the right wing up, or vice versa).

Wings
The aircraft had a wingspan of 40 ft 4 in (12.3 m).

Support wires
Strong metal wires helped the wooden structure of the plane keep its shape.

First flights

Efforts to fly date back as far as 1000 BCE when the Chinese strapped people to huge kites, but the first flight carrying a person that wasn't tied to something on the ground didn't take place until the late 18th century.

Early attempts at flight

Taking to the skies was an extremely risky business. Over the centuries, in attempts to copy the flight of birds, people strapped "wings" made of wood or feathers to their arms. They then launched themselves off high structures, often with disastrous results.

Water stored in a tank next to the pilot
kept the *Flyer*'s engine from **overheating**.

Later on in the **day of its first flight**,
the *Flyer* was **damaged beyond repair**.

159

Powering the propellers
A bicycle chain connected the engine to the propellers so it could turn them.

Engine
A homemade gas engine powered two propellers mounted behind the wings, driving the plane forward.

Pilot controls
To steer the plane Orville Wright lay flat in a cradle and moved his hips from side to side to pull on wires connected to the wing tips and rudder.

Elevator control
The pilot controlled the plane's pitch (up and down movement) with a lever connected by a pulley system to the elevators.

Elevators
Movable horizontal surfaces called elevators angled the aircraft nose up and down.

First balloon
Two paper-makers from France, the Montgolfier brothers, noted that heated air flowing into a paper bag made the bag rise. In 1783, they demonstrated this with a sensational hot-air balloon flight carrying a sheep, a duck, and a rooster as passengers. The first manned flight took place later that year with Jean-Francois Pilatre de Rozier and François Laurent d'Arlandes on board.

THE MONTGOLFIER
BROTHERS' BALLOON

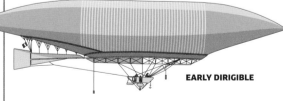

EARLY DIRIGIBLE

Dirigible
Many inventors sought ways to steer "lighter than air" vehicles. In the 19th century, French engineer Jules Henri Giffard built a "dirigible", a type of airship; a canvas bag that was 143 ft (44 m) long and could hold 113,000 cubic feet (3,200 cubic meters) of the gas hydrogen, which is lighter than air. In 1852, steered by a pilot and powered by an engine, Giffard's airship proved that controlled flight was possible.

The Flying Man
German aviation pioneer Otto Lilienthal made more than 2,000 flights in gliders in the late 19th century, taking off from the top of an artificial hill he had built especially for the purpose near Berlin. His gliders had no tail and were little more than a pair of wings, controlled by the movements he made with his body. A hero of the Wright brothers, Lilienthal became known as "the Flying Man." He died in 1896, from injuries he suffered when one of his creations crashed to the ground.

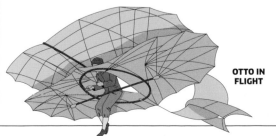

OTTO IN
FLIGHT

THE MODERN WORLD

From the beginning of the 20th century, innovations in travel and communications connected humans across the world like never before. Conflicts became global, with many nations involved in wars far away. But in the late 20th and early 21st centuries, this connection has also given people new opportunities, allowing ideas of freedom and equality to spread around the world.

1961: The Berlin Wall
The East German government built a barrier to prevent people escaping Soviet-controlled East Germany for democratic West Berlin. The wall was torn down in 1989.

WATCHTOWER ALONG THE BERLIN WALL

1960S ELECTRIC GUITAR

1969: Woodstock
At the end of the 1960s, a decade of change in music and fashion, the Woodstock Music and Art Fair took place in the US. Half a million people showed up to listen to the most famous musicians of the day.

LOCKHEED F-117A NIGHTHAWK STEALTH FIGHTER

1990–1991: The Gulf War
Saddam Hussein of Iraq invaded the oil-rich nation of Kuwait. Allied forces, led by the US, attacked the Iraqis in Operation Desert Storm.

1955: The bus boycott
In Montgomery, Alabama, Rosa Parks, an African American woman, refused to give up her bus seat to a white passenger, inspiring a boycott of the city's buses to protest against the separation of black and white people on public transportation.

1960: The Year of Africa
The process of decolonization in Africa reached its peak in 1960, when 17 countries, including 14 former French colonies, declared their independence.

REPLICA MONTGOMERY BUS

Timeline of the modern world

World War I, and later World War II, brought many nations into global conflict. Millions of people from all over the world, both soldiers and civilians, were killed.

In the 1920s, people tried to forget the horrors of World War I. New music and dances became popular, and cinema developed into a form of entertainment. But the next decade was hard for many, as the world economy crashed and dictators began to take power in Europe, leading to another global war. In the aftermath of World War II, weakened empires lost control of their overseas territories. The US and the Soviet Union emerged as rival superpowers, struggling for dominance by involving themselves in regional wars. Yet the end of the war also brought new optimism and freedoms, with young people creating new ways to express themselves through fashion and music. In the 21st century, thanks to advances in communication technology, there is a greater awareness of the discrimination faced by many people in their daily lives, as well as the damage humans have caused to the environment.

1942: The Final Solution
German dictator Adolf Hitler finalized plans to murder the Jewish population of Europe. Millions of people were forced into concentration camps where they lived in terrible conditions until they were killed.

STAR OF DAVID IDENTIFICATION BADGE

USS *ENTERPRISE* CV-6

1941: The US enters the war
Until 1941, the US refused to take sides, but when Japanese forces attacked Pearl Harbor, a naval base in Hawaii, the US responded by declaring war. Germany then declared war on the US. For Britain, the US was a welcome ally.

1914: World War I
After Austria-Hungary invaded Serbia, other countries joined in, and the war became global. Millions were killed as new inventions, such as tanks and poison gas, made conflict deadlier than ever before.

WORLD WAR I BRITISH TANK

A HAMMER AND SICKLE, A SYMBOL OF SOVIET COMMUNISM

1917: The Russian Revolution
For 300 years the Romanov family had controlled Russia, but they were overthrown by a communist revolution that established the Soviet Union.

1920s: The Jazz Age
After the hardships of World War I, the US enjoyed a period of optimism, as people sought fun and frivolity. Jazz music became very popular, along with exciting new dances.

1920S SAXOPHONE

NELSON MANDELA
ON A SOUTH AFRICAN
BANKNOTE

1994: President Nelson Mandela
Nelson Mandela became the first black president of South Africa, ending decades of apartheid—a system of discrimination against black people within the country.

2001: The War on Terror
On September 11, 2001, the Islamic terrorist group Al-Qaeda carried out attacks in New York and Washington, D.C. The US declared a "war on terror," launching wars in Afghanistan and later Iraq.

2014: Pepper the robot
SoftBank Robotics revealed their new robot, Pepper. The robot can recognize faces, and can analyze a person's expressions and tone of voice to detect emotion.

PEPPER

US CHINOOK CH-47

1955–1973: The Vietnam War
War erupted between North and South Vietnam. The US entered the war in 1965 on the side of South Vietnam, while the Soviet Union and China supported the North. People protested worldwide about US involvement.

1949: The People's Republic of China
Chinese communist leader Mao Zedong proclaimed the communist People's Republic of China. Mao led the country as chairman until his death in 1976.

最高指示

BOOK OF QUOTATIONS FROM
CHAIRMAN MAO ZEDONG

1945: End of World War II
After five years of brutal fighting, World War II ended when the US dropped two atomic bombs on Japan. Tens of thousands of people were killed instantly, and Japan surrendered shortly afterward.

"FAT MAN"
ATOMIC BOMB

1947: The Partition of India
At its independence, India was divided in two: a Muslim-majority Pakistan and a Hindu-majority India. Millions of people found themselves on the wrong side of the new borders.

1948: Creation of Israel
After the horrors faced by Jews during World War II, a Jewish homeland was created in Palestine in the Middle East. The Palestinian Arabs were angry at the arrival of millions of Jews and years of conflict followed.

SPANISH MAUSER 1893 RIFLE

1939: World War II begins
Adolf Hitler invaded Poland, prompting Britain and France to declare war on Germany. Hitler quickly conquered much of Europe, including France, although Britain remained an obstacle to his domination.

1936-1939: The Spanish Civil War
Spanish General Francisco Franco led his forces to victory in the Spanish Civil War. He became the military dictator of Spain, and went on to rule the country for the next 40 years.

1934-1945: Adolf Hitler
In Germany, Adolf Hitler became Führer (leader). He persecuted Jews across Europe and his ambitions led to the outbreak of World War II.

CLAPPER BOARD

1927: The "Talkies"
The first feature film to include sound, The Jazz Singer marked a new era in cinema. Clapper boards were used to synchronize the action in a scene with separately recorded sound.

1929: The Wall Street Crash
After the optimism of the 1920s, the US economy crashed, causing the Great Depression. The effects were felt around the world. In 1933, President Franklin D. Roosevelt introduced his New Deal to help the US economy recover.

ROOSEVELT
MEMORIAL TO THE
GREAT DEPRESSION

World War I

In July 1914, war broke out in Europe. As countries rushed to support their allies, they were drawn into a fight that soon escalated into a global war that is now known as World War I.

The Central Powers–Germany, Austria-Hungary, and Turkey – battled against the Entente Powers (who later became known as the Allies)–Britain, France, and Russia, joined by Italy in 1915 and the US in 1917. Equally matched, each side tried to grind down the other, inflicting high numbers of casualties using huge, unprecedented amounts of firepower. Most of the fighting took place in trenches dug by the armies, as each side fought to gain and defend territory from their enemy.

RECRUITMENT

When war broke out, each country involved had a national army, but few were ready for such a long, drawn-out war. Armies needed more soldiers, and lots of them. Many civilians were conscripted–forced to join the armed forces by law. Others volunteered to fight, driven by a sense of national duty. All governments used inspiring posters to create support for the war.

Poster campaign
This French poster is encouraging people to raise money for the war effort.

LEAD UP TO THE WAR

At the start of the 20th century, European countries grew increasingly hostile toward each other. Germany had only become a unified nation in 1871, but its ruler, Kaiser Wilhelm II, began building up its navy, kick-starting an arms race with Britain. With the aim of supporting each other if conflict did arise, France and Russia joined together in a military alliance against their rivals Germany and Austria–Hungary. Britain drew close to France and Russia as one of the Entente Powers. Only a spark was needed to start a war.

"The lamps are going out all over Europe."

Sir Edward Grey, British Foreign Secretary, 1914

A continent at war
Eventually, the war was fought on three fronts in Europe–the Western Front, the Eastern Front, and the Balkan Front.

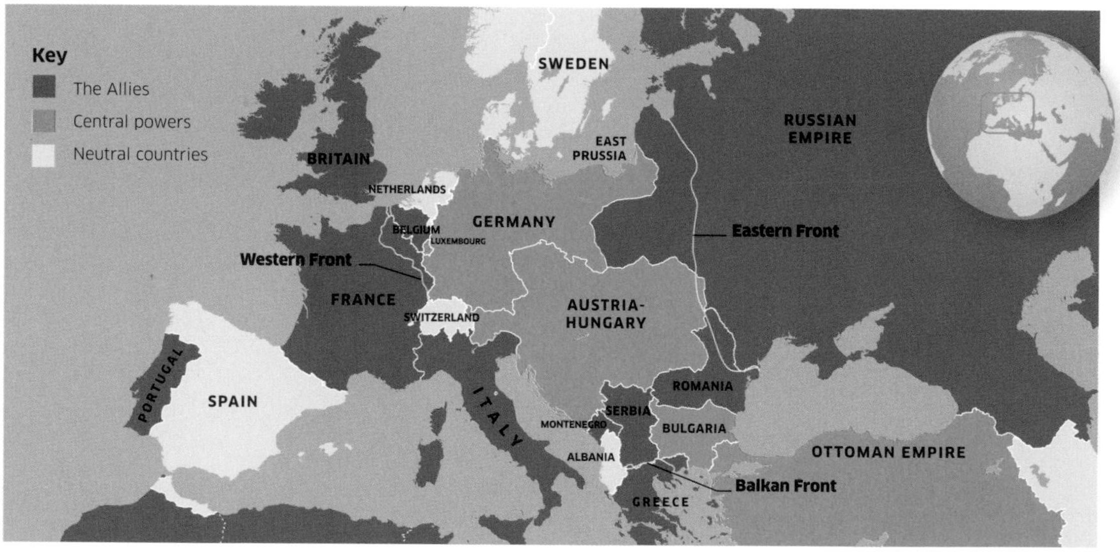

SUBMARINE WARFARE

From 1915, German U-boats (short for *Unterseeboot*, meaning "submarine boat") took the war underwater. They attacked unarmed merchant ships carrying supplies, including food, to Britain–almost starving the country into submission by 1917. Germany's new naval tactics horrified the world. Submarine warfare was seen as uncivilized and against the rules of combat that had been followed in the past.

German U-boat
Throughout the war, German U-boats sank 5,554 Allied merchant ships and warships. Conditions on board the U-boats were hot and cramped.

Map Key
- The Allies
- Central powers
- Neutral countries

(Map labels: SWEDEN, RUSSIAN EMPIRE, BRITAIN, NETHERLANDS, EAST PRUSSIA, BELGIUM, LUXEMBOURG, GERMANY, Eastern Front, Western Front, FRANCE, SWITZERLAND, AUSTRIA-HUNGARY, PORTUGAL, SPAIN, ITALY, MONTENEGRO, SERBIA, ROMANIA, BULGARIA, ALBANIA, OTTOMAN EMPIRE, GREECE, Balkan Front)

Timeline

A global war

When war broke out in July 1914, the Central Powers and the Allies thought it would be finished by Christmas. But World War I was to become the most brutal and destructive conflict the world had ever seen, lasting for four years and resulting in the deaths of millions of soldiers and civilians.

June 1914

Franz Ferdinand assassinated
Archduke Franz Ferdinand–heir to the Austria-Hungary Empire–and his wife were shot in Sarajevo in Bosnia. The killer belonged to a Serbian revolutionary group. Austria-Hungary blamed Serbia for the killing.

July 1914

Declarations of war
When Austria-Hungary declared war on Serbia, it was given support by its ally Germany. Russia backed Serbia and declared war on Austria-Hungary, leading Germany to declare war on Russia and on Russia's ally France. When Germany invaded neutral Belgium on its way to attack France, Britain declared war on Germany.

October-November 1914

Battle of Ypres
After Germany invaded Belgium intending to deliver a decisive blow to the French military, they encountered French and British forces in Flanders. A series of battles, known as the Battle of Ypres, were fought close to the northern coast. The fighting was savage, but the battle ended in stalemate.

February 1915–January 1916

Gallipoli campaign
British, French, Australian, and New Zealand troops launched an attack on the Gallipoli Peninsula in Turkey, aiming to take control of the country. The attack failed–about 58,000 Allied soldiers were killed.

235 Allied spies were **found guilty of espionage** by the Germans.

4.5 million artillery shells were fired during the **Battle of Passchendaele.**

165

NEW TECHNOLOGY

The invention of new technologies made World War I more deadly than any war previously fought. Each country worked to improve their fighting methods, developing new tools and techniques to gain an advantage over their enemy. For the first time, soldiers in war had to contend with powerful weaponry such as machine guns, poison gas, flamethrowers, and explosive mines, as well as tanks and aircraft.

Machine gun
This Schwarzlose machine gun automatically reloaded after firing, allowing soldiers to shoot rapidly. It was one of the main weapons of the Austro-Hungarian army.

War in the skies
As technology developed, planes became sturdier. They were used to carry out reconnaissance, drop bombs, and fight battles in the skies, with brave pilots called "aces" becoming heroes.

Fearsome tanks
First invented in Britain, tanks could travel over rough, muddy terrain, acting as a shield for Allied soldiers as they advanced. They were used for the first time in 1916 at the Battle of the Somme.

SECRET WAR

Both sides used espionage, or spying, to gain secret information about the enemy. Spies listened in on their enemy's communications, and code breakers tried to crack the codes that were used to send secret messages via telegraph and radio. Male and female secret agents worked in disguise in enemy territory to find out as much information as possible, but many were caught and imprisoned.

Pigeon with message canister
A secret message could be delivered to and from the battlefield by inserting it into a canister, then attaching the canister to the leg of a carrier pigeon.

THE HOME FRONT

World War I had a huge impact on civilians, particularly in Belgium and France, where a lot of the fighting took place on the Western Front. The effects of war were felt not just on the battlefield but also at home. On this "Home Front," many civilians faced food shortages and rationing, and as millions of men went off to fight, women took over their jobs. By the end of the war, millions of civilians had lost their lives.

Zeppelin over London
Zeppelins were huge, slow-moving German airships. Some flew in the skies over London, dropping bombs on shocked and terrified citizens.

May 1915	1916	July–November 1917	November 1918	June 28, 1919
Sinking of the Lusitania A German submarine sank the passenger liner *Lusitania*, drowning US civilians. German submarine attacks eventually led the US to join the war on the Allied side in 1917.	**Battle of Jutland** In the only full-scale naval battle of the war, German and British navies fought each other off the Jutland peninsula in Denmark. Both sides claimed victory, but Germany decided not to fight at sea again. **Battle of the Somme** Fought in northern France near the Somme River, more than a million soldiers were killed or wounded in this four-month-long battle. The Allies were unable to push through German lines and ended the attack after heavy snow made fighting difficult.	**Battle of Passchendaele** The Allies, who sought to destroy German submarine bases on the Belgian coast, attacked German forces near Ypres. But torrential rain turned the clay-soil battlefield into a muddy swamp, with tanks, troops, and horses becoming stuck. The Allies gained just 5 miles (8 km) of territory, with more than 475,000 casualties on both sides.	**Fighting ends** After losing a series of battles in 1918, Germany signed an armistice (truce) with the Allies, agreeing to end the fighting on the 11th hour of the 11th day of the 11th month.	**Treaty of Versailles** The German government signed a peace treaty at Versailles in France, but its terms were very unpopular among Germans. The treaty stated that Germany and its allies were to blame for the war and had to pay compensation.

Pillbox
Raised, concrete shelters allowed soldiers to fire machine guns at the enemy from a protected position.

Gas attack
Poison gas was used for the first time during World War I by both sides. Soldiers used gas masks to protect their eyes, noses, and throats from lethal fumes.

Sandbag reinforcement
Sandbags filled with earth prevented the walls of the trenches from falling in.

Sentry duty
Keeping watch on the enemy was dangerous—soldiers on sentry duty stood on a ledge and peered over the top of the trench to see.

Sniper attack
At night, hidden shooters called snipers prepared to launch attacks at dawn, by getting into position behind trees close to the enemy's trench.

Raiding party
Soldiers crawled on their bellies toward the enemy in surprise attacks.

Underground war
Both sides tried to place explosives into enemy trenches by tunneling deep under no-man's land.

Barbed wire
No-man's land was crisscrossed with barbed wire and traps to slow down enemy attacks.

> "What a bloodbath ... hell cannot be this
> **dreadful"**

Albert Joubaire, French soldier at Verdun, in his diary, 1916

Battlefield nurses

Women drove ambulances and worked as nurses on the Western Front, helping soldiers injured in battle. These battlefield nurses treated many types of wound, including poison gas burns, shrapnel injuries, and infections.

Christmas truce

On Christmas Day 1914, some soldiers from both sides called a cease-fire along parts of the Western Front. They crossed no-man's land to sing carols, exchange gifts, and play soccer. The army generals were angry when they heard what had happened and tried to prevent this type of truce happening again.

No-man's land at night

The German and Allied soldiers fought over an area between their trenches known as "no-man's land." Much of the action took place at night under the cover of darkness, as this was the safest time for soldiers to surprise the enemy, recover casualties, and repair trench defenses.

20,000 miles (32,200 km) of trenches had been dug by the end of World War I.

11 a.m. The time the armistice ending World War I came into effect on **November 11, 1918**.

167

Casualties
Soldiers killed in action would often lie in no-man's land for days until it was safe for their bodies to be collected.

Bright light
Flares were used to light up the enemy's trench at night.

Over the top
Soldiers used ladders to climb out of the trench and advance across no-man's land.

The Western Front

By Christmas 1914, World War I had reached a stalemate. The German advance across western Europe had been stopped by Allied troops. Both sides dug in, building a zigzagged line of deep trenches which became known as the Western Front.

The Western Front stretched 400 miles (645 km) from the coast of Belgium to the border of Switzerland. Over the next few years, the two sides fought with bullets, shells, and poison gas to capture just a few miles of territory from their enemy. Soldiers lived in constant fear of attack and suffered tough conditions in the trenches, which were cold, wet, and full of rats.

Support trench
A second trench behind the front trench provided another line of defense support.

Field telephone
Telephones were used to relay orders along the Western Front. Dogs and carrier pigeons were also used to transport messages.

Officers' dugout
An officers' shelter deep underground offered some comfort, and plans were made there for future advances.

Duckboards
Trenches were wet and muddy, so these wooden planks were laid to help keep soldiers' feet dry.

Soldiers' shelter
Soldiers took shelter and rested in holes cut into the side of the trench wall.

The Russian Revolution

By the start of the 20th century, the Romanov family had ruled over Russia for 300 years, but after years of war and famine, the people began to demand change.

Nicholas II, the ruling czar (emperor), was slow to react to calls for reform, which were led by the Bolsheviks—a communist political party that argued resources should be shared equally among the people. His poor handling of wars with Japan and Germany fueled unrest, and in 1917 two dramatic revolutions took place, eventually transforming Russia from a monarchy into the world's first communist state—the Soviet Union.

1905
Russia's humiliating defeat in the Russo-Japanese War led to strikes and protests against the rule of Czar Nicholas II who was blamed.

March 1917
After a series of public protests about food shortages and poor living conditions, Czar Nicholas II abdicated (renounced the throne).

1917–1922
Civil war between the Bolsheviks and anti-communist forces ended in a Bolshevik victory, allowing the party to consolidate its power.

December 30, 1922
The Russian Communist Party founded the Soviet Union (USSR)—the world's first communist state.

1914–1918
During World War I, Russia suffered catastrophic losses fighting against Germany. Again, Czar Nicholas II was blamed.

October 1917
The Bolsheviks seized power from the provisional government, which had been in power since March. In July 1918, Nicholas II was arrested and executed.

1918
The Bolsheviks became known as the Russian Communist Party. They signed a peace treaty with Germany, taking Russia out of World War I.

From 1924
Soviet politician Joseph Stalin took power. He used violence to eliminate his opponents and military force to occupy European countries.

Revolutionary leader
Vladimir Lenin (1870-1924) was the founder and leader of the Bolsheviks. He was a passionate public speaker and made stirring speeches to crowds of workers, soldiers, and peasants, urging them to support the ideals of the revolution.

THE ROARING TWENTIES

In the 1920s, fun, fashion, and entertainment became the order of the day. Young women known as Flappers outraged the older generations with their short skirts, bobbed hairstyles, and rebellious behavior. Although the US government banned alcohol between 1920 and 1933, illicit bars known as speakeasies emerged, where young people could socialize and enjoy new dances such as the twisting Charleston. Jazz—a new African American music style—became so popular that the decade became known as the Jazz Age.

The Jazz Age
Trumpeter and singer Louis Armstrong, playing here with King Oliver's Creole Jazz Band, was one of jazz music's biggest stars.

Boom and bust in the US

After World War I ended in 1918, many Americans greeted the 1920s with a sense of optimism. The economy grew, and people had more money to spend on luxury items and entertainment. But the good times didn't last. At the end of the decade, the economy collapsed, leaving many Americans in poverty.

At the start of the 1920s, the US recovered quickly from the war's drain on its resources, and experienced a "boom" period of economic growth. Factories switched from producing goods intended for the war effort to making consumer items, such as household appliances and cars. Newspapers and magazines were full of ads for these new goods, selling the public a glamorous lifestyle. The misery of the war made its survivors determined to have a good time, and they flocked to sporting events, dance clubs, and the cinema. But between October 24 and 29, 1929, the party came to an abrupt end when the economy went "bust". The next decade brought with it the Great Depression—a period of mass unemployment and hardship for millions of people, not just in the US but around the world.

CONSUMER GOODS

During the 1920s, factories began to mass-produce time-saving devices such as vacuum cleaners and washing machines. Banks let people pay in installments, making these new goods more affordable.

Buy it now!
Colorful, catchy ads persuaded Americans to buy new items for their homes. This poster for vacuum cleaners promised US housewives more leisure time.

RISING SKYSCRAPERS

The economic boom in the US brought with it the need for more office space. Tall buildings, or skyscrapers, were the answer. New developments in technology, especially steel, made it possible for skyscrapers to reach unprecedented heights, and architects competed to see who could build the tallest building. In the 1920s, these super-high structures were a symbol of US confidence, but they became an important source of jobs, and hope, during the troubled times of the 1930s.

Race to the top
Each day, 3,400 workers constructed the building, completing an average of four and a half floors per week. The building was finished in just 410 days.

New heights

Construction of the iconic 102-story Empire State Building in New York City began on March 17, 1930—six months after the Wall Street Crash—despite the poor state of the economy. It opened to the public on May 1, 1931, 45 days earlier than scheduled.

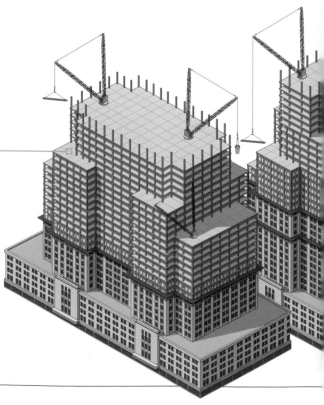

12 million The number of **Americans** unemployed in 1932.

President Franklin D. Roosevelt spoke to the US population every week during his **"fireside chats"**, which were broadcast on national radio.

171

THE GREAT DEPRESSION

For years, Americans had bought small shares in companies, or stocks, hoping to get rich from their profits. But between October 24 and 29, 1929, the New York stock market crashed. Stock prices slumped, quickly becoming worthless, in what became known as the Wall Street Crash. It triggered the Great Depression, which lasted until the late 1930s.

Hoovervilles

Unable to repay bank loans, more than two million people lost their homes during the Great Depression. In major cities, large shanty towns, or slums, sprang up. They were nicknamed Hoovervilles, after President Herbert Hoover, who was blamed for the economy's collapse.

The Dust Bowl

During the 1930s, severe droughts and dust storms hit the US, affecting 1,500 sq miles (4,000 sq km) of land from Texas to Nebraska. Soil turned to dust, causing crops and livestock to die. Unable to grow anything, 200,000 farmers migrated to California.

The New Deal

In 1933, Franklin D. Roosevelt became US president, promising a "New Deal" to help the country recover. He pledged assistance for the poor and launched huge public projects to boost the economy and create more jobs for the unemployed.

Tallest tower
To guarantee its position as the world's tallest building, architects topped the skyscraper with an aerial.

Stepped back
The building's design was stepped, to allow sunlight to reach the street below.

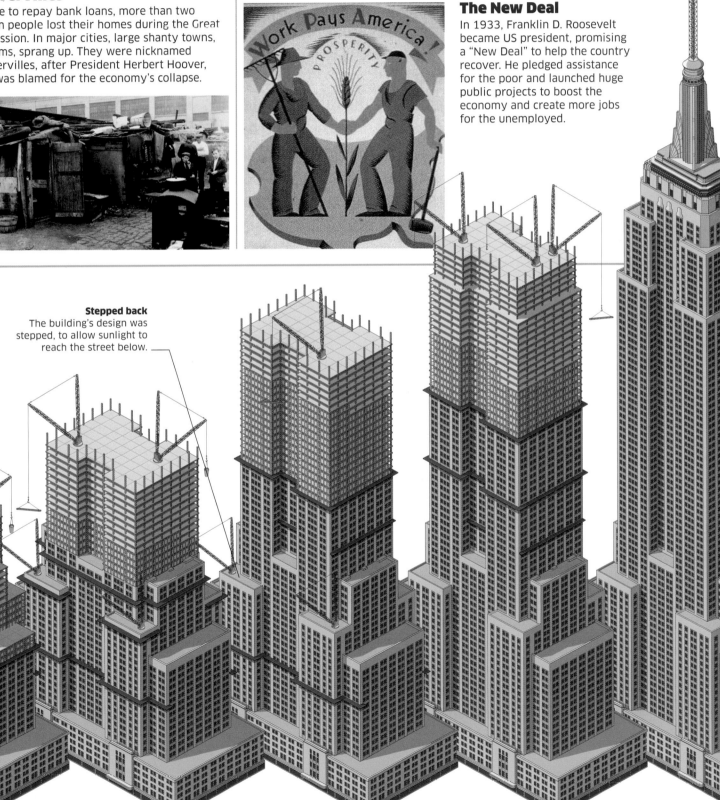

172 the modern world ○ AGE OF DICTATORS

1934 The year **Adolf Hitler and Benito Mussolini first met**, in Venice, Italy.

Political extremes
By the end of the 1930s, democracy was under threat. Dictators, many of whom were either communist or fascist, were in power in many different countries across Europe. Communist dictators believed in government control of the economy and resources, while fascist leaders were extremely nationalistic. They rejected democracy and communism.

Age of dictators

The 1930s was a time of economic hardship around the world and many people were poor, unemployed, and desperate. Across Europe, strong leaders seized control, in some cases using force. These extreme, all-powerful rulers were called dictators.

Although many of these dictators promised a better future for their citizens, their ruthless policies were responsible for the deaths of millions of people. They rejected democracy, glorified war, used violence to crush their political opponents, and stoked racial divisions.

GERMANY

FRANCE

The Spanish Civil War
General Franco led nationalist forces to victory in the Spanish Civil War, defeating the republicans and overthrowing the democratic government.

SPAIN

PORTUGAL

MADRID

LISBON

Antonio de Oliveira Salazar
Antonio Salazar became prime minister of Portugal in 1932. He went on to form a conservative, nationalist dictatorship, using censorship and the help of his secret police.

General Francisco Franco
In Spain, army leader General Franco became dictator in 1939 after three years of civil war. His fascist regime would be in power for the next 40 years.

13 The number of **five-year plans** that were developed between 1928 and 1991 to **modernize the Soviet Union's economy.**

Stalin was born **Josef Vissarionovich Dzhugashvili**. He changed his name to Stalin, meaning **"Man of steel."**

173

Reichstag fire
In 1933, Hitler used a fire at the Reichstag, the parliament building, as an excuse to declare a state of emergency, allowing him to take complete control of the country.

Five-year plans
In an effort to modernize the country's economy, Stalin introduced new policies for farmers. But they backfired, resulting in famine and the deaths of millions.

MOSCOW

BERLIN

Adolf Hitler
In Germany, economic struggles increased popular support for Adolf Hitler's fascist Nazi party. He became Führer (leader) in 1934. He persecuted Jews across Europe, and his imperial ambitions led to the outbreak of World War II.

SOVIET UNION

Engelbert Dollfuss
In 1932, Austrian Chancellor Engelbert Dollfuss established an authoritarian regime, abolishing all other political parties. He modeled his politics on Mussolini and Italian fascism.

VIENNA

AUSTRIA

BUDAPEST

HUNGARY

Joseph Stalin
Communist Joseph Stalin came to power in the Soviet Union in 1924. He seized total control of the state and the economy. He strengthened his power by using propaganda to shape public opinion.

ROME

ITALY

Fascist symbol
Mussolini chose the ancient Roman image of an eagle clutching a bundle of sticks (a symbol of collective strength) to represent Italian fascism.

General Miklos Horthy
In 1920, General Horthy's army overthrew Hungary's communist regime. Horthy was an authoritarian ruler who believed he was creating a strong, united nation. He ruled until he was arrested by invading Nazi troops in 1944.

Benito Mussolini
The founder of fascism, Benito Mussolini, became dictator of Italy in 1925. He called himself *Il Duce* (The Leader) and used his secret police to crush his opponents.

MEDITERRANEAN SEA

The Golden Age of Cinema

Lights! Camera! Action! In 1895, the Lumière brothers in France developed the cinematograph, a device to capture moving pictures. By the late 1920s—the start of the Golden Age of Cinema—their invention had inspired an industry of filmmakers determined to entertain audiences.

As technology improved, films changed from silent, black-and-white creations that were just a few minutes long to feature-length, full-color epics, gangster films, musicals, and comedies with sound. By the 1930s, film studios were producing films as fast as they could for audiences desperate for light relief from the Great Depression—a period of economic hardship for many around the world. Hollywood, once a quiet suburb of Los Angeles, became the home of the US film industry—its warm weather perfect for filming outdoors all year round.

Lights
Movable lights allowed studios to film indoors.

Studio rigging
The "grip" was the person who organized the equipment holding cameras and lighting in position.

Gaffer
The electrician in charge of the film's lighting was known as the "Gaffer."

Camera operator
Many camera operators spent 20 or 30 years at the same studio, helping create a unique studio style.

Creative vision
Directors were in charge of everything creative. They earned great recognition if their films were well received.

1930s film set
Film studios employed thousands of people who carried out all sorts of jobs, from actors and directors to costume designers and film editors. They worked tirelessly on vast sets that were built to mimic real life.

Synchronized sound
Films were silent until 1927, when the Warner Brothers studio released *The Jazz Singer*, the first "talkie," marking a new era in cinema. To synchronize the action in a scene with sound that was recorded separately, a clapper board was struck to make a noise when the camera started rolling.

Overworked
So that studios could churn out films as fast as possible, actors could be made to work up to 18 hours a day, six days a week.

Long day
Actors could wait for hours at a time to be filmed.

7,500 The number of **films released by the** Hollywood studios between 1930 and 1945.

80 million The number of people who **visited the cinema** each week during the 1930s in the US.

175

Animation

One of the first cartoons ever to feature sound was Walt Disney's *Steamboat Willie*, released in 1928. Just eight minutes long, it propelled Disney's character "Mickey Mouse" to stardom and started what became known as the Golden Age of Animation.

Pioneer of animation
American artist and producer Walt Disney (1901–1966) created many classic animated films including, *Snow White and the Seven Dwarfs* (1937) and *Cinderella* (1950).

Bollywood

The Indian film industry, popularly known as Bollywood, is based in Bombay (Mumbai). It is famous for big-budget films, vibrant song-and-dance routines, and superstar actors who are adored by their fans. The first Bollywood film was *Raja Harishchandra*, released in 1913.

BOLLYWOOD DANCERS

Special effects

As film technology advanced, Hollywood enticed people to cinemas with jaw-dropping special effects. In 1977, the film *Star Wars*, by American director George Lucas, was released. Full of incredible effects, it wowed audiences and set a new standard for thrilling films.

Green screen
Today, technology lets film editors add a background to a scene after it has been filmed.

Changing scenery
To create a background behind the actors, an image was projected onto a large canvas screen.

Star power
Some actors became household names and huge celebrities, including Shirley Temple, who began her career when she was just three years old. The public and private lives of famous stars were carefully controlled by the studio they worked for.

Quick change
Time was money, and studios kept up a relentless pace during filming, with actors changing costumes and makeup on set.

Makeup artist
Specialists used makeup to help transform actors into their characters. Actors often had to report for hair and makeup at 4 a.m. each day.

Extra
Some films had a cast of thousands, with extras playing lots of different smaller parts.

Avoiding mistakes
The script supervisor ensured that props, costumes, hair, and makeup were consistent in each scene.

Cable
Cables trailed across the floor of the set, providing power to cameras and lights.

176 the modern world ∘ **WORLD WAR II BEGINS**

6 The number of **weeks** it took for Germany to conquer France.

World War II begins

In 1939, a war erupted in Europe that would go on to span most of the globe. With hundreds of millions of people caught up in the conflict, World War II became the deadliest war in history.

Though some countries were neutral, much of the world was divided between two opposing sides: the Axis (led by Germany, Italy, and Japan) and the Allies (initially led by Britain and France, later joined by the Soviet Union, the US, and China). When Germany, under dictator Adolf Hitler, invaded Poland in 1939, the world was astonished by the ferocity of the attack. This was the beginning of a brutal six-year war, which cost millions of lives.

Hawker Hurricane
The Hawker Hurricane was the RAF's most formidable aircraft during the Battle of Britain. It was capable of inflicting serious damage on the enemy with its eight .303 in (7.7 mm) machine guns. The wings of the Hurricane were partially covered with canvas rather than metal, allowing engineers to repair a plane quickly if it was damaged.

Lethal guns
The Hurricane's eight machine guns were positioned four in a row on each wing.

The Battle of Britain

Aircraft were used throughout the war for bombing raids, aerial fights, and to support land battles. Germany planned to master the skies over Britain before launching a land invasion, but suffered its first setback in the Battle of Britain. The Luftwaffe—Germany's air force—fought Britain's Royal Air Force (RAF) in dogfights (close-up aerial battles) over southeast England, but the RAF gradually won control.

Supermarine Spitfire
Fast, light, and powerful, this supreme fighter plane played a decisive role in the Battle of Britain.

Pilot
British pilots were often young and hastily trained.

22 The average age of a **British pilot** in the **Battle of Britain**.

In **Poland**, about **5.5 million people died** during the war—**one-sixth of the country's population**.

177

Heinkel He 111
Germany's Heinkel He 111 bomber enjoyed early success in the war. It could take heavy damage and still remain airborne, but was no match for the modern fighters of the RAF and so became obsolete before the war ended. After the Battle of Britain, German Heinkel He 111 pilots switched to attacking British cities and industrial sites.

Experienced flyer
German pilots usually had more combat experience than British pilots.

Messerschmitt Bf 109
These German fighter planes were heavy and had a short range, which hampered their effectiveness.

Radar on the ground
Radar (Radio Detection And Ranging) was vital to the British. It allowed the RAF to track incoming enemy planes and take off in time to meet them.

TIMELINE

Germany advances
After World War I, European leaders were wary of more fighting, but Adolf Hitler's foreign policy made conflict inevitable. Aiming to create a Greater Germany in Europe, Hitler expanded his army, annexed German-speaking Austria in 1938, and invaded Czechoslovakia in March 1939.

Sept 1, 1939

The invasion of Poland
Hitler's tanks blasted deep into Polish territory. Poland's allies, Britain and France, declared war on Germany but failed to launch an attack, and Poland was crushed in little over a month.

1939–1945

Battle of the Atlantic
Throughout the war, Hitler tried to starve Britain by attacking ships carrying food and weapons from the US. Supply ships were bombarded constantly by aircraft and U-boats (German submarines).

May–June 1940

Blitzkrieg
In May 1940, German forces attacked Belgium, the Netherlands, and France using dive bombers, tanks, and infantry to break through weak points in Allied defenses. This aggressive tactic, called Blitzkrieg or "lightning war," shocked and overwhelmed the Allies.

May 26–June 4, 1940

Dunkirk evacuation
The German advance trapped 380,000 Allied troops on the northern coast of France. Most were rescued and returned to Britain by naval ships and hundreds of civilian volunteer vessels.

Sept 1940–May 1941

The Blitz
After losing the Battle of Britain, Hitler began a bombing campaign on British cities and ports at night, called the Blitz, but British defenses held firm. Children were evacuated away from the bombing to safety in the countryside.

June 1941

Operation Barbarossa
Hitler ordered his troops to invade the Soviet Union. He aimed to capture land for *Lebensraum* or "living space" for the German population.

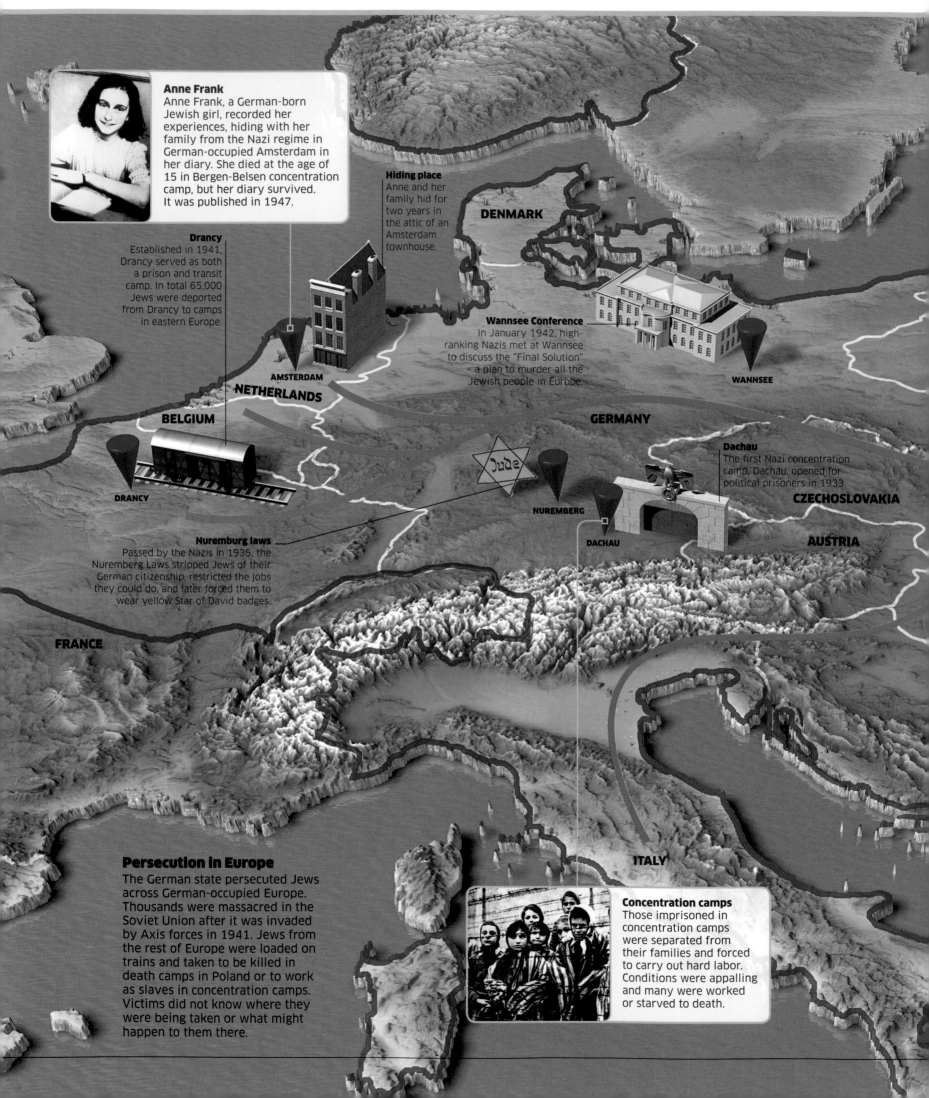

Anne Frank
Anne Frank, a German-born Jewish girl, recorded her experiences, hiding with her family from the Nazi regime in German-occupied Amsterdam in her diary. She died at the age of 15 in Bergen-Belsen concentration camp, but her diary survived. It was published in 1947.

Hiding place
Anne and her family hid for two years in the attic of an Amsterdam townhouse.

Drancy
Established in 1941, Drancy served as both a prison and transit camp. In total 65,000 Jews were deported from Drancy to camps in eastern Europe.

Wannsee Conference
In January 1942, high-ranking Nazis met at Wannsee to discuss the "Final Solution" – a plan to murder all the Jewish people in Europe.

Nuremburg laws
Passed by the Nazis in 1935, the Nuremberg Laws stripped Jews of their German citizenship, restricted the jobs they could do, and later forced them to wear yellow Star of David badges.

Dachau
The first Nazi concentration camp, Dachau, opened for political prisoners in 1933.

DENMARK

AMSTERDAM
NETHERLANDS

BELGIUM

GERMANY

WANNSEE

DRANCY

NUREMBERG

DACHAU

CZECHOSLOVAKIA

AUSTRIA

FRANCE

ITALY

Persecution in Europe
The German state persecuted Jews across German-occupied Europe. Thousands were massacred in the Soviet Union after it was invaded by Axis forces in 1941. Jews from the rest of Europe were loaded on trains and taken to be killed in death camps in Poland or to work as slaves in concentration camps. Victims did not know where they were being taken or what might happen to them there.

Concentration camps
Those imprisoned in concentration camps were separated from their families and forced to carry out hard labor. Conditions were appalling and many were worked or starved to death.

15,000 The number of **concentration camps** established across German-occupied Europe.

10,000 The number of **Nazi war criminals** imprisoned after World War II.

179

Warsaw Ghetto
When Germany invaded Poland in 1939, Jews were forced into ghettos—restricted urban areas controlled by Nazi troops. The Warsaw Ghetto held more than 300,000 people in awful conditions.

The Holocaust

During World War II (1939–1945), the German anti-Semitic (anti-Jewish) Nazi party, led by dictator Adolf Hitler, systematically imprisoned and killed Jewish people in Europe. This is known as the "Holocaust."

By 1945, about 6 million Jews, as well as 5 million Romanies, Soviet prisoners of war, political prisoners, homosexuals, and disabled people, had been murdered by the Nazis. Millions more were imprisoned in concentration camps (huge prisons). The Holocaust officially ended after Allied forces defeated Hitler and the German army in 1945. When the camps were liberated by Allied soldiers, they found victims sick and traumatized.

LATVIA

LITHUANIA

EAST PRUSSIA

TREBLINKA

CHELMNO   WARSAW

SOBIBOR   POLAND

AUSCHWITZ

MAJDANEK   SOVIET UNION

BELZEC

Auschwitz
The largest of the Nazi death camps, more than 1 million people died here.

HUNGARY

Death camps
At death camps set up in Poland, the Nazis murdered millions of Jews by gassing them to death in locked chambers. This image shows a room full of thousands of shoes collected from people killed in the gas chambers at Belzec death camp.

YUGOSLAVIA

ROMANIA

BULGARIA

Key
▼ Death camp
— Deportation route
■ Extent of Axis control, December 1941

World War II in Africa

During World War II, fighting in North Africa saw the opposing sides push each other's forces backward and forward across the desert between 1940 and 1943.

After Italy entered the war on the side of Germany in June 1940, British Prime Minister Winston Churchill dispatched troops to North Africa to support those already stationed in Egypt. There, he hoped to remove the Italians from their colony in Libya. Forces from Britain and its colonies won a decisive victory against the Italians, but then German dictator Adolf Hitler sent General Erwin Rommel to Africa. Rommel reversed some of the British gains, and extended the North African Campaign for another two years.

September 1940
Benito Mussolini, dictator of Italy, ordered the invasion of Egypt, which was occupied by the British. Within months, his troops were overwhelmed by Allied forces.

From April 1941
Australian troops captured Tobruk in eastern Libya and then resisted German attempts to take it back in an eight-month siege.

November 1942
Commanded by US General Dwight D. Eisenhower, a series of British and American landings and assaults brought reinforcements, including US tanks.

February 1941
Hitler dispatched General Erwin Rommel to North Africa. His forces drove Britain back through Libya toward Egypt.

November 1942
Lieutenant-General Bernard Montgomery, commander of the British Eighth Army, defeated Rommel at El Alamein in Egypt. It was a turning point in the war in North Africa.

May 1943
US troops eventually helped force the surrender of German and Italian forces in Tunisia after a long struggle. Almost 250,000 troops were taken prisoner, and all of North Africa was in Allied hands.

General Erwin Rommel
Rommel was nicknamed the "Desert Fox" for his capable leadership of German and Italian forces in the North African Campaign. A national hero in Germany, Rommel was highly respected by his counterparts in the British army.

Island hopping

The US navy adopted a strategy of "island-hopping." The aim was to quickly capture and control strategic islands along a path toward the Japanese mainland, bringing US bombers within range of the country in preparation for an invasion.

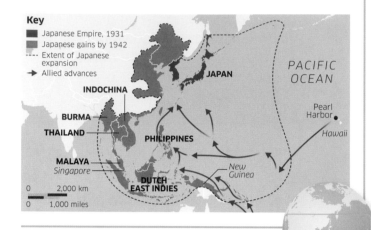

Key
■ Japanese Empire, 1931
■ Japanese gains by 1942
--- Extent of Japanese expansion
→ Allied advances

PACIFIC OCEAN

JAPAN
INDOCHINA
BURMA
THAILAND
PHILIPPINES
MALAYA
Singapore
DUTCH EAST INDIES
New Guinea
Pearl Harbor
Hawaii

0   2,000 km
0   1,000 miles

World War II becomes global

World War II began in Europe, but by late 1941, the conflict had spread worldwide. While the Allied forces fought for survival against Hitler's army in Europe, Japan began to expand its empire in Southeast Asia.

In December 1941, Japan attacked European- and US-controlled territories across Southeast Asia. But by mid-1942, Japan's advance was halted by the US, the only country powerful enough to thwart its imperial ambitions.

The control center
The Island, the ship's main control center, had a narrow base to save space on the flight deck. It held the navigation bridge and the flight deck control, which oversaw all planes taking off and landing.

Ready for anything
Planes could launch or land at either end of the ship, in case part of the flight deck was damaged.

Onboard weaponry
The aircraft carrier's machine guns were protected by shielded mounts and used to defend the ship against dive bombers.

Camouflaged hull
The USS *Enterprise* (CV-6) was painted in different shades of blue to make it harder for enemy planes and ships to spot it at sea.

Underwater protection
Upright walls, or "bulkheads," within the ship's hull were up to 2 in (4 cm) thick and made of steel to limit the damage caused by enemy torpedoes.

Crew living space
More than 2,000 people, including sailors, pilots, mechanics, and cooks, lived on board. The ship held enough supplies to last for months at sea.

Timeline

The Allies fight back

By late 1941, Hitler's domination of Europe was almost complete. But after a series of victories in the first two years of the war, Germany's military was starting to weaken. As the US joined the fighting in December 1941, the war was beginning to turn in favor of the Allies.

December 7, 1941

Pearl Harbor
Hoping to destroy the US navy's Pacific Fleet in one devastating blow, Japan launched a surprise attack on the US naval base at Pearl Harbor, Hawaii. In response, the US entered the war against Japan and Germany. It became a powerful new ally for Britain and the Soviet Union.

June 4–7, 1942

Battle of Midway
Japan suffered a huge defeat at the Battle of Midway when four of its aircraft carriers and 3,500 of its sailors and airmen were lost. The only aircraft carrier lost by the US was the USS *Yorktown*. The Japanese navy never recovered from the losses it experienced during the Battle of Midway.

August 1942–February 1943

Battle of Stalingrad
Hitler's ambition to expand into eastern Europe suffered a major setback when his troops were trapped by the Soviet army in the city of Stalingrad, Russia. Suffering from frostbite and short of food and ammunition, the German army was forced to surrender. In total, 2.2 million soldiers died during the Battle of Stalingrad.

36 The number of **days** it took **for US forces to** capture the island of Iwo Jima from Japan in 1945.

8:15 a.m. The moment the **atomic bomb struck** the city of **Hiroshima on August 6, 1945.**

183

Folded wings
When planes weren't in the air, their wings were kept folded to save space.

Flight deck
The ship's flight deck was 828 ft (250 m) in length.

Planes in position
An elevator below deck raised the aircraft one-by-one from the hangar to the flight deck.

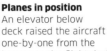

Hangar
The hangar was the height of two decks and had space to store 90 aircraft when they weren't in use.

Engine room
The engine room generated enough power for the ship to travel at 32.5 knots—about 37 mph (60 km/h).

The Gray Ghost

During World War II, the US and Japan used aircraft carriers—enormous floating air bases—to get their planes into position ready to fight. The USS *Enterprise* (CV-6) took part in more battles against Japan than any other US ship. On three occasions, the Japanese navy thought they had sunk it and announced it had gone down, earning the aircraft carrier its nickname "The Gray Ghost."

Kamikaze tactics

As Japan was forced to retreat, its military resorted to desperate tactics. The airforce filled aircraft with bombs and crashed them deliberately into the decks of US and British warships. In total, 34 US warships were sunk by these Japanese kamikaze attacks.

Ready for battle
Kamikaze pilots wore a *hachmaki*, a traditional Japanese head cloth.

Women at work

In the US, with the country's men sent abroad to fight, new job opportunities opened up for women. American women entered the workforce in huge numbers. They were encouraged to work on farms, in shipyards, railroad companies, and airplane manufacturers to support the war effort.

Recruitment campaign
Posters inspired women to take on jobs done previously by men.

June 6, 1944

D-Day landings
After two years of planning, the Allied invasion of western Europe, "Operation Overlord," began. Nearly 200,000 troops were ferried across the English Channel to capture five beaches in Normandy, France.

February 1945

Dresden
With Germany almost defeated, Britain and the US unleashed a series of devastating air raids on major German cities to stop military resistance and crush civilian morale. The bombing of Dresden in February 1945 created a huge firestorm which killed an estimated 25,000 people, most of whom were civilians or refugees.

April 1945

Germany falls
Soviet forces entered Berlin, taking control of the city after fierce street fighting with German troops. Hitler committed suicide and Germany surrendered.

August 6 and 9, 1945

Atomic bombs
The war had ended in Europe but Japan refused to surrender. On August 6, 1945, the world's first atomic bomb to be used in war, nicknamed "Little Boy," was dropped over Hiroshima in Japan. Three days later, a second atomic bomb, "Fat Man," was released over Nagasaki. Tens of thousands were killed immediately and thousands more died later from the effects of radiation. Japan finally surrendered on August 14, 1945.

Decolonization

World War II was the final blow for colonialism (powerful countries or empires controlling other regions around the world). Weakened by years of conflict, empires could not control their overseas territories as the people of Asia, Africa, and the Caribbean called for independence.

By 1945, the Japanese, Italian, and German empires had fallen, and their colonies were occupied by other powers or came back under local control. But many other colonies, mostly under British, French, or Dutch rule, still wanted to govern themselves. Some colonies gained independence through peaceful means, but often the European powers refused to let go. The process of decolonization— giving a colony its own political independence— also coincided with the Cold War between the US and the Soviet Union. Both of these powers interfered in newly independent states.

◉ SOUTH ASIA

The campaign to end British rule over the vast Indian subcontinent started long before World War II. The Indian National Congress, founded in 1885, was the main opposition movement against British rule. The All-India Muslim League was formed in 1906 to protect the rights of Indian Muslims. In 1947 India gained independence and was divided into two independent states: India and Pakistan.

◉ AFRICA

From the 1950s onward, many African countries gained independence from colonial rule. For some African nations the transition to independence was violently opposed by the ruling colonizers, such as in Algeria where France was determined to keep control. In the 1970s, Portugal also fought bitter wars to maintain control of Angola and Mozambique.

A false start

Egypt had gained independence from Britain in 1922, but Britain still interfered in the government and controlled the Suez Canal (an important waterway in Egypt used by many countries to trade with each other). In 1956, the Egyptian president, Gamal Abdel Nasser, declared the Suez Canal to be the property of Egypt. Britain, France, and Israel responded with force, but withdrew after pressure from the US, the Soviet Union, and the United Nations.

GAMAL ABDEL NASSER

Ghana independence

The Gold Coast, a British colony in West Africa, had been demanding independence since 1947. In 1949, nationalist Kwame Nkrumah formed the Convention People's Party (CPP), an organization fighting for self-governance. Nkrumah began a campaign of nonviolent opposition. Independence was proclaimed for the new nation of Ghana on March 6, 1957, with Nkrumah becoming prime minister.

Kwame Nkrumah
As prime minister, Nkrumah improved education, roads, and health facilities.

MAURITANIA · MALI · NIGER · CHAD · SENEGAL · REPUBLIC OF UPPER VOLTA · IVORY COAST · TOGO · DAHOMEY · CAMEROON · NIGERIA · GABON · CENTRAL AFRICAN REPUBLIC · REPUBLIC OF THE CONGO · DEMOCRATIC REPUBLIC OF CONGO

Year of Africa

In 1960, 17 countries, including 14 former French colonies, declared their independence in what became known as the Year of Africa. By 1990, every country in Africa was independent.

Timeline

Southeast Asia

Japan had invaded Southeast Asia during World War II, driving out the old colonial powers. After the war, these colonial powers returned, but many countries did not want them back. Nationalist movements (groups supporting political independence), stirred up by Japanese occupation, demanded self-rule.

1946

The Philippines
Since the 1930s, the Philippines had been pushing for independence, but World War II interrupted the fight for self-governance. The Philippines was the first Southeast Asian country to gain its freedom after World War II, when the US granted its formal independence on July 4, 1946.

1949

Indonesia
In 1945, the leader of Indonesia's nationalist movement proclaimed the independent Republic of Indonesia. In 1949, the Dutch recognized Indonesian independence after four years of war.

INDONESIAN INDEPENDENCE FIGHTER

1954

French Indochina
In the late 1940s, the French struggled to control their colonies in Indochina—Vietnam, Laos, and Cambodia. Nationalist uprisings against French rule began to take their toll, and a French military defeat at Dien Bien Phu in Vietnam prompted peace negotiations. After an agreement was reached in 1954, French Indochina came to an end.

1957

Malaya
Part of the Malayan Communist Party declared war on Britain in 1948. Independence was not given to the Federation of Malaya until 1957. In 1963, the British colonies of Sabah, Sarawak, and Singapore joined the Federation to form Malaysia. In 1965, Singapore became an independent state.

10 cent stamp
A stamp sold in Malaya on Independence Day.

21 days—the length of Gandhi's longest fast in peaceful protest.

54 internationally recognized nations were created in Africa after decolonization.

150,000 The estimated death toll in the French-Algerian conflict.

185

Civil disobedience

The campaign for independence in India was led by Mohandas Gandhi. He used a campaign of civil disobedience (nonviolent defiance) called *satyagraha*. From 1917 he organized protests, made inspiring speeches, disobeyed British laws, and called on Indians to stop buying British goods. He was jailed many times, but his insistence on not using violence gained him the name "Mahatma" meaning "Great Soul."

Mohandas Gandhi
Gandhi encouraged Indians to weave their own clothes by spinning cotton instead of buying British products.

Refugee camp in Delhi, India
During the "Great Migration," tens of thousands were driven into refugee camps all over the continent.

The Partition of India

After independence in 1947 the British divided India in two: a Muslim-majority Pakistan and a Hindu-majority India. Pakistan itself was split into two regions on either side of India: West Pakistan and East Pakistan (East Pakistan later became the nation of Bangladesh). Millions of Hindus, Sikhs, and Muslims found themselves on the wrong side of the new borders. During the "Great Migration" 6 million Muslims crossed into West Pakistan, and 4.5 million Sikhs and Hindus went to India.

THE CARIBBEAN

The US exerted strong political, military, and economic influence over the Caribbean throughout the 20th century. After the Spanish-American War in 1898, Spain handed control of Cuba and Puerto Rico to the US, and Puerto Rico became a US territory. In 1915, the US invaded Haiti and stayed in the country for almost 20 years. In Cuba, during a communist revolution in 1959, the US-backed president Fulgencio Batista was forced out, ending direct interference by the US in the country's affairs.

SOMALIA

MADAGASCAR

Key
Countries that gained independence in 1960

THE LEADER OF THE CUBAN REVOLUTION WAS FIDEL CASTRO WHO RULED CUBA UNTIL 2008

Jamaican independence
Norman W. Manley was the founder of the Jamaican People's National Party, seen here during Jamaica's first Independence Day celebrations.

The British Caribbean

In 1962, Jamaica and Trinidad and Tobago became politically independent. This event ushered in a period of decolonization of the British colonies in the Caribbean, including Barbados, Grenada, the Bahamas, Dominica, and St. Lucia. Many Caribbean countries joined the British Commonwealth, becoming self-governing nations while retaining Britain's monarch as their Head of State.

September 1975

New Guinea
During World War II, Japanese forces occupied New Guinea but were pushed back by Allied forces. After the war, Australia took control of the region. In 1975, Papua and New Guinea became the independent state of Papua New Guinea, one of the last colonies in the world to gain independence.

November 1975

East Timor
The Portuguese left East Timor in 1975, but it was soon occupied by Indonesia. More than 100,000 East Timorese people died in the following decades-long conflict. In a referendum run by the United Nations in 1999, Timorese people voted for independence. In 2002, the UN supervised a transition to Timorese self-government.

1997

Hong Kong and Macao
After 150 years, control of Hong Kong returned from Britain back to China in 1997. However, Hong Kong's government remained separate from that of mainland China. Control of Macao, the last colony in Asia, was returned to China in 1999.

Hand over celebrations
Victoria Harbour in Hong Kong was lit up with fireworks to mark the historic hand over to China.

Era of tension

Although the US and the Soviet Union had fought on the same side during World War II, their relationship soon broke down into rivalry and distrust. They avoided direct conflict with each other but took sides in "proxy wars" that erupted in smaller nations.

NATO and the Warsaw Pact

Western Europe and the US formed NATO, an alliance of democratic countries. The Soviet Union and its allies created a similar treaty, the Warsaw Pact in 1955, in response.

WARSAW PACT BADGE

The Korean War

With the support of the US, South Korea fought against an invasion by communist North Korea. The Soviet Union and China supported the North. The conflict ended in stalemate.

The Vietnam War

The US sent troops to support South Vietnam in its brutal fight against communist North Vietnam. The North was supported by the Soviet Union and China. The war dragged on and ended in defeat for the US.

The Hungarian Uprising

The Hungarian people rebelled against their Soviet-controlled government. Thousands were killed by Soviet troops after the US failed to intervene.

The Berlin Wall

Facing large-scale emigration, Soviet-influenced East Germany erected the Berlin Wall, dividing communist East Berlin from capitalist West Berlin.

The Cuban Missile Crisis

The world came close to nuclear war when the Soviet Union installed nuclear missiles on the island of Cuba, close to the coast of North America.

The Prague Spring

Under new leader Alexander Dubček, Czechoslovakia experienced a period of freedom. Within months, Soviet troops invaded, restoring communist control.

The fall of the Berlin Wall

Relations between the two superpowers began to thaw in the 1980s, culminating in the Berlin Wall being torn down. Germany was reunified a year later.

Timeline

- 1949
- 1950–1953
- 1955–1975
- 1956
- 1961
- 1962
- 1968
- 1989

The Iron Curtain

The Soviet Union installed communist regimes across Eastern Europe, sometimes using force. By 1950, it lay behind a wall of communist states forming an East–West divide that British politician Winston Churchill called the "Iron Curtain." It stretched 4,225 miles (6,800 km) across Europe.

SWEDEN
DENMARK
NETH.
BEL.
• Berlin
EAST GERMANY
WEST GERMANY
POLAND
CZECHOSLOVAKIA
FRANCE
SWITZ.
AUSTRIA
HUNGARY
ITALY
YUGOSLAVIA
ROMANIA
BULGARIA

WEST BERLIN — EAST BERLIN

UNION OF SOVIET SOCIALIST REPUBLICS (USSR)

Key
- ▪ Soviet controlled area
- — Iron Curtain
- 0   250   500 km
- 0   250 miles

The Death Strip

The barrier consisted of two concrete walls: the political boundary and the rear wall. The area in between was known as the "Death Strip."

Watchtower

There were more than 300 watchtowers along the length of the Berlin Wall.

High-intensity lights

Floodlights gave border guards a better chance of spotting anyone trying to escape at night.

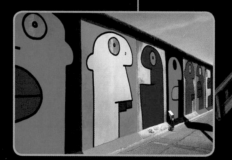

Viewing platform

Western tourists stood on observation platforms to see into the "Death Strip."

Wall graffiti

The concrete face on the western side of the wall was used as a blank canvas for paintings and protest messages. This painting is called *Some heads* by Thierry Noir, but much of the artwork was anonymous. The eastern side of the wall remained blank, because people were forbidden to approach it.

Political boundary

The western side of the wall was made up of 45,000 concrete panels, each reinforced with steel and topped with tubing.

Anti-vehicle ditch

V-shaped ditches were dug all along the East German border. Sometimes reinforced with concrete, they could stop almost any type of vehicle.

8 The number of **countries** that were members of the Warsaw Pact.

5,000 The number of **people** thought to have fled East Germany across the wall.

187

Guarding the wall
Armed East German border guards watched the wall constantly for people trying to escape to West Berlin. Guards had permission to shoot anyone attempting to flee; more than 130 East Germans died trying to get across the wall.

The Cold War

In the aftermath of World War II, the world's two most powerful nations, the US and the Soviet Union, contested for military, cultural, and political supremacy.

The superpowers were divided over their political beliefs: the Soviet system was based on communism (in which a central government controls and distributes property) while the US favored capitalism (a system that encourages private ownership of property). The two countries competed for dominance in many ways, from space exploration to sports and technology. They raced to develop more effective nuclear weapons, eventually stockpiling enough to destroy the planet. The threat of nuclear war prevented a direct battle, but their rivalry played out in a "cold war" of propaganda and fear that affected the entire globe.

The Berlin Wall
The most visible symbol of the Cold War was the Berlin Wall in Germany. Erected by East Germany in 1961, the 97-mile- (156-km-) long barrier prevented people from escaping Soviet-controlled East Germany for democratic West Berlin. The wall divided families and friends until it was torn down in 1989.

The rear wall
On the eastern side, there was a rear wall built of reinforced concrete and topped with barbed wire.

Spike mats
Sharp spikes at the bottom of the wall deterred potential escapees.

Patrols
Border guards worked in pairs. Only the most trusted guards worked in the "Death Strip."

Signal fence
Touching the fence triggered a silent alarm to alert the guards in the watchtower.

Dogs
Guard dogs were leashed to stakes and could alert the guards to any escapees.

Czech hedgehogs
These X-shaped steel beams acted as a barrier against vehicles.

Fight for influence

The US aimed to stop South Vietnam from falling under the control of communist North Vietnam, but despite the superior military power of the US, it was defeated.

Timeline

The end of colonialism

Communist leader Ho Chi Minh's troops defeated the French army at Dien Bien Phu, ending 67 years of French control. The country was divided into two zones–communist-controlled North Vietnam and anti-communist South Vietnam.

1954

Declaration of war

Ho Chi Minh declared a "People's War" in South Vietnam, intending to eventually reunite the two zones of the country under his leadership.

March 1959

The Ho Chi Minh trail

North Vietnamese forces began to create the Ho Chi Minh trail–a network of routes leading from North Vietnam, Laos, and Cambodia into South Vietnam, which they used to transport soldiers and weapons.

May 1959

Naval attack

In the Gulf of Tonkin, a clash between the US destroyer USS *Maddox* and North Vietnamese torpedo boats led to the US pledging more military support for South Vietnam.

1964

"Operation Rolling Thunder"

In March, US President Lyndon Johnson ordered "Operation Rolling Thunder," a huge bombing campaign against North Vietnam. The first US Marines landed in South Vietnam, with army ground troops arriving two months later.

1965

The Tet Offensive

During the festival of Tet, communist forces struck targets in towns and cities across South Vietnam. US and South Vietnamese troops defeated the offensive, but suffered a high number of casualties.

1968

Changing policy

As US public opinion turned against the war, US President Nixon announced a policy of strengthening the South Vietnamese forces in order to reduce the number of US troops in the country.

1969

Kent State shootings

Four students at Kent State University in Ohio were killed when the Ohio National Guard opened fire on a crowd protesting the war.

1970

US withdrawal

In January, peace talks in Paris between the US and representatives of the North Vietnamese government ended in agreement to withdraw US troops by March.

1973

Vietnam reunited

North Vietnamese troops marched into Saigon, reuniting the country and ending the war.

1975

The Vietnam War

In 1959, conflict broke out in South Vietnam between pro-communist forces and the anti-communist government. Eventually the US became involved, with the conflict becoming the 20th century's longest war.

The communist North Vietnamese government encouraged the unrest in South Vietnam, increasing its support gradually by sending in the North Vietnamese Army (NVA). The US, caught up in a Cold War with the Soviet Union, feared the spread of communism in Southeast Asia. It joined the fighting in support of anti-communist South Vietnam, sending more and more troops, and resulting in the loss of more than 50,000 US lives. The US withdrew from the conflict in 1973, before the fighting ended in 1975.

Cockpit
Inside the cockpit there were seats for the pilot and copilot.

Front flank gunner
A gunner with an M60 machine gun sat in position ready to fire.

"Vietnam was lost
in the living rooms of America– not on the battlefields of Vietnam."

Marshall McLuhan, in the *Montreal Gazette*, May 16, 1975

By 1970, 18,000 tonnes of supplies were being transported along the Ho Chi Minh trail each month.

23 The **average age** of a **US soldier killed** during the Vietnam War.

189

US CH-47 Chinook

Stable, agile, and fast, the US CH-47 Chinook helicopter transported soldiers, vehicles, ammunition, and casualties quickly over Vietnam's rugged jungle terrain. It had a hook underneath that allowed it to carry heavy artillery to mountain positions inaccessible by foot, and even to pick up and move lighter aircraft.

Careful design
With two rotors, front and back, the Chinook was more steady and stable in flight than other helicopters designed with just one rotor.

Cabin window
In case of emergencies, the cabin windows could be jettisoned (thrown from the aircraft) so that soldiers on board could escape.

US troops
Those personnel serving in the war were from a variety of different ethnic and social backgrounds.

Engine power
The Chinook was powered by two gas turbine engines. It was one of the US army's fastest helicopters, with a top speed of 196 mph (315 km/h).

Loading ramp
This ramp could be raised or lowered, allowing troops to load and unload cargo.

Transporting troops
The Chinook could carry up to 33 fully equipped soldiers.

Onboard vehicle
The Chinook had space to carry a Jeep on board. The Jeep was well suited to Vietnam's rugged jungle terrain.

Guerrilla warfare

The NVA and the Viet Cong, a pro-communist force in the south, used guerrilla tactics against US soldiers. Hidden by jungle, they planted booby traps or attacked US troops from a distance, then quickly disappeared. Unlike the US military, the NVA and the Viet Cong were used to the terrain and had the support of some locals.

Standing guard
Thousands of South Vietnamese women fought for the Viet Cong.

Public protests

The Vietnam War was the first conflict to be reported on television, and many Americans were deeply angered by the death and destruction they saw. Huge anti-war demonstrations were organized around the country and some young people refused the draft—the government's order to fight.

Anti-war demonstrations
In Berkeley in California, women gathered to protest against the war.

The Civil Rights Movement

In the 1950s, African Americans in the US faced daily discrimination, such as being forced to use separate areas from white people in public places and on transportation.

A growing number of African American civil rights groups took a stand against segregation (the separation of people based on skin color). Many adopted a policy of nonviolence, protesting in a peaceful manner. These activists faced attacks from those who opposed an end to segregation. Eventually, in the 1960s, laws were passed to outlaw discrimination, but many African Americans still struggle for basic rights and the ability to vote.

◎ JIM CROW LAWS

"Jim Crow" was an insulting term for a black person. The Jim Crow Laws were a series of regulations that some states used to legalize the segregation of black and white people in places such as schools, restaurants, libraries, hospitals, and on public transportation. The laws also made it difficult for black people to vote.

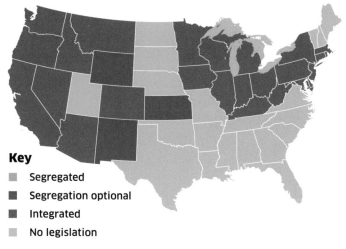

Key

- ▮ Segregated
- ▮ Segregation optional
- ▮ Integrated
- ▮ No legislation

Educational segregation in the early 1950s
Each US state had its own laws about whether black and white children could attend the same schools.

◎ MARTIN LUTHER KING, JR.

Martin Luther King, Jr., was born in 1929 in Atlanta, Georgia. He was a Baptist minister and civil rights activist. He organized many acts of nonviolent protest and gave inspirational speeches, playing a pivotal role in ending segregation in the US. King won the Nobel Peace Prize in 1964. In April 1968 he was assassinated by a white gunman.

Timeline	May 1954	1957	1957	1960
The fight for equality During the 1950s and 1960s, black and white people came together to demand equality for African Americans. This Civil Rights Movement challenged discrimination through lawsuits and nonviolent protests. The struggle for political rights and freedom was long and hard. Many participants often faced violent attacks by people who wanted a "white-only" country.	**Brown v. Board of Education of Topeka** When nine-year-old Linda Brown tried to attend an all-white school in Topeka, Kansas, her enrollment was blocked. Her parents brought a lawsuit against the Topeka Board of Education. This resulted in a landmark ruling by the US Supreme Court that segregation went against the Constitution. The Court found in favor of the Browns and banned segregation in public schools.	**Martin Luther King, Jr., and the SCLC** Martin Luther King, Jr., became founder and president of a new civil rights organization, the Southern Christian Leadership Conference (SCLC). Working with the NAACP, its aim was to unite African American churches across the South to advance the cause of civil rights using nonviolent action.	**Little Rock Nine** Nine African American teenagers enrolled at Little Rock Central High School in Arkansas, where all 1,900 students were white. They faced a hostile white crowd and had to be escorted to class by US army troops. They became known as the Little Rock Nine. 	**Greensboro sit-in** When four black college students sat down at a "whites-only" lunch counter in a department store in Greensboro, North Carolina, they were refused service. The students remained seated until closing time, and returned with 300 more students a few days later. This act of nonviolent protest, which was known as a sit-in, inspired other sit-ins across the South.

c. 21,000 people were **arrested for rioting** after the death of **Martin Luther King, Jr.**

1970 The year that **Black History Month** was first celebrated.

191

Washington speech
At the end of a march attended by 250,000 people in Washington, D.C., Martin Luther King, Jr., gave a speech on the steps of the Lincoln Memorial about his hopes for the future for African Americans.

"I have a dream
that my four little children will one day live in a nation where they will not be judged by the color of their skin"

Martin Luther King, Jr., at a speech in Washington, D.C., 1963

ROSA PARKS AND THE BUS BOYCOTTS

An African American seamstress named Rosa Parks made history in 1955 when she broke Alabama segregation laws by refusing to give up her bus seat for a white person. She was a member of the National Association for the Advancement of Colored People (NAACP), a civil rights organization founded in 1909. Her arrest led to a year-long boycott of the local bus system, led by Martin Luther King, Jr. The protest brought worldwide attention to the discrimination faced by African Americans.

Taking fingerprints
Rosa Parks was arrested when she refused to give up her bus seat for a white passenger.

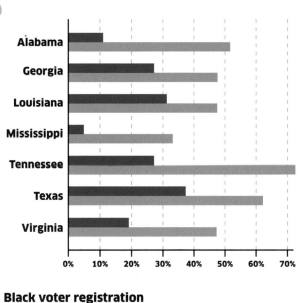

Black voter registration
■ 1956   ■ 1966

THE RIGHT TO VOTE

The Voting Rights Act of 1965 was passed by President Lyndon Johnson, with Martin Luther King, Jr. present when it was signed. It allowed black people the freedom to vote without facing restrictions such as proving that they could read and write. The Voting Rights Act was one of the greatest achievements of the Civil Rights Movement. After it was passed, the number of African Americans who showed up to vote soared, particularly in the southern states.

1961
Freedom rides
When new laws were passed banning segregation on interstate buses, college students tested the laws by taking "freedom rides" throughout the South. They encountered shocking violence when they went into "whites-only" waiting rooms and cafeterias, but eventually bus and train companies were forced to prohibit segregation.

April 3, 1964
"The ballot or the bullet"

Malcolm X was a black Muslim leader. In a speech just before the 1964 election, he said that civil rights would be attained either "by the ballot or the bullet." The speech encouraged African Americans to vote, but warned that violence was an option if the government continued to prevent equality. Malcolm X was assassinated in 1965.

July 2, 1964
1964 Civil Rights Act
After years of protests and intense international pressure, the US Senate brought America a step closer to equality by passing the Civil Rights Act of 1964. The law ended segregation on buses, in schools, and in other public places, and made racial discrimination in education and employment illegal.

March 1965
Selma-Montgomery March
Black people in southern states were often blocked from registering to vote. Protesters attempted to march 50 miles (80 km) from Selma, Alabama, to the state capital Montgomery, demanding the right to vote. They faced brutal attacks from police.

1968
1968 Civil Rights Act
After Martin Luther King, Jr., was assassinated, riots broke out across 125 US cities. President Johnson urged Congress to quickly pass the Civil Rights Act. Commonly known as the Fair Housing Act, it allowed equal housing opportunities for those attempting to buy or rent a home in the US, regardless of race, religion, or nationality.

192 the modern world ○ THE 1960S

1966 The year **Mary Quant started selling her iconic miniskirts** in London, England.

A decade of protests

Inspired by the Civil Rights Movement that started in the US in the 1950s, other protest movements began to form in the 1960s. Protesters marched for gender and racial equality, human rights, better working conditions, the environment, and the end of war in Vietnam. The turbulent decade ended with riots and social unrest.

Timeline

Women's peace protest

Women across the US marched in a one-day protest against the nuclear weapons of both the US and the Soviet Union. This demonstration led to the formation of a national organization— Women Strike for Peace (WSP)—which campaigned against nuclear weapons.

1961

March on Washington

Nearly 250,000 people traveled to Washington, D.C., to demand equal civil rights for African Americans. The March for Jobs and Freedom was one of the largest rallies in history, and where civil rights leader Martin Luther King, Jr. gave his influential "I Have a Dream" speech.

1963

Flower power

The hippie movement emerged in San Francisco. The movement's members, easily recognizable with their long hair and colorful clothes, peacefully opposed the war in Vietnam, giving flowers to soldiers and police.

1965

Summer of love

Thousands of young people traveled to San Francisco to experience hippie culture. Influenced by Eastern religions such as Buddhism, they protested against violence, and embraced peace and love.

1967

Protests in France

When student riots broke out in Paris, 10 million workers unhappy with the government joined them in a huge general strike that lasted two weeks.

1968

Stonewall riots

After a police raid sparked riots outside the Stonewall Inn, a gay bar in New York City's Greenwich Village, the US gay rights movement was formed. It protested against the social and political discrimination of gay people.

1969

The 1960s

After the hardships of World War II and the recovery afterward, the 1960s was a decade of optimism and fun, as young people found exciting new ways to express themselves through fashion, music, and art.

Young people were inspired by new British pop and rock bands such as The Beatles, The Who, and The Rolling Stones, innovative fashion designers such as Mary Quant, and stylish models including Twiggy and Jean Shrimpton. A "generation gap" between young and old began to emerge, as young people rebelled against their parents, challenging not just their tastes in fashion and music, but their political views, too.

Space Age fashion
Fashion designers were inspired by advances in space technology. They designed clothes using futuristic colors and modern materials.

Colorful patterns
Some boutiques had vivid street art on the walls outside.

5-point haircut
Working women needed an easy-to-maintain haircut. Hairdresser Vidal Sassoon revolutionized women's hair with his iconic 5-point haircut.

Miniskirts
Popularized by British designer Mary Quant, short miniskirts became a symbol of rebellious youth culture.

Jaguar XK-E
This British sports car was fun to drive and hugely popular.

Photo shoots
Fashion photographers often photographed models on location in gritty urban settings.

Fashion model
Fashion photographers turned teenage models into international stars.

600 million The number of **Beatles** records sold worldwide.

32 The number of **acts** that performed at **Woodstock** in 1969.

193

Pop art

Pop art, short for "Popular art," emerged in the 1950s but flourished in the 1960s. Artists began to reject traditional painting in favor of bold colors and simple everyday imagery. They took their inspiration from popular mass culture, comic books, and advertising. The most famous pop artists were Andy Warhol and Roy Lichtenstein, who were both based in New York.

Andy Warhol
US pop artist Andy Warhol was fascinated by Hollywood film stars. He depicted famous actresses in his work many times.

Woodstock

In 1969, the Woodstock Music and Art Fair took place on a small farm in upstate New York. The promotional poster promised "3 days of peace and music." Half a million people showed up to the festival to listen to the most famous musicians of the day, including Jimi Hendrix, The Who, and Janis Joplin.

Jimi Hendrix
Famed for his jazz-influenced guitar solos, legendary guitarist Jimi Hendrix performed on the festival's last night.

Swinging London

In the 1960s, London was at the center of fast-changing tastes in fashion, music, and art, with *Time* magazine calling it "the swinging city." Young people flocked to London's busy shopping streets to browse and buy the latest trends.

Afro hair
Inspired by the Civil Rights Movement in the US, some black British people chose to wear their hair naturally as a symbol of pride.

Mop tops
British band The Beatles popularized this floppy hairstyle, which marked a change from the more conservative male haircuts of the previous decade.

Color blocking
Bright, bold, geometric patterns became popular.

Mods and Rockers
"Mods" were people who wore parkas, polo shirts, and rode scooters. They battled with gangs of motorcycle-riding "Rockers."

MINI
The first MINI was sold in 1959. It became an iconic symbol of 1960s Britain.

Military clothing
Yves Saint Laurent's famous double-breasted pea coats ignited a trend for military-inspired fashion.

Gender-neutral clothing
Fashion designers challenged traditional ideas of femininity and masculinity by creating unisex fashion that could be worn by anyone.

194 the modern world ○ CONFLICT IN THE MIDDLE EAST

Saudi Arabia produces **10 million** barrels of oil each day.

Conflict in the Middle East

Throughout the 20th and early 21st centuries, the Middle East has experienced a series of wars between countries within and outside the region and among different religious groups.

The Middle East is made up of many different religious groups, though the majority of people are Muslim Arabs. In 1948, the state of Israel was created in Palestine, prompting anger across the Middle East, and sparking a conflict that is still ongoing today. More recently, in 2010, a series of pro-democracy uprisings, later known as the Arab Spring, led to unrest and upheaval across the region, while civil wars in Syria and Yemen have worsened divisions.

The Middle East today
The Middle East is the common term used for the region consisting today of countries in West Asia as well as Egypt in North Africa.

IRAN

After Saudi Arabia, Iran is the second largest country in the region. Iran's population is mostly made up of Shia Muslims, followers of a particular branch of Islam. Throughout the 20th century, Iran experienced regular political upheaval and war, most frequently with its neighbor, Iraq.

The Iranian Revolution

In 1941, Mohammad Reza Pahlavi came to power as Shah (king) in Iran, backed by the US. He introduced reforms inspired by the US, but this angered conservative Shia Muslims. The Shah's main opponent was Ayatollah Khomeini, a Muslim cleric (priest), who wanted to create a government based upon Islamic beliefs. In 1979, when more than a million people took to the streets in support of Khomeini, the Shah was forced to flee and Khomeini was swept into power.

Public support
In 1979, more than a million Iranians demonstrated to support Muslim cleric and leader Ayatollah Khomeini.

The Iran-Iraq War

With Iran in chaos after the revolution of 1979, Iraq's leader, Saddam Hussein, invaded the country in 1980. He blamed a dispute over a waterway between the two states for the outbreak of war. Both sides suffered terrible losses in the fighting, which saw the use of tanks, chemical weapons, and trench warfare. A cease-fire, organized by the United Nations, was declared in 1988.

Tank war
Iran used British and US tanks, such as this Chieftain, in its fight against Iraq.

Timeline

Israel and Palestine

During the Holocaust, millions of Jewish people were murdered by Germany's Nazi party. After the war, the global community was determined to find the survivors a safe and permanent homeland. They chose British-controlled Palestine, because Jewish people believe it to be the land promised to them by God. But the Arab people already living there objected, leading to years of conflict.

1948

Creation of Israel in Palestine
The United Nations proposed dividing the region of Palestine into an Arab state and a Jewish state. Despite resistance from the Muslim Arab Palestinians, the state of Israel was created.

1948-1960s

Palestinian displacement
After the state of Israel was formed, more than 700,000 Palestinian Arabs left the region. Palestinians called this their *nakba*, or catastrophe. The Palestinians claimed they were expelled, but Israel insisted the Palestinians were not forced to leave.

1964

Palestine Liberation Organization
The Palestine Liberation Organization (PLO) was established in Jordan. It aimed to bring various Arab organizations under one banner, destroy Israel, and create a liberated Palestine. The PLO carried out terrorist attacks against Israel, including bombings and aircraft hijackings.

FORMER PLO LEADER, YASSER ARAFAT

1967

The Six-Day War
Fearing an Arab attack, Israel launched a preemptive strike against Arab troops along its borders. Israeli forces seized territories from Egypt, Syria, and Jordan.

2010 The year of the **Arab Spring**—a **series of pro-democracy uprisings** in multiple Muslim countries **across the Middle East.**

5.4 million The number of people who have **fled Syria** since the **civil war began in 2011.**

195

THE GULF WAR

In 1990, Saddam Hussein of Iraq invaded oil-rich Kuwait, claiming that it was rightfully part of Iraq. He refused the United Nations' demand to withdraw, and so military forces led by the US attacked and forced the Iraqi army out of Kuwait during Operation Desert Storm in 1991. As they withdrew, Iraqi forces set fire to more than 600 Kuwaiti oil wells, destroying millions of barrels of oil and polluting the country.

Fires in the desert
US stealth aircraft, which were almost invisible to enemy radar, flew over the Kuwaiti desert where uncontrolled oil-well fires burned for more than 10 months.

Oil production

The Middle East has the largest oil reserves in the world and many Middle Eastern countries produce and export oil. Although the global demand for oil has created wealth in the Middle East, it has also led to political and economic interference by Western powers who are eager to keep oil flowing.

Oil producer
The oil is transported across the desert by long pipelines, ready for exporting abroad.

THE WAR ON TERROR

In the 1980s, an Islamic terrorist group called Al-Qaeda formed in Afghanistan. Their aim was to establish a Muslim nation worldwide. On September 11, 2001, they carried out attacks in the US, killing almost 3,000 people and prompting the US to launch a "war on terror." The US invaded Afghanistan to destroy Al-Qaeda's bases, and then Iraq, searching for weapons it thought could be used against the West.

Scanning for explosives
Thousands of explosive mines were scattered around Iraq during the 2003 war. Here a US soldier checks the ground with a metal detector.

REFUGEE CAMPS

The United Nations refugee agency estimated that in 2013, an average of more than 30,000 people a day left their homes in the Middle East because of conflict and persecution. Many refugees take shelter in camps—temporary shelters that offer safety while they wait to be resettled in other countries.

Safe space
Refugee camps offer life-saving aid like food, water, and medicine during an emergency, though conditions are extremely basic.

1973	1979	1987–1993	1993	2000–2005
The Yom Kippur War Syria and Egypt launched a surprise attack on Israeli-held lands to coincide with the Jewish holy day of Yom Kippur. They hoped to win back territory they had lost to Israel during the Six-Day War, but Israel halted the Egyptian Army's advance.	**Mutual recognition** US President Jimmy Carter worked to improve relations between Israel and Egypt. Israel withdrew its forces from the Sinai Peninsula and returned the land to Egypt, which became the first Arab country to officially recognize Israel's existence.	**The First Intifada** During the early 1980s, Jewish settlements were established on Palestinian land, causing tensions in the occupied areas to worsen. Palestinian Arabs in the West Bank and Gaza launched the Intifada (meaning "popular uprising") against Israeli occupation with riots, strikes, boycotts, and demonstrations. Israel was accused of using extreme force in response.	**Oslo Accords** Hosted by US President Bill Clinton, Israeli and Palestinian leaders signed the first of the Oslo Accords, designed to lead to a permanent peace deal with mutual recognition between Israel and the PLO.	**The Second Intifada** After Israeli Prime Minister Ariel Sharon's controversial visit to the religious site of Temple Mount in Jerusalem, Palestinian demonstrations escalated into rioting, and later suicide attacks, rocket launches, and sniper fire targeted at Israeli soldiers and citizens. Israel responded with deadly force. This Second Intifada cost more than 4,000 Israeli and Palestinian lives.

Postcolonial Africa

During the 1950s and 1960s, African countries gained independence from their colonial rulers. For some Africans, this meant new freedoms and opportunities right away, but most nations faced huge challenges over the following decades.

Many countries experienced civil wars, and different ethnic groups fought among each other. Dictators seized power and were then reluctant to let go, ruling for decades through violence and fear. In South Africa, the government favored the minority white population in a system known as Apartheid ("separateness"). Under this system, black people faced many restrictions, such as where they could live and work, and had fewer political rights than white people. However, in the 21st century, the future of Africa looks brighter, with many nations having greater political and financial stability.

1960–1965
Extreme violence erupted in the Congo (now the Democratic Republic of Congo) after the country gained independence from Belgium.

1963
The Organization of African Unity was established to encourage cooperation between African nations and to fight colonialism across the continent.

1971–1979
Idi Amin, president of Uganda, led an eight-year reign of terror with widespread violence until he was overthrown.

1975–2002
The Republic of Angola became independent of Portugal but descended into a civil war that lasted many decades.

April–July 1994
In Rwanda, up to a million Tutsis, an ethnic group, were killed by the Hutus, a neighboring ethnic group.

May 1994
Nelson Mandela became the first black president of South Africa, ending 300 years of white rule.

2004
Wangari Maathai, a Kenyan feminist, won the Nobel Peace Prize for her work to empower young women.

2018
Ethiopia became the fastest-growing economy in Africa.

The first free elections in South Africa
In an election rally, crowds show their support for Nelson Mandela, who would become the first black president of South Africa in 1994. Mandela's election marked the end of Apartheid.

Modern Asia

Since World War II, several countries in Asia have developed wealthy, thriving economies. For the first time in modern history, parts of Asia are richer than Europe and quickly catching up with the US.

After the devastation of World War II, many Asian countries needed to recover and rebuild. They set out to strengthen their economies by supporting the growth of industries that used their own natural resources, such as coal and oil, rather than relying on foreign imports. Governments put money into improving infrastructure–systems of communication, power, and transportation–then shifted their focus to high-tech industries.

BOOMING ECONOMIES

Between the early 1960s and the 1990s, many Asian countries experienced rapid economic growth and fast improvement in standards of living. They exported cheap-to-produce, high-tech goods to the rest of the world and attracted foreign investment. In 1997, the continent suffered a setback during the Asian financial crisis, when foreign investment declined, but it recovered quickly.

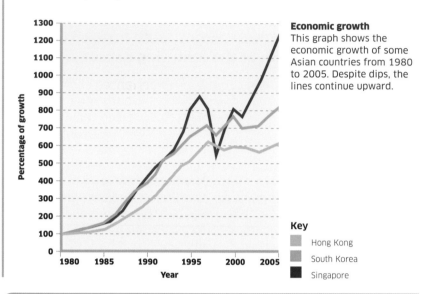

Economic growth
This graph shows the economic growth of some Asian countries from 1980 to 2005. Despite dips, the lines continue upward.

Key
Hong Kong
South Korea
Singapore

JAPAN

After World War II, Japan concentrated on producing cotton, coal, and steel to fund its recovery and rebuild its economy. The Japanese education system produced highly skilled workers, and gradually the country began to focus on making high-tech products. Japan suffered a recession in the 1990s and economic growth has since slowed, but it is still one of the richest countries in the world.

Sony Walkman
Japanese company Sony sold 200 million of these portable cassette tape players around the world after they were released in 1979.

SINGAPORE

Singapore gained its independence in 1965, after breaking away from neighboring Malaysia. Since then, the tiny nation has dramatically transformed, attracting investment from abroad and becoming a global financial center.

The Port of Singapore
Sheltered from the ocean and deep enough for large ships, Singapore's main harbor is one of the busiest ports in the world. Each year, more than 130,000 ships visit the port, with a vessel arriving or leaving every two to three minutes.

Modern technology

Japan is a world leader in technology, pioneering advances in electronics and robotics. It is home to many world-famous brands, such as electronics companies Sony and Nintendo and car companies Mitsubishi and Toyota, whose products are popular with consumers around the world.

Honda Asimo
Created in 2000, the Honda Asimo (short for "Advanced Step in Innovative Mobility") was the first robot to walk on two legs.

Nintendo Game Boy
Nintendo sold more than 18 million copies of its handheld game console, which was released in 1989.

2008 The year **Beijing in China** hosted the **Summer Olympic Games**, which were **watched by 4.7 billion people** around the world.

20 ft/s (6 m/s)—the **speed of the elevators** in the **Petronas Towers** in Malaysia.

199

MALAYSIA

Malaysia gained its independence from Britain in 1957, later becoming one of the world's fastest developing countries due to its plentiful natural resources, such as oil, gas, tin, and fertile land. To modernize the economy, the government made it easier to trade with foreign countries, invested in infrastructure, and reformed the country's health care and education.

The Petronas Towers
Standing at 1,482 ft (452 m) tall, these twin skyscrapers in Kuala Lumpur, Malaysia, were the world's tallest buildings until 2004, and a symbol of Malaysia's economic success.

SOUTH KOREA

South Korea has become one of the world's top exporters. Its popular exports include Hyundai cars and Samsung electronics, as well as cultural trends, such as K-Pop (South Korean pop music) and K-Beauty (South Korean cosmetics).

Shipping at Ulsan Port
Hyundai Motor Company produces a new vehicle every 10 seconds. From this port close to its factories, it ships its cars to consumers around the world.

CHINA

In 1978, Chinese leader Deng Xiaoping approved new policies to open up China's tightly controlled economy to the world. He invited foreign companies to invest in the country, for the first time in many years. With the labor of its gigantic population, China produced and sold more goods than any other country in the world, turning it into an economic superpower.

Modern factories
China modernized its factories by introducing new technologies. Workers were paid lower wages than in the West, which helped attract financial investment from foreign companies.

A greener future

At the start of the 21st century, as human activity takes its toll on the environment, experts are calling for urgent action to prevent a global crisis.

Since the Industrial Revolution, people have relied on fossil fuels such as oil and coal for power, but burning these fuels releases carbon dioxide into the atmosphere. Carbon dioxide is a type of greenhouse gas. It acts like a blanket around Earth, trapping in the sun's heat—a phenomenon known as the Greenhouse Effect. Earth's increasing temperature is causing the polar ice caps to melt, sea levels to rise, and natural disasters such as hurricanes and floods to become more extreme. As scientists and politicians search for technological solutions to these environmental issues, many campaigners insist that the only way to save the planet is to dramatically change the way we live.

Reduce, reuse, recycle
Every day humans produce three million tons of waste, which is buried in the ground, burned, or recycled. Concerned about the environmental damage caused by huge mounds of waste, campaigners are encouraging people to limit how much they create in the first place, by buying less and reusing items where possible.

Solar panels
These panels absorb enough energy from the sun to meet the energy needs of the inhabitants.

Green roof
The plants take carbon dioxide from the air and turn it into life-giving oxygen.

Rainwater collection
The gutters collect rainwater, channeling it into a barrel, where it is ready to be used in the garden.

Heat-proof glass
Triple-glazed windows prevent heat loss during winter and keep the house cool in summer.

Wildlife-friendly garden
Having a variety of trees and plants encourages wildlife to an area, reduces noise pollution, and improves air quality.

Compost bin
Cut grass and food scraps can be left to rot, becoming compost that provides valuable nutrients for the garden.

Beehive
A single beehive contains an average of 40,000 honeybees. Bees help plants reproduce by transferring pollen between them, but habitat destruction means the number of bees is decreasing.

Garden plot
As well as being a space to grow fruit and vegetables, a garden provides a habitat for many different insect species.

Feeding the population
One-third of the planet's land is already used for farming, but with an expanding population to feed, more and more land is needed to grow crops and rear animals. Extreme weather and natural disasters such as drought and flooding are making farming less predictable, while overfishing the oceans has reduced fish stocks.

Rainwater tank
A large underground tank stores rainwater and pipes it into the house, where it is used to wash clothes and flush the toilet.

Recycling bins
Glass, paper, plastic, and aluminum waste is collected to be recycled into new materials.

4°F (2°C)—the temperature rise beyond which climate change will become irreversible, according to scientists.

1.6 billion The global population at the start of the 20th century. Today it is more than 7 billion.

201

Home turbine
Vertical axis wind turbines work well in built-up areas.

Renewable energy
Technological advances have now made it possible to obtain large amounts of energy from natural resources. At sea, wind is plentiful and free. Unlike oil and coal, wind is a renewable resource, which means it won't run out. The wind's energy turns the blades of this turbine, which are connected to a generator. The generator converts this energy into electricity to power homes, schools, and offices.

Rising sea levels

As sea levels rise, low-lying countries are in danger of being overwhelmed by water. Most of the Marshall Islands, a collection of 12,000 islands in the Pacific Ocean, are just a few feet above sea level. Wave-driven floods are becoming more frequent, threatening homes, crops, and fresh water supplies.

Under water
Inhabitants of the Marshall Islands may be forced to leave their homes if sea levels continue to rise.

Endangered wildlife

From corals in Australia to penguins in Antarctica, wildlife across the world is disappearing at an alarming rate. Habitat destruction caused by human activity is the main reason that so many species are at risk of extinction.

Under threat
The number of orangutans in the wild is falling due to habitat loss.

Insulation
A layer of insulation prevents heat from escaping.

Living green walls
Walls covered with carbon dioxide-absorbing plants act as a natural air filter.

Low-energy lighting
These light bulbs are more efficient than traditional bulbs, with less energy lost as heat.

Eco-friendly paint
This water-based paint doesn't contain any substances harmful to the environment.

Brick walls
Brick absorbs heat and then releases it slowly, meaning that less energy is required to heat the home.

Household appliances
White goods such as washing machines, fridges, and dishwashers are now being designed to use less water and electricity.

Heat exchanger
Cold water flows through pipes underground, absorbing heat, before it is returned to the house to heat radiators, or to be used for showers and baths.

Electric car
An electric car does not emit greenhouse gases like gas- or diesel-powered cars.

"We are facing a man-made disaster of global scale. Our **greatest threat** in thousands of years. Climate change."

David Attenborough, British broadcaster, to the UN Conference on Climate Change, 2018

Eco-friendly house

Houses of the future will have as many eco-friendly features as possible in order to reduce their carbon footprint—the amount of carbon dioxide they release into the atmosphere. This house is powered by the sun and the wind. Its roof is covered in plants, which absorb carbon dioxide from the surrounding air, and it is well insulated to prevent heat loss.

Glossary

ABDICATION
Formally handing over power or responsibility to another.

ABOLITION
The movement to end the slave trade. More generally, it means the act of doing away with something.

ALLIES/ALLIED FORCES
People or countries working together. In World War I and World War II, the Allies or Allied forces were the countries fighting against Germany.

ANTI-SEMITISM
Prejudice and hostility toward Jewish people.

APARTHEID
In South Africa, a government policy of racial segregation that lasted from 1948 to 1994.

ARMISTICE
An agreement that is reached to end a conflict.

ASSASSINATION
The murder of a key figure by surprise attack, carried out for political or religious reasons.

AUTHORITARIAN
Term applied to leaders or governments who exercise power with little or no regard for democracy or other constraints.

AXIS POWERS
Nations on Germany's side in World War II, including Italy and Japan.

BARBARIAN
The name given by the Romans to tribes outside the Roman Empire.

BCE
Before Common Era. The years before 1 CE (Common Era). This abbreviation has largely replaced BC (before Christ)

BOLSHEVIK
A faction within the Russian Social Democratic Party, which later became the Communist Party in 1918.

BUDDHISM
A major world religion based on the teachings of Buddha.

CALIPH
The title of a political and religious leader of an Islamic empire, or caliphate.

CAPITALISM
An economic system based on the private ownership of property and free competitive conditions for business.

CASUALTIES
People killed or injured as a result of war or an accident.

CAVALRY
Military troops riding on horseback or in armored vehicles.

CE
Common Era. The years from 1 CE to the present day. This abbreviation has largely replaced AD (Anno Domini, which is Latin for "in the year of our lord").

CITIZEN
A person who belongs to a city or a bigger community such as a state or country.

CITY-STATE
A city and its surrounding territory, that has its own independent government.

CIVIL RIGHTS
The rights of citizens to be socially and politically equal.

CIVIL WAR
A war fought by opposing inhabitants of the same country.

CIVILIZATION
The culture and way of life of people living together in an organized and developed society.

COLD WAR, THE
The period of hostility between the West and the communist countries dominated by the Soviet Union. It lasted from shortly after World War II until 1989.

COLONIZATION
The act of sending settlers to establish a colony in another country, sometimes involving taking political control over the people already living there.

COLONY
An area under the political control of another state, usually in a foreign country. The people that settled there are called colonists.

COMMUNISM
The political belief in a society in which ownership of property and wealth is shared.

CONCENTRATION CAMP
A prison camp for nonmilitary prisoners. At Nazi concentration camps, prisoners included Jews and other groups considered to be enemies of the state.

CONFUCIANISM
A Chinese religion based on the teachings of Confucius. Followers are taught to respect people who are above them in rank.

CONQUISTADOR
One of the Spanish conquerors of Native American civilizations.

CONSTITUTION
A set of laws that determine the political principles of a government.

COUNTER-REFORMATION
The period of change in the Roman Catholic Church after the Protestant Reformation. This included internal reform and opposition to Protestantism.

CRUSADES, THE
Military expeditions of the 11th to 13th centuries, in which Christian knights tried to seize the city of Jerusalem from the Muslims.

CULTURE
The customs, beliefs, and behavior shared by a society.

CZAR
The title of the rulers of Russia from the 15th century until 1917.

DAIMYO
A lord in medieval Japan who owed allegiance to the shogun.

DECOLONIZATION
The process of giving back political control to a former colony, resulting in its independence.

DEMOCRACY
A political system in which people have power to control their government, usually by electing politicians to represent their views.

DICTATOR
A leader who rules a country alone, with no restrictions on the extent of their power.

DOMESTICATION
The taming of wild animals to make them useful to humans, or wild plants to make them more suitable to eat.

DYNASTY
A royal family ruling a country for successive generations.

EASTERN ORTHODOX CHURCH
A form of Christianity, strongest in Eastern Europe and West Asia, that split from the Roman Catholic Church in 1054 CE.

EMPIRE
A group of lands or peoples brought under the rule of one government or person.

EXTINCT
Describes a species that has no living members.

FASCISM
A political movement stressing nationalism, which places the strength of the state above individual citizens' welfare.

FEUDALISM
A social system that developed in medieval Europe and Japan, in which people of the serving classes (such as laborers and peasants) pledged support to their overlord in return for their protection.

GREAT DEPRESSION, THE
A period of drastic decline in economic activity, marked by widespread unemployment and hardship, in the 1930s.

GUERRILLA WARFARE
A war fought by people who are not part of regular uniformed armies and who use tactics such as ambush and sabotage.

HERESY
Beliefs that are considered to be in conflict with a religious group's established beliefs.

HOLOCAUST
The mass murder of the Jews by the German state in World War II.

HOMININ
A member of the biological group that includes humans and their extinct relatives.

IMMIGRANT
A person who moves to a new country to settle there permanently.

INDIGENOUS
When applied to people, the word indigenous describes the original settlers of a country or region.

ISLAM
A religion based on the teachings written in the Quran. Followers believe in one God, who revealed his message to the prophet Muhammad in the 7th century CE.

MAUSOLEUM
A large tomb, or an impressive building for housing several tombs.

MESOPOTAMIA
The region of modern-day Iraq lying between the Tigris and Euphrates rivers, where many of the earliest civilizations began.

MISSIONARY
A religious person who seeks out and persuades others to adopt their religion.

MONARCHY
A type of government in which a king or queen is recognized as the head of state, whether or not they hold real power.

MUSLIM
A follower of Islam.

NATION
An independent country, or a group of people who share historical or cultural ties.

NATIONALISM
Loyalty and devotion to a nation, and the political belief that a nation's interests should be pursued as the primary goal of a political policy.

NEANDERTHAL
An extinct species of hominin closely related to our own species.

NOMADIC
Describes people who move from place to place without establishing a permanent settlement.

PEASANT
A worker on the land of low status, usually an agricultural laborer.

PERSECUTE
To oppress or harass a person or group because of their origins or beliefs.

PHARAOH
Title given to a king in Ancient Egypt. People believed that the pharaohs had sacred powers.

PHILOSOPHY
A set of ideas or beliefs. Can also refer to the study of knowledge.

PILGRIM
A religious person who makes a journey to a holy place.

PREHISTORIC
Dating from prehistory—the time before the invention of writing.

PROPAGANDA
Method used to change and control how people think and behave It may take the form of posters, broadcasts, or air-dropped leaflets, for example.

PROTESTANTISM
A form of Christianity that is separate from the Roman Catholic Church, resulting from the Reformation.

RECONNAISSANCE
Taking a preliminary look at an area before sending in troops, usually in order to locate an enemy or to scout a location.

REFORMATION, THE
A religious movement of the 16th century, in which many Christians broke away from the traditions of the Roman Catholic Church.

RENAISSANCE, THE
A period of European history, beginning in the 14th century, when art and literature were influenced by the rediscovery of knowledge from the ancient world.

REPUBLIC
A country without a monarch or emperor. Modern republics are usually led by presidents.

REVOLT
An organized uprising intended to overthrow whoever is in authority.

REVOLUTION
A sudden and fundamental change in society brought about by an organized group of protestors. Can also mean a change in the way that people do or think about things.

ROMAN CATHOLIC CHURCH
The largest group within the Christian faith, led by the Pope and based in Rome.

SAMURAI
A Japanese warrior who owes allegiance to a daimyo and follows a strict code of honor.

SCRIPT
The written characters that make up a writing system, such as an alphabet.

SEGREGATION
Separation, particularly of one race from another within a racist social system.

SERF
A peasant who is obligated to undertake agricultural work on their lord's land.

SHOGUN
A military leader who ruled Japan in the name of the emperor.

SIEGE
To surround a city or fortress with the intention of capturing it.

SLAVE
A person who is held as the property of another.

SPECIES
A group of organisms that are similar to, and can breed with, each other.

STALEMATE
A situation in a conflict where further action by either side appears impossible.

STATE
A country—or a region within a country—and its people. A state is ruled by a government.

STOCK EXCHANGE
An organization that allows trading in shares of companies and other financial assets.

SUB-SAHARAN AFRICA
The part of Africa to the south of the Sahara desert.

SUBCONTINENT
A large landmass that forms part of a bigger continent.

SULTAN
The title given to a ruler in some Islamic empires and kingdoms.

SUPERPOWER
A country with great political and military power, capable of influencing international politics.

TREASON
The crime of betraying one's own country or its leaders.

TREATY
An official, written agreement between warring parties to bring hostilities to an end.

TRENCH
A ditch dug by soldiers for protection against enemy fire.

TRIBUTE
Money or goods paid to a state or monarch in recognition of their superior status.

UNITED NATIONS
A global organization set up after World War II to help maintain international peace, security, and cooperation.

WEST, THE
Europe and North America, or their ideals and culture when seen in contrast to other civilizations.

Index

Acknowledgments

The publisher would like to thank the following people for their assistance in the preparation of this book: Edward Aves, Ben Ffrancon Davies, Abigail Morgan, and Mani Ramaswamy for editorial assistance; Jane Ewart, Govind Mittal, and Sadie Thomas for design assistance; Simon Mumford for cartographic assistance; Stephen Haddelsey for additional text contributions; Reg Grant for additional consultancy; William Collins and Lynne Murray for additional picture research; Steve Crozier at Butterfly Creative Solutions and Tom Morse for picture retouching; Victoria Pyke for proofreading; Helen Peters for the index.

Smithsonian Enterprises:
Kealy E. Gordon, Product Development Manager
Ellen Nanney, Licensing Manager
Jill Corcoran, Director, Licensed Publishing Sales
Brigid Ferraro, Vice President,
Education and Consumer Products
Carol LeBlanc, President

Reviewers for the Smithsonian:
Dr. F. Robert van der Linden, Curator of Air Transportation and Special Purpose Aircraft, National Air and Space Museum, Smithsonian

The publisher would like to thank the following for their kind permission to reproduce photographs:
(Key: a-above; b-below/bottom; c-center; f-far; l-left; r-right; t-top)

8 Alamy Stock Photo: Artokoloro Quint Lox Limited (crb); robertharding (cra); Georgios Kollidas (ca); Puwadol Jaturawutthichai (fbl). **Bridgeman Images:** Archaeological Museum, Sarnath, Uttar Pradesh, India / Dinodia (tl). **Getty Images:** SSPL (tr). **9 123RF.com:** Daniel Schidlowski / acanthurus (tc). **Alamy Stock Photo:** Jose Lucas (br); BibleLandPictures.com (bc); Peter Horree (crb); Granger Historical Picture Archive (tr). **Bridgeman Images:** National Museums Scotland (ca); Vatican Museums and Galleries, Vatican City (cra). **Dreamstime.com:** Xiaoma (clb). **12 Alamy Stock Photo:** The Natural History Museum (bl); Ariadne Van Zandbergen (bc). **Science Photo Library:** Sputnik (tc). **13 Science Photo Library:** S. Entressangle / E. Daynes (bc, bl). **14 Alamy Stock Photo:** Heritage Image Partnership (br). **15 Getty Images:** CM DIxon / Print Collector (tr). **16 Dreamstime.com:** Irinabelokrylova (bc/pig, cow, horse, bc/goat, sheep, bc/llama); just_regress (not the chicken silhouette). **iStockphoto.com:** Vectorig (cra). **17 123RF.com:** Coroiu Octavian / taviphoto (cl); Victoriia Parnikova / 21kompot (cra/Sun burst). **Alamy Stock Photo:** BibleLandPictures.com (tc); Maurice Savage (ca). **Dorling Kindersley:** South of England Rare Breeds Centre, Ashford, Kent (clb). **18 Alamy Stock Photo:** Jerónimo Alba (bl); robertharding (bc); MNStudio (br). **19 Alamy Stock Photo:** Ian Dagnall (bc); Duby Tal / Albatross (bl). **Getty Images:** Eric Lafforgue / Art in All of Us / Corbis (br). **20 Alamy Stock Photo:** BibleLandPictures.com (bc). **21 Alamy Stock Photo:** Peter Horree (bl); Graham Mulrooney (fbl). **22 Alamy Stock Photo:** Jose Lucas (br); Petr Bonek (br); World History Archive (cra); Anka Agency International (cr). **23 Alamy Stock Photo:** Artokoloro Quint Lox Limited (ftl); Ivy Close Images (tr); Incamerastock (tl); Prisma Archivo (tc); World History Archive (bl); Dan Breckwoldt (cra); Loop Images Ltd (bc); Science History Museum (br). **24 123RF.com:** Tatyana Borozenets (fcla, fcl, clb); Vladimir Zadvinskii / zadvinskiy (fclb); Tatyana Borozenets / tatyana (cla). **iStockphoto.com:** Getty Images Plus (cl). **25 Alamy Stock Photo:** Liquid Light (bl); NDP (tr). **26 Alamy Stock Photo:** Artokoloro Quint Lox Limited (tc). **Bridgeman Images:** Metropolitan Museum of Art, New York, USA (br). **26-27 TurboSquid:** 3d_molier International / Dorling Kindersley (bull); macrox / Dorling Kindersley (wheat field); SmartCGArt / Dorling Kindersley (Egyptian farmers); 3Dhedgehog / Dorling Kindersley (papyrus plants, bulrushes); Dzejsi Models / Dorling Kindersley (water Lily); 3dsam79 / Dorling Kindersley (tilapia); Pbr Game Ready / Dorling Kindersley (well); Torttuga / Dorling Kindersley (catfish). **27 Alamy Stock Photo:** Artokoloro Quint Lox Limited (tl); Oksana Mitiukhina (bl). **29 Dreamstime.com:** Sergio Bertino (bc); Xiaoma (bl). **30 Alamy Stock Photo:** The Picture Art Collection (ca). **Bridgeman Images:** De Agostini Picture Library (cb). **31 Bridgeman Images:** De Agostini Picture Library (ftl, cl); Granger (tl); Fitzwilliam Museum, University of Cambridge, UK (tc); Louvre, Paris, France (tr); Kunsthistorisches Museum, Vienna, Austria (ftr). **Dreamstime.com:** Marcorubino (cr). **32-33 CGTrader:** l3production / Dorling Kindersley (ship). **32 Alamy Stock Photo:** Heritage Image Partnership Ltd (bl). **33 akg-images:** Erich Lessing (bc). **Alamy Stock Photo:** Ancient Art and Architecture (bl); BibleLandPictures.com (br). **34-35 Bridgeman Images:** State Hermitage Museum, St. Petersburg, Russia (c). **36 Alamy Stock Photo:** robertharding (bc). **Bridgeman Images:** De Agostini Picture Library / A. De Gregorio (bl, cl); De Agostini Picture Library / G. Dagli Orti (br). **37 Alamy Stock Photo:** Atlaspix (bl); Hemis (tl); Heritage Image Partnership Ltd (cr); James Hadley (br). **39 Alamy Stock Photo:** Hemis (bl). **Bridgeman Images:** National Museums Scotland (br). **40 Alamy Stock Photo:** Georgios Kollidas (clb). **Bridgeman Images:** Louvre, Paris, France / De Agostini Picture Library / G. Dagli Orti (br). **42-43 Getty Images:** Maremagnum (c). **44 Dorling Kindersley:** University of Pennsylvania Museum of Archaeology and Anthropology (cl). **46 akg-images:** (cl). **Alamy Stock Photo:** Hans-Joachim Schneider (bl). **Bridgeman Images:** British Library, London, UK (tr). **Getty Images:** SSPL (c, bc). **47 Alamy Stock Photo:** age fotostock (crb); View Stock (br); Art Collection 2 (c). **Bridgeman Images:** Bibliothèque Nationale, Paris, France (bl); Pictures from History (tr); People's Republic of China (tl). **Dorling Kindersley:** The Trustees of the British Museum (tc). **48 Alamy Stock Photo:** GL Archive (cr); Peter Horree (tr). **Bridgeman Images:** Costa (bc). **49 Alamy Stock Photo:** Ruslan Gilmanshin (fcr); Loop Images Ltd (bc); Lautaro (cb). **Bridgeman Images:** Naples National Archaeological Museum, Naples (cr); Ny Carlsberg Glyptotek Museum, Copenhagen (fcra). **Dreamstime.com:** Kmiragaya (crb); Krzysztof Slusarczyk (bl/Trajan's column). **52 Dreamstime.com:** Floriano Rescigno (tc). **53 Alamy Stock Photo:** Jack Aiello (bl). **54-55 123RF.com:** ermess (bc). **54 123RF.com:** Daniel Schidlowski (cr). **Alamy Stock Photo:** Chronicle (bl); United Archives GmbH (bc). **Getty Images:** Werner Forman / UIG (cl). **55 Alamy Stock Photo:** Falksteinfoto (br). **Bridgeman Images:** Musée Picardie, Amiens, France (tr). **Dorling Kindersley:** Canterbury City Council, Museums and Galleries (bl). **Getty Images:** Universal Images Group (bc). **Rex by Shutterstock:** (tc). **58 Alamy Stock Photo:** Granger Historical Picture Archive (bl); Peter Horree (crb); Seyed pedram Mireftekhari (cr); George H.H. Huey (tc); Interfoto (c). **Bridgeman Images:** American Museum of Natural History, New York, USA / Photo © Boltin Picture Library (tl); Photo © Dirk Bakker (bc); Photo © Heini Schneebeli (ca). **59 Alamy Stock Photo:** Frederick Wood Art (cr); John Warburton-Lee Photography (tc); Peter Horree (tr). **Bridgeman Images:** Universitetets Oldsaksamlingen, University of Oslo, Norway / Photo © AISA (clb). **Dorling Kindersley:** University Museum of Archaeology and Anthropology, Cambridge (tl); University of Pennsylvania Museum of Archaeology and Anthropology (bl, c). **60 Bridgeman Images:** Ognissanti, Florence, Italy (tc). **61 Alamy Stock Photo:** Interfoto (tl). **Dorling Kindersley:** Glasgow Museums (tr). **62-63 Alamy Stock Photo:** Susana Guzman (c). **64 123RF.com:** Serhil Borodin / seregasss435 (bc/Emperor icon on panel); Christos Georghiou / Krisdog (bc/warrior mask icon on panel); Sergei Vidineev / ss1001 (bc/weapons icon on panel); Ivan Ryabokon / ylivdesign (bc/man in hat icon on panel). **akg-images:** Archives CDA / St-Genès (clb/figure). **Alamy Stock Photo:** The Picture Art Collection (bl). **Getty Images:** Kyodo News (cla). **65 Alamy Stock Photo:** Art Collection 2 (bl); Granger Historical Picture Archive (c/both masks). **Bridgeman Images:** American Museum of Natural History, New York, USA / Photo © Boltin Picture Library (cl); Pictures from History (br, bc). **66 Alamy Stock Photo:** Science History Images (br). **67 Alamy Stock Photo:** age fotostock (ftl); World History Archive (tr); Lebrecht Music & Arts (tc). **Bridgeman Images:** Bibliothèque Nationale, Paris, France / Archives Charmet (cb). **Dorling Kindersley:** Ashmolean Museum, Oxford (ftr). **69 Bridgeman Images:** Universitetets Oldsaksamlingen, University of Oslo, Norway / Photo © AISA (cr); Werner Forman Archive (br). **70 Bridgeman Images:** Biblioteca Nazionale, Turin, Italy / Index Fototeca (tl). **Dorling Kindersley:** Royal Armouries, Leeds (tc). **71 123RF.com:** Dusan Loncar / Iddesign (cb/crown); Ivan Ryabokon (crb/sword). **Bridgeman Images:** Kupferstichkabinett, Berlin, Germany / Pictures from History (tr). **72 akg-images:** Heritage-Images / The Museum of East Asian Art (bc). **Alamy Stock Photo:** Eike Leppert (c). **Avalon:** Craig Lovell (cb). **Bridgeman Images:** Pictures from History / David Henley (bl); Luca Tettoni (clb). **74 Alamy Stock Photo:** Granger Historical Picture Archive (bl); George H.H. Huey (cl). **Bridgeman Images:** De Agostini Picture Library (bc); Photo © Dirk Bakker (br). **75 Alamy Stock Photo:** age fotostock (br); George Ward (bc). **76-77 Alamy Stock Photo:** The Picture Art Collection (c). **78 Bridgeman Images:** Pictures from History (bl). **The Trustees of the British Museum:** Château de Versailles (cla). **80 Alamy Stock Photo:** Heritage Image Partnership Ltd (cl); World History Archive (br). **The Trustees of the British Museum:** (tl). **81 akg-images:** Album / NY Metropolitan Museum of Art (bl). **Alamy Stock Photo:** John Warburton-Lee Photography (br). **Bridgeman Images:** Photo © Heini Schneebeli (tr). **The Trustees of the British Museum:** (bc). **82 Dreamstime.com:** Theo Malings (clb). **Getty Images:** De Agostini / V.Giannella (crb). **83 Dorling Kindersley:** Rowan Greenwood Collection (br). **84-85 Bridgeman Images:** Pictures from History. **86 Alamy Stock Photo:** peace portrait photo (tl). **Getty Images:** DeAgostini (br). **87 Alamy Stock Photo:** Konstantin Kalishko (br); World History Archive (tr). **Getty Images:** Louis Acosta / AFP (cr). **88 Alamy Stock Photo:** Heritage Image Partnership (cl); avada (tr). **89 Alamy Stock Photo:** UK Alan King (ca); trevellinglight (tr); Pictures Now (cla); Peter Horree (fcla). **Dreamstime.com:** Pixattitude (cr). **92 Bridgeman Images:** © Michael Graham-Stewart (tl); Yale Center for British Art, Paul Mellon Collection, USA (cb). **Dorling Kindersley:** Durham University Oriental Museum (cr); Board of Trustees of the Royal Armouries (bc). **93 akg-images:** Heritage Images (cla). **Alamy Stock Photo:** Artokoloro Quint Lox Limited (bl); Nick Fielding (br); The Picture Art Collection (clb). **Dorling Kindersley:** Science Museum, London (tc); Whipple Museum of History of Science, Cambridge (cr, tr). **94 123RF.com:** sborisov (bl). **Alamy Stock Photo: Artokoloro Quint Lox Limited (bc). Bridgeman Images:** Nicolò Orsi Battaglini (c). **94-95 The Metropolitan Museum of Art:** (cb). **95 Alamy Stock Photo:** Artexplorer (tl). **Bridgeman Images:** Christie's Images (tr). **96 Alamy Stock Photo:** Historic Images (cla). **97 Alamy Stock Photo:** motive56 (tr). **Bridgeman Images:** Pictures from History (cr). **98 akg-images:** Interfoto / Hermann Historica GmbH (bc). **Bridgeman Images:** Lebrecht History (tr); Topkapi Palace Museum, Istanbul, Turkey / Sonia Halliday (tc, ftr). **Dorling Kindersley:** Board of Trustees of the Royal Armouries (bl, clb, crb, br). **98-99 Alamy Stock Photo:** Alex Segre (bc). **99 akg-images:** Roland and Sabrina Michaud (br). **Bridgeman Images:** Topkapi Palace Museum, Istanbul, Turkey (tr, ftr); Topkapi Palace Museum, Istanbul, Turkey / Sonia Halliday (ftl). **Dorling Kindersley:** Durham University Oriental Museum (fcl); University of Pennsylvania Museum of Archaeology and Anthropology (cl). **Getty Images:** Historica Graphica Collection / Heritage Images (tl). **101 Bridgeman Images:** Universitatsbibliothek, Gottingen, Germany / Bildarchiv Steffens (tr). **102 akg-images:** Heritage Images / Fine Art Images (cl, fbr). **Bridgeman Images:** Tarker (crb). **Dreamstime.com:** Vladimir Sazonov / Sazonoff (br). **103 akg-images:** Heritage Images (bc). **Alamy Stock Photo:** Chronicle (cr). **Bridgeman Images:** Scott Polar Research Institute, University of Cambridge, UK (tc). **Dreamstime.com:** Vasily Pakhomov (bl). **104-105 Bridgeman Images:** Index Fototeca (c). **106 Alamy Stock Photo:** Interfoto (bl). **Bridgeman Images:** Granger (c). **Getty Images:** Print Collector (br). **107 Alamy Stock Photo:** Lanmas (tl); Pictures Now (tr). **Bridgeman Images:** British Library, London, UK / © British Library Board (bc); Universal History Archive / UIG (cr); Tarker (ftr); Castillo Chapultepec, Museo Nacional de Historia, Mexico (tc). **Getty Images:** De Agostini / G. Dagli Orti (bl). **108 Alamy Stock Photo:** gameover (bl). **Bridgeman Images:** Germanisches Nationalmuseum, Nuremberg (tr). **109 Alamy Stock Photo:** Archivart (tr); Granger Historical Picture Archive (tl). **Bridgeman Images:** Bibliothèque Nationale, Paris, France (bc); Granger (tc). **111 Alamy Stock Photo:** Anders Blomqvist (br); Historical Images Archive (tc); Dinodia Photos (cr). **112-113 Alamy Stock Photo:** Science History Images (c). **114 Bridgeman Images:** Archives de la Manufacture, Sevres, France / Archives Charmet (tr). **115 Alamy Stock Photo:** National Geographic Image Collection (cr). **116 Bridgeman Images:** Pictures from History (cl). **116-117 Getty Images:** Heritage Images (tc). **117 akg-images:** Historic Images (bc). **Alamy Stock Photo:** Stefano Ravera (cr). **119 Alamy Stock Photo:** Granger Historical Picture Archive (ca, cra); The Picture Art Collection (tr). **120 Alamy Stock Photo:** North Wind Picture Archives (bc). **121 Alamy Stock Photo:** Chronicle (tr). **Bridgeman Images:** © Michael Graham-Stewart (cla); Werner Forman Archive (tl); Granger (bc); Wilberforce House, Hull City Museums and Art Galleries, UK (c, cl). **122-123 akg-images:** (c). **126 akg-images:** (bl). **Alamy Stock Photo:** Harvy Matters (cr). **Dorling Kindersley:** Powell-Cotton Museum, Kent (tl); Gettysburg National Military Park, PA (cra); Science Museum, London (bc). **127 Alamy Stock Photo:** Granger Historical Picture Archive (tl). **Bridgeman Images:** Musée Carnavalet, Musée de la Ville de Paris, Paris, France (br). **Dorling Kindersley:** National Railway Museum, York (c); Adrian Shooter (ca). **Dreamstime.com:** Klausmeierklaus (tc). **128 Alamy Stock Photo:** Niday Picture Library (tr). **Bridgeman Images:** (bl); Washington National Gallery of Art, Washington DC, USA (cl). **129 Alamy Stock Photo:** Niday Picture Library (cr); World History Archive (bl). **Bridgeman Images:** Kunsthistorisches Museum, Vienna, Austria (tl); Schloss Sanssouci, Potsdam, Brandenburg, Germany (ftl); Odessa Fine Arts Museum, Ukraine (tc). **130 Alamy Stock Photo:** Archive Pics (bl). **131 Dorling Kindersley:** National Railway Museum, York (br); Steve Noon (tr). **132-133 Alamy Stock Photo:** World History Archive (c). **134 Alamy Stock Photo:** Granger Historical Picture Archive (tl, bl); Pictorial Press Ltd (cl). **136 Alamy Stock Photo:** Historic Collection (bl). **Bridgeman Images:** Natural History Museum, London, UK (bc). **137 Bridgeman Images:** Alexander Turnbull Library, Wellington, New Zealand (bl); The Stapleton Collection (br); Granger (cr). **138 Bridgeman Images:** Musée Carnavalet, Musée de la Ville de Paris, Paris, France (tl, tc). **139 Alamy Stock Photo:** GL Archive (tr, cr); Granger Historical Picture Archive (br). **Bridgeman Images:** Bibliothèque Nationale, Paris, France (crb). **140-141 Alamy Stock Photo:** Niday Picture Library (tr). **140 Alamy Stock Photo:** Heritage Image Partnership (bc). **Bridgeman Images:** Walker Art Gallery, National Museums Liverpool (br). **141 Alamy Stock Photo:** Interfoto (br). **Bridgeman Images:** Agra Art, Warsaw, Poland (bl); British Library, London, UK / © British Library Board (fbl). **142-143 Getty Images:** DeAgostini (c). **145 Alamy Stock Photo:** Aclosound Historic (tr). **146 Getty Images:** SSPL (bc). **147 Bridgeman Images:** Edinburgh University Library, Scotland / With kind permission of the University of Edinburgh (br); National Museum of Damascus, Syria / Photo © Luisa Ricciarini (tr); Granger (crb). **Getty Images:** Christophel Fine Art / UIG (cr). **148 Alamy Stock Photo:** Archive Images (bl). **Bridgeman Images:** Peter Newark American Pictures (crb); The Stapleton Collection (cr). **Dorling Kindersley:** Museum of Artillery, The Rotunda, Woolwich, London (cra). **149 Alamy Stock Photo:** Hemis (br); North Wind Pictures Archives (cb). **Bridgeman Images:** (tr); Massachusetts Historical Society, Boston, MA, USA (bl). **150 Bridgeman Images:** Peter Newark American Pictures (tl). **Getty Images:** Bettmann (clb, bl). **151 Alamy Stock Photo:** Granger Historical Picture Archive (br). **152-153 TurboSquid:** Next Image / Dorling Kindersley (Benz automobile). **153 Alamy Stock Photo:** Science History Images (cra). **Bridgeman Images:** Michelin Building, London, UK (br). **154-155 Alamy Stock Photo:** Gado images. **156 Alamy Stock Photo:** M&N (br). **Bridgeman Images:** Roy Miles Fine Paintings (bc). **Dorling Kindersley:** Adrian Shooter (bl). **162 Alamy Stock Photo:** Mark Scheuern (cra). **Dorling Kindersley:** Bate Collection (br); Imperial War Museum, London (c). **163 Alamy Stock Photo:** Charles O. Cecil (tl); Gunter Kirsch (bl); Design Pics Inc (br). **Dorling Kindersley:** Board of Trustees of the Royal Armouries (cb). **164 Bridgeman Images:** British Library, London, UK / © British Library Board (tr); Look and Learn (bl, br); SZ Photo / Scherl (cr). **165 Bridgeman Images:** Buyenlarge Archive / UIG (br); Universal History Archive / UIG (fbr); Look and Learn (crb). **Dorling Kindersley:** National Museums of Scotland (cb); Roger Symonds (tr). **166 Alamy Stock Photo:** akg-images (bl). **Bridgeman Images:** Universal History Archive / UIG (bc). **Getty Images:** SSPL (tl). **168-169 Alamy Stock Photo:** Pictorial Press Ltd (c). **170 Bridgeman Images:** Granger (bl). **Getty Images:** Stefano Blanchett / Corbis (tl); Lewis Hine / National Archive / Newsmakers (bc). **171 Getty Images:** American Stock (cl); MPI (c). **172-173 TurboSquid:** nikopol_c4d / Dorling Kindersley (Reichstag). **172 Bridgeman Images:** Granger (br); SZ Photo / Scherl (bl). **173 Bridgeman Images:** (bl, cr); De Agostini Picture Library (bc); SZ Photo / Scherl (ca, tl). **174 Alamy Stock Photo:** Gunter Kirsch (bl). **175 Getty Images:** Leonard Ortiz / Digital First Media / Orange County Register (tr); ullstein bild (tl, cra); Taxi (tc). **176-177 TurboSquid:** 3d_molier International / Dorling Kindersley (Hawker Hurricane, Spitfire); machine_men / Dorling Kindersley (aviator helmet); SANCHES_1985 / Dorling Kindersley (German fighter). **176 Bridgeman Images:** Granger (tc). **177 Alamy Stock Photo:** Nigel J Clarke (tl); dpa picture alliance (cr); Granger Historical Picture Archive (crb). **Getty Images:** Express / Archive Photos (br). **178 Alamy Stock Photo:** Shawshots (bc). **Bridgeman Images:** Granger (tl). **179 Bridgeman Images:** Buyenlarge Archive (tl); Tallandier (c). **180-181 Bridgeman Images:** Everett Collection (c). **182-183 TurboSquid:** chipbasschao / Dorling Kindersley (Grumman TBM-3 Avenger); file404 / Dorling Kindersley (SBD-3 Dauntless); PerspectX / Dorling Kindersley (Wildcat); xtrusion / Dorling Kindersley (crew). **182 Bridgeman Images:** Look and Learn (fbr); Peter Newark Military Pictures (bc). **183 akg-images:** (bl). **Alamy Stock Photo:** Shawshots (bc). **Bridgeman Images:** Granger (crb); PVDE (br, cb). **184 Alamy Stock Photo:** Everett Collection Inc (bc); RBM Vintage Images (cl); World History Archive (c). **184-185 Bridgeman Images:** SZ Photo / Scherl (tc). **Dreamstime.com:** Neezhom (bc). **185 Alamy Stock Photo:** TAO Images Limited (br); World History Archive (tc). **Getty Images:** George Freston / Fox Photos (cr). **186 Alamy Stock Photo:** A. Astes (c); FLHC (tl). **188-189 TurboSquid:** 3d_molier International / Dorling Kindersley (Chinook helicopter , FN magazine and stand, Howitzer); SANCHES_1985 / Dorling Kindersley (German bomber); HCGremlin / Dorling Kindersley (helmet); Glen Harris / Dorling Kindersley (paratrooper); PROmax3D / Dorling Kindersley (c/jeep); Omegavision / Dorling Kindersley (USS *Enterprise*). **188 Alamy Stock Photo:** Everett Collection Inc (cl). **Getty Images:** Keystone France / Gamma-Keystone (cla); STF / AFP (clb). **Rex by Shutterstock:** Sipa (bl). **189 Bridgeman Images:** Pictures from History (bl). **Getty Images:** Ted Streshinsky / Corbis (br). **190-191 Getty Images:** Central Press (c). **190 Getty Images:** The LIFE Picture Collection / A. Y. Owen (br). **191 Alamy Stock Photo:** Ian Dagnall (br); Granger Historical Picture Archive (bl); Everett Collection Historical (tr). **192 Alamy Stock Photo:** History Collection 2016 (cl). **Getty Images:** Reg Lancaster (bl); Harvey Lloyd / Photolibrary (clb). **193 Alamy Stock Photo:** MediaPunch (tr). **Getty Images:** Santi Visalli (tc). **194 Bridgeman Images:** Pictures from History (br); Tallandier (bl); Universal History Archive / UIG (fbr). **Dorling Kindersley:** Tank Museum, Bovington (crb). **Getty Images:** Kaveh Kazemi / Hulton Archive (cr). **195 Bridgeman Images:** Everett Collection (tr); Pictures from History (br, cla). **Getty Images:** Wayne Eastep (clb); Gokhan Sahin (crb); David Rubinger / The LIFE Collection (bl). **196-197 Getty Images:** Tom Stoddard. **198 Alamy Stock Photo:** Matt Naylor (bc). **Dorling Kindersley:** Museum of Design in Plastics, Bournemouth Arts University, UK (c). **Getty Images:** Kyodo News (br); Stone (bl). **199 Getty Images:** AFP (br); Stone (cl); Bloomberg (tr). **200 Alamy Stock Photo:** BrazilPhotos (bl). **Getty Images:** China Photos (cra). **201 Alamy Stock Photo:** Peter Adams Photography Ltd (tc). **Dorling Kindersley:** Thomas Marent (cr). **Getty Images:** Brandi Mueller (tr).

All other images © Dorling Kindersley
For further information see: www.dkimages.com

31901065058234